HOOKS-ONLY
CROCHET
FROM START TO FINISH™

Edited by Carol Alexander

HOUSE of
WHITE
BIRCHES

PUBLISHERS
SINCE 1947

Hooks-Only Crochet From Start to Finish™

Editor: Carol Alexander
Art Director: Brad Snow
Publishing Services Manager: Brenda Gallmeyer

Associate Editor: Lisa M. Fosnaugh
Assistant Art Director: Nick Pierce
Copy Supervisor: Michelle Beck
Copy Editor: Judy Weatherford
Technical Editor: Agnes Russell

Graphic Arts Supervisor: Ronda Bechinski
Book Design: Edith Teegarden
Graphic Artists: Erin Augsburger, Joanne Gonzalez
Production Assistants: Cheryl Kempf, Marj Morgan, Judy Neuenschwander

Photography: Tammy Christian, Don Clark, Matthew Owen, Jackie Schaffel
Photo Stylists: Tammy Nussbaum, Tammy Smith

Publishing Director: David McKee
Marketing Director: Dan Fink
Editorial Director: Gary Richardson

Printed in China
First Printing: 2006

Library of Congress Control Number: 2005931753
Hardcover ISBN-10: 1-59217-102-8 ISBN-13: 978-1-59217-102-6
Softcover ISBN-10: 1-59217-103-6 ISBN-13: 978-1-59217-103-3

1 2 3 4 5 6 7 8 9

A Note From the Editor

If you're like me, you just hate to sew crochet projects together. I may be quite skilled at crochet, but when it comes to sewing with needle and thread (or yarn), it's usually not pretty.

That's why my favorite crochet projects have always been those that require no sewing. Projects consisting of motifs that join as you go or pieces that can be crocheted together nearly always rank higher on my project "to do" list than others requiring even the most minimal sewing.

Knowing that there are many of you who share this preference, we thought it would be a fun to create a book of patterns based on the interesting (and at times challenging!) "hooks only" concept with absolutely no sewing involved. Of course, many of these projects could employ needle and thread if one so wishes, but for us sewing-challenged crocheters, we're good to go with just our trusty crochet hooks!

Until we began work on this book, I had no idea that so many different types of crochet projects could be made without having to sew. To my surprised delight, our designers came up with an amazing variety of designs that could be made from beginning to end with just the use of a crochet hook.

From stunning fashions and cute designs for babies and kids to beautiful home accessories and fun holiday accents, *Hooks-Only Crochet From Start to Finish* presents a colorful and creative collection of projects guaranteed to keep your crochet hooks flying—with no needles required!

With warm regards,

Contents

Spotlight on Style

Fabulous Finishing Touches

Toddlers to Teens

Haven-ly Home Accents

Treasures in Thread

Hooked on Holidays

Spotlight on Style

Step out in style with a dozen dazzling wearables from kicky little tank tops to comfy, cozy jackets to sophisticated evening wear. The spotlight will be focused directly on you when you wear these contemporary, eye-catching fashions.

Flirty Skirted Halter Top

Design by Eleanor Miles-Bradley

Keep cool when the mercury rises with this fun, flirtatious halter top. The loopy, lacy skirt sports a slit down the back that adds just the right amount of kick.

EASY

Finished Size
Small (medium, large, X-large)
Finished chest: 32 (36, 40, 44) inches
Pattern is written for smallest size with changes for larger sizes in brackets.

Gauge
Size 0 hook: 24 sc = 4 inches; 32 sc rows = 4 inches
Size G hook: 16 sc sts = 4 inches; 28 sc rows = 4 inches
Check gauge to save time.

Pattern Notes
Weave in loose ends as work progresses.

Materials
- Aunt Lydia's Classic Crochet size 10 crochet cotton (350 yds per ball): 3 (3, 4, 5) balls #495 wood violet
- Size 0/2.50mm steel crochet hook or size needed to obtain gauge
- Sizes G/6/4mm and K/10½/6.5mm crochet hooks or size needed to obtain gauge

Join rounds with a slip stitch unless otherwise stated.
Halter top is meant to be stretchy and fit snugly.

Ribbed Bodice Band
Row 1 (RS): With size 0 steel hook, ch 48 (60, 72, 84), sc in 2nd ch from hook, sc in each rem ch across, turn. *(47 (59, 71, 83) sc)*
Row 2: Ch 1, working in **back lp** *(see Stitch Guide)* sc in each st across, turn.
Rows 3–86 (3–102, 3–118, 3–134): Rep row 2.
Row 87 (103, 119, 135): Ch 120 *(strap)*, sc in 2nd ch from hook, sc in each rem ch across, working in back lps, sc in each rem st across, turn. *(166 (178, 190, 202) sc)*
Rows 88–97 (104–113, 120–129, 136–145): Rep row 2.
Row 98 (114, 130, 146): Rep row 2 across 47 (59, 71, 83) sc, turn.
Rows 99–151 (115–167, 131–183, 147–199): Rep row 2.
Row 152 (168, 184, 200): Rep row 87 (103, 119, 135).
Rows 153–162 (169–178, 185–194, 201–210): Rep row 2.
Row 163 (179, 195, 211): Rep row 2 across 47 (59, 71, 83) sc, turn.

Rows 164–248 (180–280, 196–312, 212–344): Rep row 2. At the end of last rep, fasten off.

Edging
Rnd 1 (RS): Now working in rnds, with size 0 steel hook, attach wood violet with a sl st to corner along bottom edge, ch 1, sc in same st as beg ch-1, sc in each row to next corner, (sc, ch 2, sc) in corner st, sc in each st along edge, (sc, ch 2, sc) in corner st, sc in each rem st around, sk 1 st at each inner corner of each strap, working (sc, ch 2, sc) in each rem corner, join in beg sc, turn.
Rnd 2: Ch 1, sc in each sc around, working (sc, ch 2, sc) in each corner ch-2 sp, sk 1 sc at each inner corner of each strap, join in beg sc, fasten off.

Skirted Bottom Edge
Note: Size G hook is used only for row 1 to enlarge the sts for size K hook. If the G hook is still too large, use a smaller size, then work row 2 with a larger hook and finally size K hook.

Row 1 (RS): Now working in rows, with size G hook, attach wood violet with sl st to the ch-2 sp at corner bottom, ch 1, sc in same ch-2 sp, sc in each st across bottom edge to opposite corner ch-2 sp, turn.
Row 2: With size K hook, ch 1, sc in each sc of row 1, turn.
Row 3: Ch 3 (*counts as first dc throughout*), dc in each sc across, turn.
Rows 4–12: Ch 3, dc in each dc across, turn. At the end of last rep, fasten off.

Finishing
With RS facing, with size 0 steel hook, attach wood violet in corner ch-2 sp at top back, ch 1, working through both thicknesses, sl st down back opening across Ribbed Bodice Band only, fasten off. Turn RS out. ✂

Pretty in Pink Jacket & Purse

Designs by Svetlana Avrakh

Create a timeless plaid effect with charcoal novelty yarn accenting the classic pink of this boxy, Jackie O-inspired cardigan and handbag set.

 INTERMEDIATE

 4 MEDIUM

Finished Size

Jacket: Small (medium, large, X-large) 32–34 (36–38, 40–42, 44–46) inches

Finished bust: 36 (40, 44, 48) inches

Purse: 10 x 6 inches, excluding handles

Pattern is written for smallest size with changes for larger sizes in brackets.

Materials

- Bernat Satin medium (worsted) weight yarn (3½ oz/163 yds/100g per ball):
    10 (10, 11, 11) balls of #04420 sea shell (A)
- Bernat Bling Bling bulky (chunky) weight yarn (1¾ oz/90 yds/50g per ball):
    3 (3, 5, 5) balls #65040 night club (B)
- Size H/8/5mm crochet hook or size needed to obtain gauge
- Stitch markers
- 6-inch-wide purse handles
- 5 shank ⅞-inch buttons
- 2 pieces cardboard 1¼ x 8¾ inches

Gauge

19 sts = 4 inches; 19 rows = 4 inches
Take time to check gauge.

Pattern Notes

Weave in loose ends as work progresses.

Join rounds with a slip stitch unless otherwise stated.

Rows 2 and 3 of Jacket Back establish the pattern.

Rows 2–13 of Jacket Back establish the color pattern.

Purse is crocheted vertically.

Special Stitch

Reverse single crochet (reverse sc): Working from left to right, insert hook in next st to right, yo, draw up lp on hook, yo, draw through 2 lps on hook.

Jacket

Back

Row 1 (RS): With A, ch 82 (94, 104, 116), sc in 2nd ch from hook, *ch 1, sk next ch, sc in next ch, rep from * across, turn. *(81 (93, 103, 115) sts)*

Row 2: Ch 1, sc in first sc, sc in next ch-1 sp, *ch 1, sk next sc, sc in next ch-1 sp, rep from * across, ending with sc in last sc, turn.

Row 3: Ch 1, sc in first sc, *ch 1, sk next sc, sc in next ch-1 sp, rep from * across to last 2 sc, ch 1, sk next sc, sc in last sc, turn.

Rows 4–9: Rep rows 2 and 3.

Row 10 (WS): With B, rep row 2.

Rows 11 & 12: With A, rep rows 3 and 2.

Row 13: With B, rep row 3.

Rows 14–18: Work 5 rows in pat.

Row 19: Ch 1, 2 sc in first sc, pat to last sc, 2 sc in last sc, turn. *(83 (95, 105, 117) sts)*

Rows 20–28: Work 9 rows even in pat.

Row 29: Rep row 19. *(85 (97, 107, 119) sts)*

Rows 30–39: Rep rows 20–29.

Continue even in pat until Back measures 10½ inches, ending with a WS row, turn.

Armhole Shaping

Row 1: Sl st in first 5 (5, 7, 11) sts, ch 1, sc in same st as last sl st, pat to last 4 (4, 6, 10) sts, leaving rem sts unworked, turn. *(79 (91, 97, 101) sts)*

Row 2: Ch 1, sc in first sc, **sc dec** *(see Stitch Guide)* in next 2 sts, pat across row to last 3 sts, sc dec over next 2 sts, sc in last st, turn.

Rows 3–5 (3–5, 3–9, 3–9): Rep row 2. *(71 (79, 81, 85) sts)*

Row 6 (6, 10, 10): Work even in pat.

Row 7 (7, 11, 11): Ch 1, sc in first sc, sc dec over next 2 sts, pat across to last 3 sts, sc dec over next 2 sts, sc in last sc, turn. *(69 (77, 79, 83) sts)*

Rows 8–11 (8–17, 12–21, 12–23): Rep rows 6 and 7 (6 and 7, 10 and 11, 10 and 11). *(65 (67, 69, 71) sts)*

Continue in pat until armhole measures 7 (7½, 8, 8½) inches, ending with a WS row.

First Shoulder

Row 1: Pat across 14 (15, 15, 16) sts, sc dec over next 2 sts, leaving rem sts unworked, turn. *(15 (16, 16, 17) sts)*

Row 2: Work in pat across, fasten off.

2nd Shoulder

Row 1: With RS facing, sk next 33 (33, 35, 35) sts, attach yarn with a sl st in next st, ch 1, sc dec over same st and next st, pat across rem sts, turn. *(15 (16, 16, 17) sts)*

Row 2: Work in pat across, fasten off.

Left Front

Row 1 (RS): With A, ch 44 (50, 54, 60), sc in 2nd ch from hook, *ch 1, sk next ch, sc in next ch, rep from * across, turn. *(43 (49, 53, 59) sts)*

Rows 2–18: Work in pat.

Row 19: Ch 1, 2 sc in first sc, pat to end of row, turn. *(44 (50, 54, 60) sts)*

Rows 20–28: Work 9 rows even in pat.

Row 29: Ch 1, 2 sc in first sc, pat to end of row, turn. *(45 (51, 55, 61) sts)*

Rows 30–39: Rep rows 20–29. *(46 (52, 56, 62) sts)*

Continue even in pat until Left Front measures 10½ inches, ending with a RS row.

Armhole Shaping

Row 1: Work in pat across to last 4 (4, 6, 10) sts, leaving rem sts unworked, turn. *(42 (48, 50, 52) sts)*

Row 2: Ch 1, sc in first sc, sc dec over next 2 sts, pat across row, turn. *(41 (47, 49, 51) sts)*

Row 3: Work in pat across row to last 3 sts, sc dec over next 2 sts, sc in last sc, turn. *(40 (46, 48, 50) sts)*

Rows 4 & 5 (4–7, 4–9, 4–9): Rep rows 2 and 3. *(38 (42, 42, 44) sts)*

Row 6 (8, 10, 10): Work even in pat.

Row 7 (9, 11, 11): Ch 1, sc in first sc, work in pat across to last 3 sts, sc dec over next 2 sts, sc in last sc, turn.

Rows 8–11 (10–19, 12–21, 12–24): Rep rows 6 and 7 (8 and 9, 10 and 11, 10 and 11).

Continue even until armhole measures 5 (5½, 5½, 6) inches, ending with WS row, turn.

Neck Shaping

Row 1: Pat across 16 (17, 18, 18) sts, sc dec over next 2 sts, leaving rem sts unworked, turn. *(17 (18, 19, 19) sts)*

Row 2: Ch 1, sc dec over next 2 sts, pat across row, turn. *(16 (17, 18, 18) sts)*

Row 3: Pat across row to last 2 sts, sc dec over next 2 sts, turn. *(15 (16, 17, 17) sts)*

Continue even in pat until armhole measures same length as Back, fasten off.

Right Front

Rows 1–18: Rep rows 1–18 of Left Front.

Row 19: Ch 1, pat across row to last st, 2 sc in last st, turn. *(44 (50, 54, 60) sts)*

Rows 20–28: Work 9 rows even in pat.

Row 29: Ch 1, pat across row to last st, 2 sc in last st, turn. *(45 (51, 55, 61) sts)*

Rows 30–39: Rep rows 20–29. *(46 (52, 56, 62) sts)*

Continue even in pat until Right Front measures 10½ inches, ending with a WS row.

Armhole Shaping

Rows 1–5 (1–7, 1–9, 1–9): Rep rows 1–5 (1–7, 1–9, 1–9) of Left Front.

Row 6 (8, 10, 10): Ch 1, sc in first sc, sc dec over next 2 sts, pat in each rem st across, turn.

Row 7 (9, 11, 11): Work even in pat.

Rows 8–11 (10–19, 12–21, 12–24): Rep rows 6 and 7 (8 and 9, 10 and 11, 10 and 11). Continue even until armhole measures 5 (5½, 5½, 6) inches, ending with RS row.

Neck Shaping

Rows 1–3: Rep rows 1–3 of Left Front Neck Shaping.

Continue even in pat until armhole measures same length as Back, fasten off.

Sleeve

Make 2.

Row 1 (RS): With A, ch 46, sc in 2nd ch from hook, *ch 1, sk next ch, sc in next ch, rep from * across, turn. *(45 sts)*

Row 2: Ch 1, work in pat across row, turn.

Row 3 (inc row): Ch 1, 2 sc in first sc, pat across to last sc, 2 sc in last sc, turn.

Continue in pat, working inc row on every following 10th (8th, 6th, 4th) row to 63 (67, 73, 59) sts.

Size X-large only: Continue in pat, work inc row on every following 6th row to 77 sts.

All sizes: Continue even in pat until Sleeve measures 18 inches, ending with a WS row.

Shoulder Shaping

Row 1: Sl st in first 4 (4, 4, 5) sts, ch 1, sc in same st as last sl st, work in pat to last 3 (3, 3, 4) sts, turn. *(57 (61, 67, 69) sts)*

Row 2: Work in pat across row, turn.

Row 3: Ch 1, sc in first sc, sc dec over next 2 sts, work in pat across to last 3 sts, sc dec over next 2 sts, sc in last sc, turn. *(55 (59, 65, 67) sts)*

Rows 4–11 (4–17, 4–17, 4–21): Rep rows 2 and 3. *(47 (45, 51, 59) sts)*

Row 12 (18, 18, 22): Ch 1, sc in first sc, sc dec over next 2 sts, work in pat across to last 3 sts, sc dec over next 2 sts, sc in next sc, turn. *(45 (43, 49, 57) sts)*

Rows 13–26 (19–30, 19–32, 23–34): Rep row 12 (18, 18, 22), at the end of last rep, fasten off. *(17 (19, 21, 23) sts)*

Finishing

Block garment pieces and cover with damp cloth, leaving cloth to dry.

To join shoulder seams, with RS of Back and Front facing tog, join A with sl st to top right corner, ch 1, working through both thicknesses, 1 sc in same sp as sl st, *ch 1, 1 sc in next ch-1 sp, rep from * to end of shoulder, fasten off. Rep for opposite shoulder.

To set in Sleeve, with RS of Body and Sleeve facing, set in Sleeve, join A with sl st at underarm side seam, ch 1, working through both thicknesses, 1 sc in same sp as sl st, *ch 1, sk next st, sc in next st, rep from * to opposite side of sleeve, fasten off.

To close side and sleeve seams, with RS of Back and Front facing, attach A with sl st to bottom of side seam, ch 1, working through

Continued on page 30

Mango Lace Top

Design by Belinda "Bendy" Carter

You'll stay cool no matter how steamy the weather gets when you're dressed in this tasty, tropical tank top crocheted with colorful fine weight yarn.

INTERMEDIATE

3 LIGHT

Finished Size

Small (medium, large, X-large)
Finished chest: 36 (40, 44, 48) inches
Pattern is written for smallest size with changes for larger sizes in brackets.

Materials

- Red Heart Lustersheen Yarn fine (sport) weight yarn (4 oz/335 yds/ 113g per ball):
  3 balls #0257 persimmon
- Sizes D/3/3.25mm and E/4/3.5mm crochet hooks or size needed to obtain gauge

Gauge

Size E hook: 35 sts = 9 inches; 36 rows = 9 inches
Check gauge to save time.

Pattern Notes

Weave in loose ends as work progresses. Join rounds with a slip stitch unless otherwise stated.

Always begin each row with chain 1 *(this does not count as a stitch)*. To maintain established pattern on rows, always work single crochet stitches in tall single crochet stitches of previous row and work tall single crochet stitches in single crochet stitches of previous row.

Special Stitches

Tall single crochet (tsc): Insert hook in indicated st, yo, draw up a lp, yo, draw through first lp on hook, yo, draw through 2 lps on hook.
Tall sc dec (tsc dec): (Insert hook in next st, yo, draw up a lp) twice, (yo, draw through 2 lps on hook) twice.

Pattern

Pat Row A: Ch 1, (sc in next tsc, tsc in next sc) across, turn.

13 (14, 15, 16)"

7"

3½"

4 (4½, 5, 5)"

7½ (8, 8½, 8½)"

11"

18 (20, 22, 24)"

Pat Row B: Ch 1, (tsc in next sc, sc in next tsc) across, turn.

Back armhole Shaping

Row 1 (RS): With size E hook, ch 61 (67, 73, 79), working in back bar of ch, sc in 2nd ch from hook, **tsc** *(see Special Stitches)* in next ch, *sc in next ch, tsc in next ch, rep from * across, turn. *(60 (66, 72, 78) sts)*

Row 2: Ch 1, **tsc dec** *(see Special Stitches)* over first 2 sts, *sc in next st, tsc in next st, rep from * across to last 2 sts, **sc dec** *(see Stitch Guide)* over next 2 sts, turn. *(58 (64, 70, 76) sts)*

Row 3: Work pat row B.

Row 4: Ch 1, sc dec over next 2 sts, *tsc in next st, sc in next st, rep from * across to last 2 sts, tsc dec over last 2 sts, turn. *(56 (62, 68, 74) sts)*

Row 5: Rep pat row A.

Rep rows 2–5 until 50 (54, 58, 62) sts rem, ending with row 2 (4, 2, 4).

Back Yoke

Work pat row B (A, B, A) for 18 (18, 18, 16) rows.

Right Shoulder & Right Front Neck Opening

With RS facing, work pat row B (A, B, A) for 12 (14, 16, 18) sts.

Work pat row B (A, B, A) 7 times.

Working in established pat, at the same time, inc 1 st at neck edge on next 7 rows, last row will be a RS row and will end at neck edge, fasten off. *(19 (21, 23, 25) sts)*

Left Shoulder & Left Front Neck Opening

With RS facing, sk next 26 sts on Back Yoke, with size E hook, attach yarn in next st, rep Right Shoulder and Right Front Neck Opening. Last row will be a RS row, will end at Left Shoulder, turn. *(19 (21, 23, 25) sts)*

Front Yoke

Row 1 (WS): Work pat row B (A, B, A) across

left front, do not turn, ch 12, work pat row A (B, A, B) across right front.

Row 2: Work pat row B (A, B, A) working in each st and each ch across, turn. *(50 (54, 58, 62) sts)*

Work pat row B (A, B, A) 6 (6, 6, 4) times.

Continued on page 32

Midsummer Dream Skirt

Design by Dora Ohrenstein

A dreamy shade of pale moss green is accented with tape-yarn flowers atop long, lean multicolor stems.

INTERMEDIATE

MEDIUM

BULKY

Finished Size

X-small (small, medium, large)

Waist: 25¾ (28½, 34¼, 37) inches

Hips: 33 (36, 42, 45) inches

Pattern is written for smallest size with changes for larger sizes in brackets.

Materials

- TLC Cotton Plus medium (worsted) weight yarn (3½ oz/186 yds/100g per skein): 3 (3, 4, 5) skeins #3503 spruce
- S. Charles Rondo bulky (chunky) weight ribbon yarn (88 yds/ 50g yds per ball): 2 balls color #608
- Sizes G/6/4mm and J/10/6mm crochet hooks or size needed to obtain gauge
- 8 (10, 10, 10) safety pins

Gauge

Size G hook: 11 sts = 3 inches; 1 tr row = 1 inch; hdc, tr and hdc rows = 1½ inches Take time to check gauge.

Pattern Notes

Weave in loose ends as work progresses. Join rounds with a slip stitch unless otherwise stated.

Continued on page 34

Teen Tube Top

Design by Katherine Eng for Lion Brand Yarn

This versatile little top, worked in vibrant jewel-tone stripes and accented with sparkling silver trim, is a cute, go-with-anything addition to a teenager's wardrobe.

INTERMEDIATE

4 MEDIUM

Finished Size

Woman's size small (medium, large)

Finished bust: 30 (32, 34) inches, excluding laces

Back length: 11½ inches, excluding straps

Pattern is written for smallest size with changes for larger sizes in brackets.

Materials

- Lion Brand Wool-Ease medium (worsted) weight yarn (3 oz/197 yds/85g per ball):
    1 ball each #175 green (A) and #176 spring green (B)
- Lion Brand Microspun medium sport (weight) yarn (2½ oz/168 yds/70g per ball):
    1 ball each #147 purple (C) and #146 fuchsia (D)
- Lion Brand Glitterspun medium (worsted) weight soft metallic yarn (1¾ oz/115 yds/50g per ball):
    1 ball #150 silver (E)
- Size G/6/4mm crochet hook or size needed to obtain gauge
- 16 glittery pony beads

Gauge

Rows 1–3 = 1¼ inches; 16 sts = 4 inches

Take time to check gauge.

Pattern Notes

Weave in loose ends as work progresses.

Join rounds with a slip stitch unless otherwise stated.

Work in vertical rows on each side of center from back around to front.

Left Side

Foundation row (RS): With A, ch 47, working in **back lp** (*see Stitch Guide*) of ch (*the hump*), sc in 2nd ch from hook, sc in each ch across, turn. (*46 sc*)

Row 1: Ch 1, sc in first sc, (ch 2, sk next 2 sc, sc in next sc) across, turn. (*15 ch-2 sps*)

Row 2: Ch 3 (*counts as first dc throughout*), dc in same st as beg ch-3, (3 dc in next sc) 14 times, 2 dc in last sc, turn, fasten off. (*46 sts*)

Row 3: Attach D in first dc, ch 1, sc in first dc, (ch 2, sk next 2 dc, sc in next dc) across, turn. (*15 ch-2 sps*)

Rows 4–11: Rep rows 2 and 3 in the following color sequence: 1 more row with D, 2 rows B, 2 rows C and 3 rows A.

Row 12: With A, ch 1, sc in first sc, (2 sc in next ch-2 sp, sc in next sc) across, turn. (46 sc)

Row 13: With A, rep row 2.

Row 14: With A, rep row 3, fasten off A.

Rows 15–26: Rep rows 3–14.

Rows 27–36 (27–38, 27–40): Rep rows 3–12 (3–14, 3–16). At the end of last rep, fasten off.

Right Side

Row 1: With WS of Left Side facing, working across opposite side of foundation ch, attach A in first ch, ch 1, sc in same ch, (ch 2, sk next 2 chs, sc in next ch) across, turn. *(15 ch-2 sps)* Rep rows 2–36 (2–38, 2–40) of Left Side.

Border

Rnd 1 (RS): Now working in rnds, attach E in first row end sc to the left of the foundation row on top edge of tube top, ch 1, *sc in same row end sc, working in row end sts across top edge, work 2 sc in each row end sc** to next corner, (sc, ch 2, sc) in corner st, working across front edge, sc in each dc across to next corner, (sc, ch 2, sc) in next corner st, rep from * around, ending last rep at **, join in beg sc.

Rnd 2: Ch 1, (sc, ch 2, sc) in first sc, *(sk next sc, (sc, ch 2, sc) in next sc) across to next corner, (sc, ch 4, sc) in next corner ch-2 sp, working across front edge, sc in next sc, (ch 1, sk next 2 sc, (sc, ch 2, sc) in next sc) across to within 3 sts of next corner, sk next 2 sts, sc in next sc, (sc, ch 4, sc) in next corner ch-2 sp, rep from * once, (sk next sc, (sc, ch 2, sc) in next sc) across to beg, join in beg sc, fasten off.

Lace Chain

With 2 strands of E held tog, leaving a 4-inch length at beg, ch 250, leaving a 4-inch length at end, fasten off.

Designate top and bottom. Beg at bottom, going over ch-4 sps, lace ch to top through rem ch-2 sps *(shoelace style)*, ending at top ch-4 sp. Tie ends in a bow. Pull 2 beads onto each end of lace ch, pushing first up partway onto ch. Pull an 8-inch length through

end of each lace ch and tie tails in an overhand knot. Pull 1 bead down to knot. Clip tails to 1½ to 2 inches.

Strap
Make 2.

With 2 strands of E held tog, ch 60 *(or to desired length)*, place 6 beads onto strap. With crochet hook and E, sl st other end to corresponding position on top edge of back. Attach rem strap on opposite side edge. ✂

Funky Fringe-Sleeve Jacket

Design by Svetlana Avrakh

This one-of-a-kind jacket stitched from fabulously soft fuchsia novelty yarn in a stylish, shorter length is a must-have for the young and the young at heart.

INTERMEDIATE

5 BULKY

Finished Size
Small, (medium, large, X-large)

Bust: 32–34 (36–38, 40–42, 44–46) inches

Finished bust: 36 (40, 44, 48) inches

Pattern is written for smallest size with changes for larger sizes in brackets.

Materials
• Patons Carmen soft bulky (chunky) novelty yarn (1¾ oz/64 yds/50g per ball):
  10 (11, 12, 13) balls #07310 violet
• Size K/10½/6.5mm crochet hook or size needed to obtain gauge
• Stitch markers
• 6 clear ⅝-inch shank buttons

Gauge
13 sts = 4 inches; 13 rows = 4 inches

Check gauge to save time.

Pattern Notes
Weave in loose ends as work progresses.

Join rounds with a slip stitch unless otherwise stated.

Rows 2 and 3 of Back establish pattern.

Sleeves are crocheted vertically.

Back
Row 1 (RS): Ch 60 (68, 76, 84) sc in 2nd ch from hook, *ch 1, sk next ch, sc in next ch, rep from * across, turn. *(59 (67, 75, 83) sts)*

Row 2: Ch 1, sc in first sc, *sc in next ch-1 sp, ch 1, sk next sc, rep from * across, ending with sc in last ch-1 sp, sc in last sc, turn.

Row 3: Ch 1, sc in first sc, *ch 1, sk next sc, sc in next ch-1 sp, rep from * across to last 2 sc, ch 1, sk next sc, sc in last sc, turn.

Rep rows 2 and 3 until Back measures 9½ inches, ending with a WS row, turn.

Armhole Shaping
Row 1: Sl st in first 4 (4, 4, 6) sts, ch 1, sc in same st as last sl st, work in pat across to last 3 (3, 3, 5) sts, turn. *(53 (61, 69, 73) sts)*

Row 2: Ch 1, sc in first sc, **sc dec** *(see Stitch Guide)* over next 2 sts, work in pat across to rem 3 sts, sc dec over next 2 sts, sc in last sc, turn. *(51 (59, 67, 71) sts)*

Rows 3 (3–5, 3–7, 3–7): Rep row 2. *(49 (53, 57, 61) sts)*

Row 4 (6, 8, 8): Work even in pat.

Row 5 (7, 9, 9): Rep row 2. *(47 (51, 55, 59) sts)*

Rows 6 & 7 (8–13, 10–15, 10–17): Rep rows 4 and 5 (6 and 7, 8 and 9, 8 and 9) 1 (3, 3, 4) times. *(45 (45, 49, 51) sts)*

Continue even in pat until armhole measures 7 (7½, 8, 8½) inches, ending with a WS row, turn.

Shoulder Shaping
Row 1: Ch 1, work in pat across 10 (11, 11, 12) sts, sc dec over next 2 sts, turn. *(11 (12, 12, 13) sts)*
Row 2: Pat across 11 (12, 12, 13) sts, fasten off.
Row 3: With RS facing, sk next 21 (19, 23, 23) sts of last row before Shoulder Shaping, ch 1, attach yarn in next st, ch 1, sc dec over same st as beg ch-1 and next st, pat in next 10 (11, 11, 12) sts across, turn. *(11 (12, 12, 13) sts)*
Row 4: Rep row 2 of Shoulder Shaping.

Left Front
Row 1 (RS): Ch 32 (36, 40, 44) sc in 2nd ch from hook, *ch 1, sk next ch, sc in next ch, rep from * across, turn. *(31 (35, 39, 43) sts)*
Rep rows 2 and 3 of Back in pat until Left Front measures 9½ inches, ending with a RS row, turn.

Armhole Shaping
Row 1: Ch 1, work in pat across to last 3 (3, 3, 5) sts, turn. *(28 (32, 36, 38) sts)*
Row 2: Ch 1, sc in first sc, sc dec over next 2 sts, work in pat across rem of row, turn. *(27 (31, 35, 37) sts)*
Row 3: Ch 1, work in pat across to last 3 sts, sc dec over next 2 sts, sc in last sc, turn. *(26 (30, 34, 36) sts)*
Rows 0 (4 & 5, 4–7, 4–7): Rep rows 2 and 3. *(26 (28, 30, 32) sts)*
Row 4 (6, 8, 8): Work even in pat.
Row 5 (7, 9, 9): Ch 1, pat across to last 3 sts, sc dec over next 2 sts, sc in last st, turn. *(25 (27, 29, 31) sts)*
Rows 6 & 7 (8–13, 10–15, 10–17): Rep rows 4 and 5 (6 and 7, 8 and 9, 8 and 9) 1 (3, 3, 4) times. *(24 (24, 26, 27) sts)*
Continue in pat until armhole measures 5 (5½, 5½, 6) inches, ending with a WS row facing, turn.

Neck Shaping
Row 1: Work in pat across 12 (13, 13, 14) sts, sc dec over next 2 sts, turn. *(13 (14, 14, 15) sts)*
Row 2: Ch 1, sc dec over next 2 sts, work in pat across row, turn. *(12 (13, 13, 14) sts)*
Row 3: Work in pat across to last 2 sts, sc dec over next 2 sts, turn. *(11 (12, 12, 13) sts)*
Continue in pat until Left Front measures the same length as Back, fasten off.

Right Front
Rows 1 (RS): Rep row 1 of Left Front. *(31 (35, 39, 43) sts)*
Rep rows 2 and 3 of Back in pat until Right Front measures 9½ inches, ending with WS row, turn.

Armhole Shaping
Rep the same as Armhole Shaping for Left Front.

Neck Shaping
Rep the same as Neck Shaping for Left Front.

Sleeve
Make 2.
Row 1: Ch 59, dc in 4th ch from hook, dc in each of next 25 chs, tr in each of next 20 chs, dtr in each of next 10 chs, turn. *(57 sts)*
Note: *Place a marker at the end of row 1 to mark as top of Sleeve.*
Row 2: Ch 1, sc in first st, *ch 10, sk next 10 sts, sc in each of next 2 sts, rep from * 3 times, leaving rem sts unworked, ch 9, turn.
Row 3: Hdc in 3rd ch from hook, hdc in each of next 6 chs, *dc in each of next 2 sts, dc in each of next 10 chs, rep from * to last st, dc in last st, turn.
Row 4: Rep row 2.
Row 5: Hdc in 3rd ch from hook, hdc in each of next 6 chs, (dc in each of next 2 sts, dc in each of next 10 chs) twice, tr in each of next 2 sts, tr in each of next 10 chs, 1 dtr in each of next 2 sts, 1 dtr in each of next 10 chs, dtr in last st, turn.

Continued on page 31

Amethyst Shell

Design by Kim Guzman

Top off a pretty skirt or your favorite worn-out jeans with this simple and sleek little shell for a look that can go from shabby chic to sensational.

INTERMEDIATE

Finished Size

X-small (small, medium, large)

Finished bust: 32 (36, 40, 44) inches

Pattern is written for smallest size with changes for larger sizes in brackets.

Materials

- TLC Amore medium (worsted) weight yarn (6 oz/290 yds/170g per skein):
    2 (2, 2, 2) skeins #3536 grape (A)
    1 (1, 1, 1) skein #3908 raspberry (B)
- Moda Dea Kickx (bulky) chunky yarn (1¾ oz/68 yds/50g per skein):
    1 (1, 1, 1) skein #3530 stellar (C)
- Size I/9/5.5mm crochet hook or size needed to obtain gauge
- Stitch markers

Gauge

14 sts = 4 inches; 12 rows = 4 inches
Check gauge to save time.

Pattern Notes

Weave in loose ends as work progresses. Join rounds with a slip stitch unless otherwise stated.

Continued on page 33

Desert Diva Crisscross Top

Design by Cindy Carlson

The muted colors of a Southwestern evening add a dramatic flair to this ultra-chic top that can be dressed up with pearls and heels or dressed down with jeans and sandals.

EASY

Finished Size

X-small (small, medium, large)

Finished bust: 32 (36, 40, 44) inches

Pattern is written for smallest size with changes for larger sizes in brackets.

Materials

- South West Trading Company Diva medium (worsted) weight yarn (56 yds/ 50g per ball):
    4 (4, 5, 5) balls Sahara
- South West Trading Company Optimum fine (sport) weight wool yarn (154 yds/ 50g per ball):
    2 (2, 3, 3) balls desert
- Size H/8/5mm crochet hook or size needed to obtain gauge
- ¾-inch novelty shank button

Gauge

Sahara yarn, 1 row = 1 inch; 3 cross-sts = 2 inches;

Desert yarn, 6 sc = 2 inches; 4 rows = 1½ inches

Check gauge to save time.

Continued on page 34

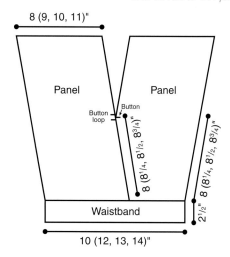

8 (9, 10, 11)"

Panel Panel

Button loop Button

8 (8¼, 8½, 8¾)" 8 (8¼, 8½, 8¾)"

Waistband

2½"

10 (12, 13, 14)"

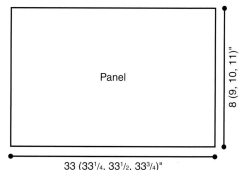

Panel

8 (9, 10, 11)"

33 (33¼, 33½, 33¾)"

Black Magic Pullover

Design by Dora Ohrenstein

No tricks here, just a treat for that special evening under the stars. Dramatic diagonal lines of gold add sparkle to this flattering black top.

EXPERIENCED

Finished Size
Small (medium, large, X-large)
Finished chest: 32–34 (36–38, 40–42, 44–46) inches
Pattern is written for smallest size with changes for larger sizes in brackets.

Materials
* Berroco Cotton Twist medium (worsted) weight yarn (1¾ oz/85 yds/50g per hank):
    7 (10, 13, 16) hanks #8390 black (A)
* Berroco Metallic FX (chunky) novelty weight yarn (⅞ oz/85 yds/25g per hank):
    2 (3, 3, 3) hanks #1003 gold/black (B)
* Berroco Lavish bulky (chunky) weight yarn (1¾ oz/55 yds/50g per ball):
    16 (20, 25, 30) balls #7319 Donatella (C)
* Sizes G/6/4mm and J/10/6mm crochet hooks or size needed to obtain gauge
* Straight pins
* Stitch markers

Gauge
Size G hook and A: 4 dc = 1 inch; 3 dc rows = 1¾ inches
Take time to check gauge.

Pattern Notes
Weave in loose ends as work progresses.
Join rounds with a slip stitch unless otherwise stated.
When **changing yarn color** *(see Stitch Guide)* from A to B, do not fasten off A, carry A along edge throughout. Do not carry B along edge; leave a small length, fasten off.

Body
Make 2.
Row 1 (WS): With size G hook and A, ch 52 (68, 68, 88), dc in 4th ch from hook, dc in each of next 21 (31, 31, 41) chs, 2 dc in next ch, ch 1, 2 dc in next ch, dc in each rem ch across, turn. *(25 (35, 35, 45) sts each side of center ch-1)*
Row 2: Ch 3 *(counts as first dc throughout)*, dc in same st as beg ch-3, dc in each st across to center ch-1 sp, (2 dc, ch 1, 2 dc) in ch-1 sp, dc in each st across to last st, 2 dc in end ch, turn.

Row 3: Ch 3, working in **front lp** *(see Stitch Guide)* of each st, dc in same st as beg ch-3, dc in each st across to ch-1 sp, (2 dc, ch 1, 2 dc) in ch-1 sp, dc in each st across to last st, 2 dc in last st, turn. *(31 (41, 41, 51) sts each side of center ch-1)*

Row 4: Draw up a lp of B, ch 1, sc in first dc, ch 1, sk 1 dc, sc in next dc, (ch 1, sk next dc, sc in next dc) across to ch-1 sp, ch 1, (sc, ch 2, sc) in ch-1 sp, sc in next dc, (ch 1, sk next dc, sc in next dc) across, turn.

Row 5: Ch 1, sc in first sc, ch 1, (sc in next ch-1 sp, ch 1) across to center ch-2 sp, (sc, ch 2, sc) in ch-2 sp, ch 1, (sc in next ch-1 sp, ch 1) across, ending with sc in last sc, turn. *(34 (44, 44, 54) sts each side of center ch-2 sp)*

Row 6: Draw up a lp of A, ch 3, dc in same st as beg ch-3, dc in each st across to ch-2 sp, (2 dc, ch 1, 2 dc) in center ch-2 sp, dc in each rem st across, ending with 2 dc in last st, turn.

Row 7 (sizes small & medium): Ch 3, working in front lps only, **dc dec** *(see Stitch Guide)* over next 3 sts, dc in front lp of each st to center ch-1 sp, (2 dc, ch 1, 2 dc) in ch-1 sp, dc in front lp of each st across to last 3 sts, front lp dc dec over next 2 sts, leaving last st unworked, turn.

Row 8 (sizes small & medium): Ch 3, dc dec over next 3 sts, dc in each st to center ch-1 sp, (2 dc, ch 1, 2 dc) in ch-1 sp, dc in each st across to last 3 sts, dc dec over next 2 sts, leaving last st unworked, turn.

Row 7 (sizes large & X-large): Rep row 3.
Row 8 (sizes large & X-large): Rep row 2.
Row 9 (all sizes): Draw up a lp of B, ch 1, sc in first st, (ch 1, sk next st, sc in next st) across to ch-1 sp, (sc, ch 2, sc) in ch-1 sp, sc in next st, (ch 1, sk 1 st, sc in next st) across, turn.

Row 10: Ch 1, sk first sc, (sc in next ch-1 sp, ch 1) across to center ch-2 sp, (sc, ch 2, sc) in ch-2 sp, (ch 1, sc in next ch-1 sp) across, leaving last sc unworked, turn.

Row 11: Draw up a lp of A, ch 3, dc dec over next 3 sts, dc in each st across to center ch-2 sp, (dc, ch 1, dc) in ch-1 sp, dc in each st across to last 3 sts, dc dec over next 2 sts, leaving last st unworked, turn. *(37 (47, 53, 63) sts each side of center ch-1 sp)*

Row 12: Rep row 8.
Row 13: Rep row 7.
Rows 14 & 15: With B, rep rows 9 and 10.
Row 16: With A, rep row 11.
Row 17: Rep row 7.
Row 18: Rep row 11.
Rows 19 & 20: With B, rep rows 9 and 10.
Row 21: With A, rep row 11.
Row 22: Ch 3, dc dec over next 3 sts, dc in each st to center ch-1 sp, (dc, ch 1, dc) in ch-1 sp, dc in each st across to last 3 sts, dc dec over next 2 sts, leaving last st unworked, turn. *(36 (42, 52, 63) sts on each side of center ch-1 sp)*

Row 23: Ch 3, working in front lps only, dc dec over next 3 sts, dc in front lp of each st to center ch-1 sp, (dc, ch 2, dc) in ch-1 sp, dc in front lp of each st across to last 3 sts, dc dec over next 3 sts, turn.

Row 24: Draw up a lp of B, ch 1, (sc in next dc, ch 1) across to ch-2 sp, (sc, ch 2, sc) in center ch-2 sp, (sc in next dc, ch 1) rep across, ending with sc in last st, turn.

Row 25: Ch 1, sk first sc, (sc in next ch-1 sp, ch 1) across working (sc, ch 2, sc) in center ch-2 sp, (ch 1, sc in next ch-1 sp) across, turn.

Rows 26–28: Rep rows 21–23.
Rows 29 & 30: Rep rows 24 and 25.
Rows 31–33: Rep rows 21–23. At the end of last rep, fasten off.

Sleeve
Make 2.
Row 1: With A, ch 4, (2 dc, ch 1, 3 dc) in 4th ch from hook, turn.

Row 2: Ch 3, dc in same st as beg ch-3, dc in each dc to center ch sp, (2 dc, ch 1, 2 dc) in center ch-1 sp, dc across to last dc, 2 dc in last dc, turn.

Row 3: Ch 3, working in front lps, dc in same st as beg ch-3, dc in each st across, (2 dc, ch 1, 2 dc) in ch-1 sp of center, dc in each st across ending with 2 dc in last st, turn.

Row 4: With B, ch 1, sc in first dc, ch 1, sk next dc, (sc in next dc, ch 1, sk next dc) across to center ch-1 sp, (sc, ch 2, sc) in center ch-1 sp, (ch 1, sk next dc, sc in next dc) across, turn.

Row 5: Ch 1, sc in first sc, ch 1, (sc in next ch-1 sp, ch 1) across to center ch-2 sp, (sc, ch 2, sc) in center ch-2 sp, (ch 1, sc in next ch-1 sp) across to last sc, ch 1, sc in last sc, turn.

Row 6: With A, ch 3, dc in same st as beg ch-3, dc in each st to center ch-2 sp, (2 dc, ch 1, 2 dc) in center ch-2 sp, dc in each rem st across, ending with 2 dc in last st, turn.

Row 7: Ch 3, working in front lps, dc in same st as beg ch-3, dc in each st across to center ch-1 sp, (2 dc, ch 1, 2 dc) in center ch-1 sp, dc in each st across, turn.

Row 8: Ch 3, dc in same st as beg ch-3, dc in each dc to center ch-1 sp, (dc, ch 1, dc) in center ch-1 sp, dc in each rem dc across, ending with 2 dc in last st, turn.

Rows 9 & 10: Rep rows 4 and 5.

Row 11: Rep row 6.

Row 12: Rep row 8.

Row 13 (size small): Ch 3, working in front lps, dc dec over next 2 dc, dc in each st to center ch sp, (dc, ch 1, dc) in center ch sp, dc in each st across to last st, sk last st, turn.

Row 13 (sizes medium, large & X-large): Rep row 8.

Row 14 (sizes small & medium): With B, sk first dc, (sc in next dc, ch 1, sk next dc) across to center ch sp, ch 1, (sc, ch 2, sc) in center ch sp, (ch 1, sk next dc, sc in next dc) across to last dc, sk last dc, turn.

Row 14 (sizes large & X-large): Rep row 4.

Row 15 (sizes small & medium): Ch 1, sk first sc, (sc in next ch-1 sp, ch 1, sk next sc) across to center ch sp, (sc, ch 2, sc) in ch-2 sp, (ch 1, sk next sc, sc in next ch-1 sp) across, turn.

Row 15 (sizes large & X-large): Rep row 5.

Row 16 (sizes small & medium): With A, ch 3, dc dec over next 2 dc, dc in each st to center, (dc, ch 1, dc) in center ch sp, dc in each st across to last st, sk last st, turn.

Row 16 (sizes large & X-large): Rep row 6.

Row 17 (sizes small, medium & large): Ch 3, working in front lps, dc dec over next 2 dc, dc in each st to center ch sp, (dc, ch 1, dc) in center ch sp, dc in each st across to last st, sk last st, turn.

Row 17 (size X-large): Ch 3, working in front lps, dc in same st as beg ch-3, dc in each st across to center ch sp, (dc, ch 1, dc) in center ch sp, dc in each st across to last st, 2 dc in last st, turn.

Row 18: Ch 3, dc dec over next 2 sts, dc in each st across to center ch sp, (dc, ch 1, dc) in center ch sp, dc in each dc across to last dc, sk last dc, turn.

Row 19: With B, sc in first dc, ch 1, sk next dc, (sc in next dc, ch 1, sk next dc) across to center ch sp, (sc, ch 2, sc) in center ch sp, (ch 1, sk next dc, sc in next dc) across, turn.

Row 20: Ch 1, sk first sc, (sc in next ch-1 sp, ch 1) across to center ch sp, (sc, ch 2, sc) in center ch sp, (ch 1, sc in next ch-1 sp) across, turn.

Row 21: With A, ch 3, dc dec over next 2 sts, dc in each st to center ch sp, (dc, ch 1, dc) in center ch-1 sp, dc in each st to last st, sk last st, turn.

Row 22: Ch 3, dc dec over next 2 sts, dc in each dc to center ch sp, (dc, ch 1, dc) in center ch sp, dc in each dc across to last dc, sk last dc, turn.

Row 23: Ch 3, working in front lps, dc dec over next 2 sts, dc in each st across to center ch sp, (dc, ch 1, dc) in center ch sp, dc in each st across to last st, sk last st, turn, *(sizes small and medium)* fasten off.

Rows 24–28: Rep rows 19–23. At the end of last rep, fasten off.

Assembly

Measure from row 1 of Body down 7½ (8½, 9½, 10½) inches and place a st marker to mark underarm.

Attach A at bottom edge of Body, working through both thicknesses catching 1 strand each side, sc up edge to marker at underarm, fasten off. Rep body joining on opposite edge.

With WS facing, matching color rows of pattern, pin Sleeve into armhole opening. With A, sc shoulder seam from neckline edge down to Sleeve, sc Sleeve into armhole opening. Rep Sleeve and shoulder on opposite edge.

Trim

Rnd 1: With RS facing and size J hook, attach C in neckline opening between any 2 dc sts, ch 2, hdc into every other sp between sts around neckline opening, join in beg ch-2, fasten off.

Rnd 2: With RS facing and size J hook, attach C near sleeve seam between 2 sts, ch 2, hdc into every other sp between sts around Sleeve opening, join in beg ch-2, fasten off. Rep rnd 2 on opposite Sleeve edge. ✂

Pretty in Pink Jacket & Purse
Continued from page 13

Continued from page 13

both thicknesses, 1 sc in same sp as sl st, *ch 1, sk next st, sc in next st, rep from * along sleeve and side seam, fasten off.

For buttons, mark position of 5 buttons on Left Front, with top button ½ inch down from top edge, last button 1 inch up from bottom edge and rem 3 buttons sp evenly between. For buttonholes on Right Front place markers opposite button markers, pat to marker, ch 2, sk next 2 sts, pat to next marker across edge.

Body Edging

Rnd 1: Attach A with a sl st at bottom of left seam, ch 1, sc in same sp as sl st, *ch 1, 1 sc in next ch-1 sp of foundation ch, rep from * to right front corner, (sc, ch 1, sc) in next corner, (ch 1, sk next st, sc in next st) 39 (40, 40, 41) times up front edge to corner Neck Shaping (ch 1, sc) in same corner st, work (ch 1, sc) around neckline (sc, ch 1, sc) into opposite neckline corner, (ch 1, sk next st, sc in next st) 39 (40, 40, 41) times down left edge to bottom corner, (ch 1 sc) in same corner st, *ch 1, sc in next ch-1 sp of foundation ch, rep from * across bottom edge, ending with ch 1, sl st to join, attach B with sl st in first sc.

Rnd 2: With B, sl st in next ch-1 sp, ch 1, sc in same sp as last sl st, *ch 1, sk next sc, sc in next ch-1 sp, rep from * around, working (sc, ch 1, sc) in each corner ch-1 sp, join in beg sc.

Rnd 3: With A, sl st in next ch-1 sp, ch 1, sc in same sp as last sl st, *ch 1, sk next sc, sc in next sc, rep from * around, working (sc, ch 1, sc) in each corner ch-1 sp and working buttonholes opposite markers up Right Front, join in beg sc.

Rnd 4: With A, sl st in next ch-1 sp, ch 1, sc in same sp as last sl st, *ch 1, sk next sc, sc in next ch-1 sp, rep from * around, working (sc, ch 1, sc) in corner ch-1 sps and work in pat across ch sts of buttonholes, join in beg sc.

Rnd 5: Ch 1, **reverse sc** *(see Special Stitch)* in each evenly sp around, join in beg sc, fasten off.

Fold a double length of A and pass through shank of button, secure buttons opposite buttonholes by passing double strands through edging, knot ends to secure.

Weave

With crochet hook and B, weave running st in groups of 2 vertical lines 14 sts apart over entire jacket.

Purse

Side
Make 2.

Row 1 (RS): With A, ch 50, sc in 2nd ch from hook, *ch 1, sk next ch, sc in next ch, rep from * across, turn. *(49 sts)*

Row 2: Ch 1, sc in first sc, *sc in next ch-1 sp, ch 1, sk next sc, rep from * across to last ch-1 sp, sc in next ch-1 sp, sc in last sc, turn.

Row 3: Ch 1, sc in first sc, *ch 1, sk next sc, sc in next ch-1 sp, rep from * to last 2 sc, ch 1, sk next sc, sc in last sc, turn.

Rows 4–9: Rep rows 2 and 3.

Row 10: With B, rep row 2.

Rows 11 & 12: With A, rep rows 3 and 2.

Row 13: With B, rep row 3.

Rep rows 2–13 until side measures 11½ inches, ending with a WS row, fasten off.

Finishing
Place markers on each side 2½ inches down from side edge. With RS facing, attach A at right marker, working through both thicknesses, ch 1, sc in same sp as beg ch-1, *ch 1, sk next st, sc in next st, rep from * along side, bottom and opposite side to next marker, fasten off. The rem of crocheted section above markers is for handle extensions. Turn Purse RS out. Holding a section of cardboard next to top opening of Purse on inside edge, fold top edge over cardboard, with a length of yarn, sl st opening closed around cardboard. Sl st rem piece of cardboard on opposite Purse edge of opening. Sl st handles into position. ✄

Funky Fringe-Sleeve Jacket
Continued from page 22

Continued from page 22

Rep rows 2–5 until top of Sleeve measures approximately 12 (13, 14, 15) inches, ending with a row 3 or row 5, do not fasten off.

Sleeve Shaping
Row 1 (RS): Working across top wide edge, ch 1, (sc, ch 1) 19 (21, 23, 25) times across edge, ending with sc in last st, remove stitch marker, turn. *(39 (43, 47, 51) sts)*

Row 2: Ch 1, sc in first sc, sc in next ch-1 sp, *ch 1, sk next sc, sc in next ch-1 sp, rep from * across, ending with sc in last sc, turn.

Row 3: Sl st in each of next 3 (3, 3, 5) sts, ch 1, sc in same st as last sl st, work in pat across to last 2 (2, 2, 3) sts, turn. *(35 (39, 43, 45) sts)*

Row 4: Work in pat across row, turn.

Row 5: Ch 1, sc in first sc, sc dec over next 2 sts, work in pat across row to last 3 sts, sc dec over next 2 sts, sc in last sc, turn. *(33 (37, 41, 43) sts)*

Rows 6–11 (6–9, 6–11, 6–11): Rep rows 4 and 5. *(27 (33, 35, 37) sts)*

Row 12 (10, 12, 12): Ch 1, sc in same st as beg ch-1, sc dec over next 2 sts, work in pat to last 3 sts, sc dec over next 2 sts, sc in last sc, turn. Rep row 12 (10, 12, 12) until 7 (9, 11, 33) sts rem, fasten off.

Finishing
To join shoulder seams, with RS of Back and Front facing, attach yarn with a sl st to top right corner, ch 1, working through both thicknesses, sc in same sp as sl st, *ch 1, sc

in next ch-1 sp, rep from * across to end of shoulder, fasten off.

With RS of body and Sleeve facing, attach yarn with sl st at underarm side seam, ch 1, working through both thicknesses, sc in same sp as beg st, *ch 1, sk next st, sc in next st, rep from * to opposite side of sleeve, fasten off. For side and Sleeve seam, with RS of Back and Front facing, attach yarn with a sl st at bottom of side seam, ch 1, working through both thicknesses, sc in same sp as sl st, *ch 1, sk next st, sc in next st, rep from * along body and Sleeve, fasten off.

Mark position of 6 buttons on Left Front, top button at top edge and last button 1 inch up from bottom edge and rem 4 buttons evenly sp between.

Edging

Rnd 1: Attach yarn with sl st at bottom of left seam, ch 1, sc in same sp as sl st, *ch 1, sc in next ch-1 sp of foundation ch, rep from * to right front corner, (sc, ch 1, sc) in corner st, (ch 1, sk 1 st, sc in next st) 27 (27, 28, 28) times up Right Front edge to neck corner, (ch 1, sc) in same corner st, (ch 1, sc) around neck edge, working (sc, ch 1, sc) in opposite neckline corner, (ch 1, sk next st, sc in next st) 27 (27, 28, 28) times down Left Front to bottom corner, (ch 1, sc) in same st as last sc, (ch 1, sc in next ch-1 sp of foundation ch) across rem foundation ch, ch 1, join in beg sc.

Rnd 2: Sl st in next ch-1 sp, ch 1, sc in same sp as beg ch-1, *ch 1, sc in next ch-1 sp, rep from * around, working (sc, ch 1, sc) in each corner sp and work buttonholes on Right Front at each marker working (ch 2, sk next 2 sts, sc in next st) for each buttonhole, join in beg sc.

Rnd 3: Sl st into ch-1 sp, ch 1, sc in same sp, *ch 1, sc in next ch-1 sp, rep from * around, working (sc, ch 1, sc) in each corner ch-1 sp and working in pat across each ch-2 sp of each buttonhole, join in beg sc, fasten off. Fold a double strand violet, pass through shank of button, pass strands through left edge opposite buttonholes, secure ends on WS. ✄

Mango Lace Top
Continued from page 15

Front Armhole Shaping

Working in established pat, inc 1 st at each end of next row, then every other row 4 (5, 6, 7) times, ending with a WS row. *(60 (66, 72, 78) sts)*

Body

Rnd 1 (RS): Now working in rnds, ch 1, *sc in next st, tsc in next st, rep from * across front, ch 10 (12, 14, 16), working across back *(working sts in unused lps of beg ch)*, (sc in next st, tsc in next st) across, ch 10 (12, 14, 16), do not join.

Rnd 2: Working in each st and ch around, work *sc in next st, tsc in next st, rep from * around. *(140 (156, 172, 188) sts)*

Rnd 3: *Sc in next st, tsc in next st, rep from * around.

Rep rnd 3 until body is 11 inches from beg, do not fasten off.

Bottom Edging

Rnd 1: Ch 1, (sc, ch 3, dc) in next st, sk next 1 (2, 3, 1) sts, *(sc, ch 3, dc) in next st, sk next 2 sts, rep from * around, join in beg sc, fasten off.

Neck & Armhole Edging

Rnd 1 (RS): With size D hook, attach yarn at opening, ch 1, sc evenly sp around opening, working in multiples of 3 sts, join in beg sc.

Rnd 2: Ch 1, *(sc, ch 3, dc) in next st, sk next 2 sts, rep from * around, join in beg sc, fasten off. ✄

Amethyst Shell
Continued from page 23

Body

Rnd 1: Beg at bottom edge, with A, ch 114 (126, 138, 150) using care not to twist ch, sl st to join in first ch to form a ring, ch 1, sc in each ch around, join in beg sc, turn. *(114 (126, 138, 150) sc)*

Rnd 2: Ch 1, *sc in **front lp** *(see Stitch Guide)* of next st, sc in **back lp** *(see Stitch Guide)* of next st, rep from * around, join in beg sc, turn.

Rnds 3 & 4: Rep rnd 2. At the end of last rep, fasten off.

Rnd 5 (RS): With B, rep rnd 2.

Rnd 6: With C, rep rnd 2.

Rnd 7: With B, rep rnd 2.

Rnd 8: With C, rep rnd 2, fasten off C.

Rnd 9: With B, rep rnd 2, fasten off B.

Rnds 10-14: With A, rep rnd 2.

Rnds 15-19: Rep rnds 5-9.

Rnds 20-35 (20-37, 20-41, 20-43): With A, rep rnd 2, at the end of last rep, fasten off. Place Body on flat surface with the beg of rnds at center facing. Using st markers, mark the center back 47 (51, 55, 59) sts for shell Back, make 10 (12, 14, 16) sts on each side of Back for armholes, the rem 47 (51, 55, 59) sts are for the shell Front.

Back

Row 1: Now working in rows, attach A with sl st in first marked st for back placement, ch 1, working in established pat of sc in front lp, sc in back lp of sts, work across next 46 (50, 54, 58) sts, turn. *(47 (51, 55, 59) sc)*

Row 2: Ch 1, working in established pat, **sc dec** *(see Stitch Guide)* over next 2 sc, work in pat across to last 2 sts, sc dec over next 2 sts, turn. *(45 (49, 53, 57) sc)*

Rows 3-9 (3-10, 3-11, 3-12): Rep row 2 a total of 7 (8, 9, 10) rows. *(31 (33, 35, 37) sc)*

Rows 10-19 (11-22, 12-25, 13-27): Ch 1, working in established pat of sc in front lp, sc in back lp, work even in pat on rem sts, turn. At the end of last rep, fasten off.

Front

Rep instructions for Back.
At the end of last rep, do not fasten off.

Turtleneck

Rnd 1: Now working in rnds, working across front, ch 1, turn, work in established sc pat across front, pick up back and work in pat across back, join in beg sc, turn. *(62 (66, 70, 74) sc)*

Rnds 2-19: Ch 1, work in established pat of sc in front lp, sc in back lp around, join in beg sc, turn. At the end of rnd 19, fasten off.

Armhole Edging
Make 2.

Rnd 1 (RS): Attach A at center underarm, ch 1, sc evenly sp around armhole opening, join in beg sc, fasten off.

Bottom Edging
Rnd 1 (RS):

Attach A in opposite side of foundation ch, ch 1, sc in same st as beg ch-1, sc evenly sp around bottom edge of shell, join in beg sc, fasten off. ✂

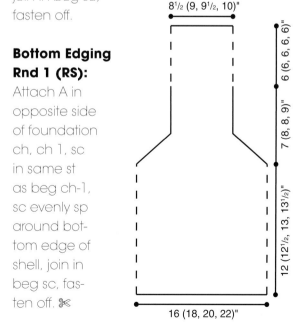

8¹/₂ (9, 9¹/₂, 10)"

6 (6, 6, 6)"

7 (8, 8, 9)"

12 (12¹/₂, 13, 13¹/₂)"

16 (18, 20, 22)"

Dotted lines indicate section worked in rnds.

Desert Diva Crisscross Top
Continued from page 24

Pattern Notes
Weave in loose ends as work progresses. Join rounds with a slip stitch unless otherwise stated.

Special Stitch
Cross-stitch (cross-st): Sk next st, dc in next st, dc in sk st.

Panel
Make 2.
Row 1: With desert, ch 103 (105, 107, 109) sc in 2nd ch from hook, sc in each rem ch across, turn. *(102 (104, 106, 108) sts)*
Row 2: Ch 1, sc in each st across, fasten off, turn.
Row 3: Attach Sahara with a sl st in first st, ch 3 *(counts as first dc throughout)*, [**cross-st** *(see Special Stitch)* over next 2 sts] 50 (51, 52, 53) times, dc in last st, fasten off, turn. *(50 (51, 52, 53) cross-sts)*
Row 4: Draw up a lp of desert in first dc, ch 1, sc in each dc across, turn. *(102 (104, 106, 108) sc)*
Row 5: Rep row 2.
Row 6: Rep row 3.
Rows 7–18 (7–21, 7–24, 7–27): Rep rows 4–6.

Row 19 (22, 25, 28): Draw up a lp of desert, ch 1, sc in same dc as beg ch-1, sc in each dc across, turn.
Row 20 (23, 26, 29): Ch 1, sc in each sc across, fasten off.

Waistband
Make 2.
Row 1: With desert, ch 11, sc in 2nd ch from hook, sc in each rem ch across, turn. (10 sc)
Row 2: Ch 1, working in **back lp** *(see Stitch Guide)* of each st only, sc in each st across, turn. Rep row 2 until Waistband measures 11 (12, 13, 14) inches unstretched. At the end of last rep, fasten off.

Assembly
Using diagram as a guide, with desert, overlap short ends of Panels at center front to fit width of Waistband, sl st Waistband to Panels. Cross Panels at center back to fit Waistband, sl st Waistband to Panels. Fold RS tog and sl st side seams following diagram. Turn RS out and attach button according to diagram. Attach desert with sl st across from button and 1 st down, ch 4, sk 1 st, sl st in next st, fasten off. ✄

Midsummer Dream Skirt
Continued from page 16

Special Stitches
Extended double crochet (edc): Yo, insert hook in indicated st, yo, draw up a lp, yo, draw through 2 lps on hook, yo, draw through 1 lp, yo, draw through rem 2 lps on hook.
Surface chain stitch (surface ch st): With RS facing, holding ribbon yarn on WS, insert hook in indicated sp, draw up a lp, (insert hook in next sp between sts, yo, draw up a lp and draw through st on hook) across edge.

Skirt Body
Note: *Skirt total length is 15 inches, the Hip Band measures 3½ inches and Skirt Body 12 inches. Skirt Body is crocheted vertically. To make skirt body longer, using gauge as a guide, add desired number of chs. Always maintain the 4 edc and 10 tr on the bottom edge of the skirt body. The treble section of the body of the skirt is the bottom edge.*

Skirt Body

Row 1 (RS): With size G hook and spruce, ch 40, hdc in 3rd ch from hook, hdc in each rem ch across, turn. *(39 hdc)*

Row 2: Ch 3 *(counts as first dc throughout)*, dc in each of next 24 sts, **edc** *(see Special Stitches)* in each of next 4 sts, tr in each of next 10 sts, turn.

Row 3: Ch 2 *(counts as first hdc throughout)*, working in **front lp** *(see Stitch Guide)* of each st, hdc in each st across, turn.

Row 4: Ch 2, hdc in each st across, turn.

Row 5: Ch 4 *(counts as first tr throughout)*, working in front lp of each st, tr in each of next 9 sts, edc in each of next 4 sts, dc in each rem st across, turn.

Row 6: Ch 2, hdc in each st across, turn.

Row 7: Ch 2, working in front lp of each st only, hdc in each st across, turn.

Rows 8-66 (8-72, 8-84, 8-90): Rep rows 2-7. At the end of last rep, fasten off.

Hip Band

Row 1 (WS): With size G hook and spruce, ch 91 (101, 121, 131) hdc in 3rd ch from hook, hdc in each rem ch across, turn. *(90 (100, 120, 130) hdc)*

Row 2: Ch 3, dc in each st across, turn.

Row 3: Ch 2, working in front lps only, hdc in same st as beg ch-2 *(hip inc)*, hdc in each st across to halfway point, 2 hdc in each of next 2 sts *(hip inc)*, hdc in each st across to last st, 2 hdc in last st *(hip inc)*, turn. *(94 (104, 124, 134) hdc)*

Row 4: Ch 3, dc in same st as beg ch-3, dc in each st across to hip inc, 2 dc in each of next 2 sts, dc in each rem st across to last st, 2 dc in last st, turn. *(98 (108, 128, 138) dc)*

Rows 5 & 6: Rep Rows 3 and 4. *(106 (116, 136, 146) sts)*

Row 7: Rep row 3, fasten off. *(110 (120, 140, 150) hdc)*

Joining

With size G hook, sl st row 7 to top edge of skirt. Beg at row 3 of Hip Band and working downward, sl st down side of rem Hip Band and down Skirt Body.

Bottom Trim

Rnd 1 (RS): With size G hook, attach spruce at bottom side seam of Skirt Body, ch 1, sc evenly sp around bottom edge of skirt, join in beg sc, fasten off.

Drawstring Belt

Measure waistline of skirt and add 24 inches to the length. With size J hook and 1 strand each spruce and ribbon yarn, make ch length needed, fasten off.

Starting at hip opening, weave drawstring over and under dc sts of row 2 of Hip Band. Tie drawstring in a bow.

Ribbon Surface Crochet

Working around bottom of skirt, position 8 (10, 10, 10) safety pins evenly sp around. Cut 8 (10, 10, 10) 4-yd lengths of ribbon yarn. If skirt is longer, add 3 inches of ribbon yarn per inch of skirt.

Beg at bottom edge of Skirt Body with size J hook and 1 strand of ribbon yarn, leaving a 4-inch tail at beg, work loose **surface ch st** *(see Special Stitches)* starting at skirt bottom working 1 surface ch st per st on row. At final st just below Hip Band, do not make surface ch, draw entire rem length of ribbon yarn through to RS to use rem for flower. *ch 4, sl st in rem free lp of row 6 of Hip Band directly above, ch 4, sl st in same st as last surface ch was worked on skirt body, rep from * twice, draw rem length to WS of Skirt Body and secure. Weave rem beg length into Bottom Trim or into WS of surface ch and remove safety pin. Rep ch and flower beg at each safety pin. ✂

Fabulous Finishing Touches

You'll be polished to perfection when you step out to greet the day (or night!) wearing one of these fabulous accessories. There are capelets for evening wear, ponchos for casual wear and scarves for any time! From your head to your feet, you'll be ready for any occasion in fashionable style.

Gold Nugget Skirt-cho

Design by Fredricka Schuh

Whether you wear it around the shoulders or hips, you'll sparkle like spun gold when you jazz up an evening outfit with this glittering cover-up.

INTERMEDIATE

5 BULKY

Finished Size

Child: small (medium, large)

Adult: (small, medium, large)

Pattern is written for child's small size with changes for child's larger sizes and adult sizes within brackets.

Materials

- Berroco Quest bulky (chunky) weight yarn (1¾ oz/82 yds/50g per hank):

    2 (3, 4, 4, 5, 6) hanks #9812 polished copper

- Size H/8/5mm crochet hook or size needed to obtain gauge

Gauge

10 sc = 2 inches; 7 rows = 2 inches
Check gauge to save time.

Pattern Notes

Weave in loose ends as work progresses.
Join rounds with a slip stitch unless otherwise stated.
Adjust neck ribbing to fit tightly enough to stay on when wearing off the shoulders.

Continued on page 58

Mixed Media Wrap

Design by Katherine Eng

Varied textures and harvest colors make this charming little wrap the perfect accompaniment to autumn's fabulous fashions.

INTERMEDIATE

Finished Size

23 inches long x 49 inches wide

5 BULKY

Materials

- Lion Brand Lion Suede bulky (chunky) weight yarn (3 oz/122 yds/85g per skein):
    2 skeins #133 spice
- Lion Brand Homespun bulky (chunky) weight yarn (6 oz/185 yds/ 170g per skein):
    1 skein #377 harvest
- Lion Brand Incredible bulky (chunky) weight ribbon yarn (1¾ oz/110 yds/50g per ball):
    2 balls oz #207 purple party
- Sizes G/6/4mm and H/8/5mm crochet hooks or size needed to obtain gauge
- 2 decorative ⅞-inch glass beads

Gauge

Size H hook: rnds 1 and 2 = 3¼ inches; completed square = 4 inches
Check gauge to save time.

Pattern Notes

Weave in loose ends as work progresses.
Join rounds with a slip stitch unless otherwise stated.
Size G hook is used for final border round only.
After first square, join squares while working round 3.

Square

Make 45.

Rnd 1 (RS): With size H hook and harvest, ch 4, sl st to join in first ch to form a ring, ch 3 (*counts as first dc throughout*), 2 dc in ring, (ch 2, 3 dc in ring) 3 times, ch 2, join in 3rd ch of beg ch-3, fasten off. (*12 dc, 4 ch-2 sps*)

Rnd 2: Draw up a lp of purple party in any ch-2 sp, ch 1, sc in same sp, *ch 1, sk next dc, (3 dc, ch 2, 3 dc) in next dc, ch 1**, sk next dc, sc in next ch-2 sp, rep from * around, ending last rep at **, join in beg sc, fasten off. (*24 dc, 4 corner ch-2 sps, 4 sc, 8 ch-1 sps*)

Continued on page 56

Funky Stripes Leg Warmers

Design by Mary Jane Hall

Kick it up a notch in hot fashion looks with fun, funky leg warmers that are perfect to wear with jeans and boots or a miniskirt and heels.

EASY

Finished Size
One size fits most
17 inches long

4 MEDIUM

5 BULKY

Materials
- Medium (worsted) weight yarn (3 oz/170 yds/85g per skein):
    1 skein gray
    1 oz each lilac, light raspberry, black, country blue, purple, leaf green, white and light gray
- Mohair-look bulky (chunky) weight yarn:
    1 oz each pastel yellow and rose
- Sizes F/5/3.75mm and H/8/5mm crochet hooks or sizes needed to obtain gauge

Pattern Notes
Weave in loose ends as work progresses. Join rounds with a slip stitch unless otherwise stated.

Gauge
Size F hook: 4 sc = 1 inch; 4 sc rows = 1 inch
Size H hook: 4 puff sts = 3½ inches; 4 sc rnds = 1¼ inches; 10 sc = 3 inches
Check gauge to save time.

Special Stitches

Bulky puff stitch (bulky puff st): Insert hook in indicated st, yo, draw up a lp approximately ¾-inch, (yo, insert hook in same st, yo, draw up a lp approximately ¾-inch) twice, yo, draw through all 6 lps on hook, ch 1 to lock.

Puff stitch (puff st): Insert hook in indicated st, yo, draw up a lp approximately ¾-inch, (yo, insert hook in same st, yo, draw up a lp approximately ¾-inch) 3 times, yo, draw through all 8 lps on hook, ch 1 to lock.

Top Ribbed Cuff

Row 1: With size F hook and gray, ch 11, sc in 2nd ch from hook, sc in each rem ch across, turn. *(10 sc)*

Row 2: Ch 1, working in **back lps** *(see Stitch Guide)* sc in each st across, turn.

Rows 3–39: Rep row 2.

Row 40: With WS facing, holding row 39 to opposite side of foundation ch, sl st in each st across, fasten off, turn Cuff RS out.

Leg

Rnd 1 (RS): Now working in rnds, with size F hook, attach gray in side edge of Cuff, ch 1, sc in same row as beg ch-1, sc in each of next 38 rows, join in beg sc, fasten off. *(39 sc)*

Rnd 2: With size H hook, attach pastel yellow in any sc, ch 3 *(does not counts as a st)*, **bulky puff st** *(see Special Stitches)* in same st as beg ch-3, ch 2, sk next 2 sts, (bulky puff st in next st, ch 2, sk next 2 sts) around, join in 3rd ch of beg ch-3, fasten off. *(13 bulky puff sts)*

Rnd 3: Attach purple in top of first bulky puff st, ch 1, sc in same st, 2 sc in next ch-2 sp, (sc in top of next bulky puff st, 2 sc in next ch-2 sp) around, join in beg sc. *(39 sc)*

Rnd 4: Ch 1, sc in each sc around, join in beg sc, fasten off.

Rnd 5: Draw up a lp of rose, ch 1, sc in each sc around, join in beg sc.

Continued on page 55

Newsboy Cap & Medallion Belt

Designs by Mary Jane Hall

Go retro with a funky cap and belt combo that's perfect with jeans for a casual day of shopping at the mall or hanging out with friends.

INTERMEDIATE

4 MEDIUM

Finished Sizes

Cap: One size fits most
Belt: 2 x 32 inches,
　excluding ribbon

Materials

- Red Heart Super Saver medium (worsted) weight yarn (7 oz/364 yds/198g per skein):
　2 skeins #382 country blue
- Sizes E/4/3.5mm and F/5/3.75mm crochet hooks or sizes needed to obtain gauge
- 28 inches ⅜-inch-wide off-white satin ribbon
- Straight pins

Gauge

Size F hook: 4 sts = 1 inch; 3 rows = 1 inch; medallion motif = 2 inches in diameter
Size E hook: 5 sc = 1 inch; 5 sc rows = 1 inch
Check gauge to save time.

Pattern Notes

Weave in loose ends as work progresses. Join rounds with a slip stitch unless otherwise stated.

Cap

Wedge
Make 7.
Row 1: With size F hook, ch 2, 2 sc in 2nd ch from hook, turn. *(2 sts)*

Row 2: Ch 2 (*does not count as a hdc*), hdc in first sc, (sc, hdc) in next sc, turn. (*3 sts*)

Row 3: Ch 1, sc in first hdc, hdc in next sc, (sc, hdc) in next hdc, turn. (*4 sts*)

Row 4: Ch 1, sc in first hdc, hdc in next sc, sc in next hdc, (hdc, sc) in next sc, turn. (*5 sts*)

Row 5: Ch 2, hdc in first sc, sc in next hdc, hdc in next sc, sc in next hdc, (hdc, sc) in next sc, turn. (*6 sts*)

Rows 6–23: Work in pat of hdc in sc and sc in hdc across each row and working 2 sts in last st of each row, turn. (*24 sts*)

Using diagram as a guide, with straight pins, pin 2 wedges tog, starting at row 1 center point of pieces, sl st a ¼-inch seam across edge, because corner is curved so that Cap will fit band, seam at widest point will be 1 inch. Join rem 5 Cap Wedges in same manner.

Cap Band

Row 1: Ch 5, sc in 2nd ch from hook, sc in each rem ch across, turn. (*4 sc*)

Row 2: Ch 1, sc in each sc across, turn. Rep row 2 until Cap Band measures 24 inches. Holding row 1 to last row and working through both thicknesses, sl st across forming a circle, fasten off.

With RS tog, pin Cap Band to cap, attach yarn, easing in fullness, sl st pieces tog, fasten off.

Brim

Note: *Brim is worked across 3 Wedge shapes on the hat, but the first row will be worked between the 2 seams (center) of 1 Cap Wedge.*

Row 1: With size E hook, with RS of top of Cap facing, attach yarn in line with Wedge seam in Cap Band, ch 1, **sc dec** (*see Stitch Guide*) over same st yarn was attached and next st, sc in next 6 sts, sc dec over next 2 sts, sc in next 5 sts, sc dec over next 2 sts (*14 sts between 2 seams on cap*), fasten off, do not turn.

Row 2: With RS of top of Cap facing, attach yarn in first sc of previous row, ch 1, sc in same

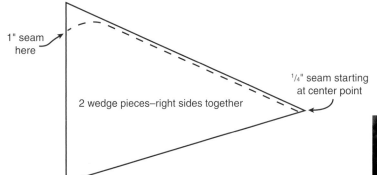

1" seam here

1/4" seam starting at center point

2 wedge pieces–right sides together

With hook, weave rem length through tops of sts of rnd 3, draw end to close opening, knot to secure. Attach to center top of Cap.

st as beg ch-1, sc in each of next 2 sts, 2 sc in next st, sc in each of next 6 sts, 2 sc in next st, sc in each of next 3 sts, fasten off. *(16 sc)*

Row 3: With RS of top of Cap facing, attach yarn 2 sts to the right of first st of previous row, ch 1, sc in each of next 2 sts, sc in each of next 16 sts of previous row, sc in each of next 2 sts, fasten off, do not turn. *(20 sc)*

Row 4: With RS of top of Cap facing, attach yarn 2 sts to the right of first st of previous row, ch 1, sc in each of next 2 sts, sc in each of next 2 sts, 2 sc in next st, sc in each of next 15 sts, 2 sc in next st, sc in next st, sc in each of next 2 sts on band, fasten off, do not turn. *(26 sc)*

Rows 5–8: Rep row 4, attaching yarn 2 sts to the right of first st of previous row, working inc above the 2 inc sts and working 2 sts beyond previous row, fasten off, do not turn. *(50 sc)*

Rows 9 & 10: With RS of top of Cap facing, attach yarn 2 sts to the right of first st of previous row, ch 1, sc in each of next 2 sts, sc in each sc across of previous row, sc in each of next 2 sts beyond sts of previous row, fasten off, do not turn. *(58 sc)*

Cap Button

Rnd 1: With hook size F, ch 3, sl st to join in first ch to form a ring, ch 2 *(counts as first hdc throughout)*, 7 hdc in ring, join in 2nd ch of beg ch-2. *(8 hdc)*

Rnd 2: Ch 2, working in back lp only, hdc in same st as beg ch-2, 2 hdc in each rem st around, join in 2nd ch of beg ch-2. *(16 hdc)*

Rnd 3: Ch 2, hdc in each hdc around, join in 2nd ch of beg ch-2, leaving a length of yarn, fasten off.

Belt

Medallion
Make 16.

Rnd 1: With size F hook, ch 3, sl st to join in first ch of ch-3 to form a ring, ch 1, 12 sc in ring, join in beg sc. *(12 sc)*

Rnd 2: Ch 1, sc in same sc as beg ch-1, ch 3, sk next sc, (sc in next sc, ch 3, sk next sc) 5 times, join in beg sc. *(6 ch-3 sps)*

Rnd 3: (Sl st, 2 sc, sl st) in each ch-3 sp around, join in first sl st, fasten off.

Join Medallions at 2 points of 2 sc groups on each Medallion to previous Medallion until all are joined in a strip.

Draw ribbon through ch-3 sp at each end of Belt, tie ends in a bow. ✀

Heart Choker

Design by Mary Jane Hall

A little goes a long way with this dainty, fashionable necklace stitched in jute and accented with an antiqued silver heart charm.

EASY

Finished Size

16 inches long, excluding ends for tying

Materials

- 6 feet waxed green fine macramé jute
- Size D/3/3.25mm crochet hook or size needed to obtain gauge
- Heart charm

Gauge

7 chs = 1½ inches; 3 picots = 1½ inches
Check gauge to save time.

Pattern Note

Weave in loose ends as work progresses.

Choker

Row 1: Leaving a 5-inch length at beg, ch 35, sl metal circle at top of heart charm through loose end of jute, ch 35, leaving a 5-inch length, fasten off.

Row 2: Attach jute on same side of ch that heart will be hanging down, *ch 2, sl st in first ch *(for picot)*, sk next 2 chs, sl st in next ch, rep from * across, eliminating the picot that would be where the heart is hanging, sl st behind heart instead of working a picot, so as not to cover the charm; when sl stitching around heart, use care not to cover heart or twist it, end with sl st in last ch, fasten off. *(22 picots)*

Finishing

Tie a knot at each end of choker next to first and last st of row to hold sts in place.
Place Choker around neckline, tie ends in a bow at center back. ✂

Mocha Tweed Purse

Design by Mary Jane Hall

Grab this trendy, go-anywhere little bag when you're headed out for a day of shopping and a tasty cup of cappuccino with your friends.

INTERMEDIATE

Finished Size
7 x 11½ inches

MEDIUM

BULKY

Materials
- Bernat Soft Bouclé bulky (chunky) weight yarn (5 oz/255 yds/140g per skein):
    - 1 skein #22927 misty shades
- Caron Perfect Match medium (worsted) weight yarn (7 oz/355 yds/198g per skein):
    - 1 skein espresso
- Sizes G/6/4mm and K/10½/6.5mm crochet hooks or size needed to obtain gauge
- 19 inches metal chain for handle
- 2 round metal 1¼-inch key rings
- 2¼-inch round metal ring
- 2-inch metal latch hook
- Stitch marker
- Straight pins

Gauge
Size K hook: 4 sts = 1½ inches; 4 rows = 1½ inches
Check gauge to save time.

Pattern Notes
Weave in loose ends as work progresses.
Join rounds with a slip stitch unless otherwise stated.

Purse Front
Row 1 (RS): Beg at bottom edge of purse, with size K hook and 1 strand of each color held tog, ch 24, sc in 2nd ch from hook, sc in each rem ch across, turn. *(23 sc)*

Row 2: Ch 1, sc in each sc across, turn.

Rows 3–14: Rep row 2.

Row 15: Ch 1, **sc dec** *(see Stitch Guide)* over next 2 sc, sc in each sc across to last 2 sc, sc dec over next 2 sc, turn. *(21 sc)*

Rows 16 & 17: Rep row 15. At the end of row 17, fasten off. *(17 sc)*

Purse Back
Rows 1–17: Rep rows 1–17 of Purse Front.

Bottom & Side Insert

Row 1: With size K hook and 1 strand each color held tog, ch 5, sc in 2nd ch from hook, sc in each rem ch across, turn. *(4 sc)*

Row 2: Ch 1, sc in each sc across, turn. Rep row 2 until Insert measures 23½ inches.

Tab

Row 1: With size G hook and espresso, ch 6, sc in 2nd ch from hook, sc in each rem ch across, turn. *(5 sc)*

Rows 2–5: Ch 1, sc in each sc across, turn.

Continued on page 57

Flowers & Lace Poncho

Design by Diane Poellot

When the weather cools, you'll have just the right minimal coverage in this lacy jewel-toned poncho. It's perfect with jeans or at the office.

INTERMEDIATE

4 MEDIUM

Finished Size
33 inches around neckline, 60 inches around bottom and 16 inches long

Materials
- Caron Simply Soft medium (worsted) weight yarn (5 oz/147g per skein):
  2 skeins #9810 brocade print
- Size I/9/5.5mm crochet hook or size needed to obtain gauge

Gauge
Flower = 2½ inches; 4 chs = 1 inch
Check gauge to save time.

Pattern Notes
Weave in loose ends as work progresses. Join rounds with a slip stitch unless otherwise stated.

Poncho
Row 1 (RS): Ch 7, (sl st in 4th ch from hook (*ring formed*), ch 3, (2 dc, ch 3, sl st, ch 3, 2 dc) in ring*, ch 10) 12 times, ending last rep at *, turn to work along top of this row.

Row 2 (RS): (Ch 3, sl st into ring (*center of flower*), ch 3, (2 dc, ch 3, sl st, ch 3, 2 dc) in ring, sk next 2 chs of foundation ch, sl st in next ch, ch 2, sk next 2 chs, sl st in next ch) across, ch 3, remove lp from hook, insert hook in 3rd ch of beg ch-3 of this row, dc in beg foundation ch to join row.

Continued on page 58

Sparkling Jewels Scarf

Design by Katherine Eng

A delicious blend of sparkling mohair and lustrous ribbon yarns creates the shimmer and shine in this soft, cozy scarf.

 BEGINNER

 5 BULKY

Finished Size
5½ x 53½ inches, excluding fringe

Materials
- Lion Brand Moonlight Mohair bulky (chunky) weight yarn (1¾ oz/82 yds/50g per ball):
    2 balls #204 rainbow falls
- Lion Brand Incredible ribbon yarn (1¾ oz/110 yds/50g per ball):
    1 ball #208 copper penny
- Size H/8/5mm crochet hook or size needed to obtain gauge

Gauge
First 3 rows = 1 inch; 3 sc = 1 inch
Check gauge to save time.

Pattern Notes
Weave in loose ends as work progresses.
Scarf is crocheted from center outward.

Continued on page 57

Evening Elegance Capelet

Design by Tammy Hildebrand

Top an elegant evening dress with this soft, shimmering capelet stitched in lustrous lightweight rayon-blend yarn and fastened with a dazzling brooch.

INTERMEDIATE

4 MEDIUM

Materials

- Patons Katrina medium (worsted) weight yarn (3½ oz/163 yds/100g per skein):
    3 skeins #10128 dawn
- Size I/9/5.5mm crochet hook or size needed to obtain gauge

Finished Size

47 inches around bottom and 13 inches long

Gauge

9 sc = 4 inches; rows 1 and 2 = ¾ inch
Check gauge to save time.

Pattern Note

Weave in loose ends as work progresses.

Special Stitch

Cross-Stitch (cross-st): Sk next st, dc in next st, working over previous dc, dc in sk st.

Capelet

Row 1: Ch 61, sc in 2nd ch from hook, sc in each rem ch across, turn. *(60 sc)*

Continued on page 59

Suede Luxury Scarf

Design by Mary Ann Sipes

Contrasting colors of suedelike yarn and a loopy chain-stitch fringe add up to luxury and style in this striking scarf with a reversible pattern.

INTERMEDIATE

5 BULKY

Finished Size
6¼ x 62 inches, excluding fringe

Materials
- Lion Brand Lion Suede bulky (chunky) weight yarn (3 oz/122 yds/85g per ball):
    2 balls each #098 ecru and #178 teal
- Size I/9/5.5mm crochet hook
- Size J/10/6mm double-ended crochet hook or size needed to obtain gauge

Gauge
Size J hook: 3 puff sts = 2 inches; 4 row pattern = ⅞ inch; 22 rows = 5 inches Check gauge to save time.

Pattern Note
Weave in loose ends as work progresses.

Special Stitch
Puff stitch (puff st): Draw up a lp in next ch sp, yo, draw up a lp in same sp.

Scarf

Row 1 (RS): With double-ended hook and ecru, ch 18, draw up a lp in 2nd ch from hook, yo, draw up a lp in same ch, (sk next ch, **puff st** *(see Special Stitch)* in next ch) across, turn. *(28 lps on hook)*

Row 2: With teal, draw through first lp on hook, (ch 1, yo, draw through 4 lps on hook) across, do not turn.

Row 3: Ch 1, (draw up a lp in next ch sp, yo, draw up a lp in same sp) across, turn.

Row 4: With ecru, rep row 2.

Row 5: Rep row 3.

Rows 6–280: Rep rows 2–5, ending with row 4, do not fasten off.

First Edging

Row 1: Ch 1, (2 sc over next lp) 9 times, turn.

Loopy Fringe

Row 1: Working across the edge with ecru and size I hook, (ch 50, sk next sc, sl st in next sc) 8 times, ch 50, sl st in last ch, fasten off. *(9 lps)*

Row 2: With size I hook, attach teal with sl st in first sk sc, (ch 50, sl st in next sk sc) 7 times, ch 50, sl st in last st, fasten off.

2nd Edging

Row 1: Working on opposite end of Scarf, with predominantly teal side facing, attach ecru with sl st in first ch, ch 1, 2 sc in same st as joining, (sk next ch, 2 sc in next ch) 8 times, turn.

Rep rows 1 and 2 of Loopy Fringe on end of Scarf. ✄

Funky Stripes Leg Warmers
Continued from page 43

Rnd 6: Rep rnd 4.

Rnd 7: Draw up a lp of light raspberry, ch 3, **puff st** *(see Special Stitches)* in same st as beg ch-3, ch 2, sk next 2 sts, (puff st in next st, ch 2, sk next 2 sts) around, join in 3rd ch of beg ch-3, fasten off. *(13 puff sts)*

Rnd 8: Attach black in top of first puff st, ch 1, sc in same st, 2 sc in next ch-2 sp, (sc in top of next puff st, 2 sc in next ch-2 sp) around, join in beg sc. *(39 sc)*

Rnd 9: Rep rnd 4.

Rnds 10 & 11: With lilac, rep rnds 5 and 6.

Rnd 12: With leaf green, rep rnd 7.

Rnds 13 & 14: With white, rep rnds 8 and 9.

Rnds 15 & 16: With country blue, rep rnds 5 and 6.

Rnd 17: Rep rnd 2.

Rnd 18: Rep rnd 5.

Rnd 19: Ch 1, sc in each sc around, join in beg sc.

Rnd 20: Rep rnd 4.

Rnds 21 & 22: With gray, rep rnds 5 and 6.

Rnd 23: Rep rnd 7.

Rnds 24 & 25: With purple, rep rnds 8 and 9.

Rnds 26 & 27: With light gray, rep rnds 5 and 6.

Rnd 28: With black, rep rnd 7.

Rnds 29 & 30: With lilac, rep rnds 8 and 9.

Rnds 31 & 32: With white, rep rnds 5 and 6.

Rnd 33: With leaf green, rep rnd 7.

Rnd 34: With gray, rep rnd 8, fasten off. *(39 sc)*

Bottom Ribbed Cuff

Rows 1–40: Rep rows 1–40 of Top Ribbed Cuff.

Joining

With RS tog of rnd 34 of Leg and edge of Bottom Ribbed Cuff, attach gray, working through both thicknesses, sl st in each st around, fasten off. ✄

Mixed Media Wrap
Continued from page 40

Rnd 3: Draw up a lp of spice in first ch-1 sp to the left of any corner, ch 1, (sc, ch 2, sc) in same sp, *sk next sc, (sc, ch 2, sc) in next ch-1 sp, ch 1, sk next 3 dc, (sc, ch 4, sc) in next ch-2 sp, ch 1, sk next 3 dc**, (sc, ch 2, sc) in next ch-1 sp, rep from * around, ending last rep at **, join in beg sc, fasten off.

Using diagram as a guide, join squares on rnd 3 on 1 or 2 sides as necessary. Connect at corner ch-4 sps and 2 ch-2 sps (*or lps*).

In pattern st of rnd 3, join ch-4 sps by ch 2, drop lp from hook, draw lp under to over through opposite ch-4 sp, ch 2 and continue. To join ch-2 sps, ch 1, drop lp from hook, draw lp under to over through opposite ch-2 sp, ch 1 and continue. To join where 4 corners meet, ch 2, drop lp from hook, draw lp under to over through opposite ch-4 sp, ch 1, drop lp from hook, sk next ch-4 sp, draw lp under to over through next ch-4 sp, ch 2 and continue.

Continue joining squares as indicated in diagram.

working across top, *(sc, ch 2, sc) in next ch-1 sp, sc in next 2 ch-2 sps and next ch-1 sp**, sc in next ch-4 sp; ch 1 (*over joining seam*), sc in next ch-4 sp, rep from * across, ending last rep at **, rep corner pattern, working across side, (rep pattern from * to **, rep corner pattern, rep from * to **, sk next ch-4 sp, sc in next (*center*) ch-4 sp, sk next ch-4 sp) 5 times. Work first 2 sides around bottom square, rep from * to **, rep former pattern, (sc, ch 2, sc) in next ch-1 sp, sc in next ch-2 sp, ch 3, sc in side of last sc worked, sc in next ch-2 sp, (sc, ch 2, sc) in next ch-1 sp, rep corner pattern, rep between ( ) 5 times, rep from * to **, join in beg sc, fasten off.

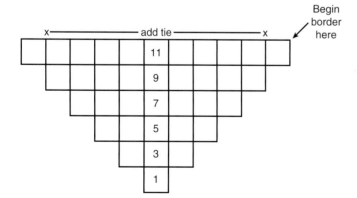

Border

Rnd 4: Working in specified sts only, sk over other sts, with size G hook, draw up a lp of spice in top right-hand corner ch-4 sp (*see Diagram*), ch 1, work corner pattern (sc, ch 2, sc, ch 3, sc, ch 2, sc) in corner ch-4 sp,

Tie
Make 2.
With a 5-yd length of spice, fold length in half and draw center fold through first ch-2 sp on side edge of 2nd square from top end square at both sides, ch out 45, leaving a 6-inch length, fasten off. Add 1 length 12 inches long to end of ch, draw bead into tails and tie tails in an overhand knot under bead. Trim ends to desired length. ✂

Mocha Tweed Purse
Continued from page 49

Row 6: Holding 2½-inch metal ring next to row 5 and working over ring, ch 1, sc in each of next 5 sc, fasten off.

Assembly

Place a st marker at bottom center of Purse Front and Purse Back. Fold Bottom and Side Insert in half, pin center of strip to bottom center of Purse Front. Pin first and last row of Bottom and Side Insert to each side of row 14 of Purse Front.

Rnd 1: With size G hook, attach espresso in side edge of row 14 of Purse Front, working through both thicknesses, ch 1, sc evenly sp down side edge, across bottom to within center 4 sts, holding lp of latch hook next to bottom center of Purse Front and working over latch, sc in each of next 4 sts, sc evenly sp across rem of bottom and up opposite side, ending at opposite side of row 14, sc up side edge of dec rows, across top edge of Purse and down opposite edge of dec section, join in beg sc, fasten off.

Rnd 2: With size G hook, attach espresso in side edge of row 14 of Purse Back, working through both thicknesses, ch 1, sc evenly sp down side edge, across bottom, up opposite side, ending at row 14, sc up side edge of dec rows, across top edge of Purse to center 5 sc, holding opposite side of foundation ch of Tab at center and working through both thicknesses, sc in each of next 5 sts, sc across rem of top edge, sc across side edge of dec rows, join in beg sc, fasten off.

Purse Handle

Attach a key ring to each end of metal ch. Holding key ring to center end of Bottom and Side Insert, with size G hook, attach espresso, ch 1, working over key ring, work 3 sc in end of Bottom and Side Insert securing key ring in place.

Rep attaching opposite end with key ring to opposite end of Bottom and Side Insert.

With size G hook and espresso, make a ch approximately 19 inches long, weave through chains of Handle, secure ends, fasten off. ✂

Sparkling Jewels Scarf
Continued from page 52

When attaching and fastening off yarn colors, leave a 6-inch length at beg and end.

Scarf

First half

Row 1 (RS): Beg at center, with rainbow falls, ch 160, sc in 2nd ch from hook, sc in each rem ch across, turn. *(159 sc)*

Row 2: Ch 1, sc in first sc, (ch 1, sk 1 sc, sc in next sc) across, fasten off, turn.

Row 3: Draw up a lp of copper penny in first sc, ch 1, sc in same sc as beg ch-1, sc in next ch-1 sp, (ch 1, sk next sc, sc in next ch-1 sp) across, ending with sc in last sc, fasten off, turn.

Row 4: Draw up a lp of rainbow falls in first sc, ch 1, sc in each sc and each ch-1 sp across, turn.

Row 5: Ch 1, sc in first sc, (ch 1, sk 1 sc, sc in next sc) across, turn.

Row 6: Ch 1, sc in each sc and each ch-1 sp across, turn.

Row 7: Rep row 2.
Row 8: Rep row 3.
Row 9: Draw up a lp of rainbow falls in first sc, ch 1, (sc, ch 2, sc) in first sc, *sk next sc, (sc, ch 2, sc) in next ch-1 sp, rep from * across, ending with sk next sc, (sc, ch 2, sc) in last sc, fasten off.

2nd half
Row 1 (RS): Working on opposite side of foundation ch, draw up a lp of rainbow falls in first ch, ch 1, sc in same ch as beg ch-1, sc in each rem ch across, turn. *(159 sc)*
Rows 2–9: Rep rows 2–9 of First Half.

Fringe
Cut 12-inch lengths of matching yarn and ribbon to add to ends of rows. Add 1 length where there are tails and 2 lengths where there are none. Draw lengths through ends of rows, fold in half and tie in an overhand knot. Trim to desired length. ✄

Gold Nugget Skirt-cho
Continued from page 38

Special Stitch
Shell: 5 dc in indicated st.

Ribbed Neck/Waistband
Row 1: Ch 11 (11, 11, 21, 21, 21) sc in 2nd ch from hook, sc in each rem ch across, turn. *(10 (10, 10, 20, 20, 20) sc)*
Row 2: Ch 1, working in **back lp** *(see Stitch Guide)* of each st, sc in each st across, turn.
Rows 3–56 (64, 72, 76, 84, 92): Rep row 2.
Row 57 (65, 73, 77, 85, 93): Holding last row to opposite side of foundation, sl st in each st across, do not fasten off.

Body
Rnd 1: Now working in rnds, working in side edge of ribbing rows, ch 1, sc in same row as beg ch-1, (ch 5, sk next row, sc in end of next row) around, ending with sk last row, ch 2, dc in beg sc. *(28 (32, 36, 38, 42, 46) ch-5 lps)*
Rnd 2: Ch 1, sc in same ch sp as beg ch-1, *shell *(see Special Stitch)* in next sc, sc in next ch lp, ch 5, sc in next lp, rep from * around, ending with ch 2, dc in beg sc. *(14 (16, 18, 19, 21, 23) shells)*
Rnd 3: Ch 1, sc in same ch sp as beg ch-1, *ch 5, sc in center dc of next shell, ch 5, sc in next ch-5 sp, rep from * around, ending with ch 2, dc in beg sc.
Rnds 4–10 (12, 14, 18, 20, 22): Rep rnds 2 and 3 or to desired length. At the end of last rep, fasten off.

Neck/Waistband Tie
Ch 150 for child's sizes and 200 for adult sizes, fasten off.
Starting at center front of Ribbed Neck/Waistband, approximately 2 sts down from top edge of ribbing, weave through ribbing rows. Tie ends in a bow at center. ✄

Flowers & Lace Poncho
Continued from page 50

Rnd 3: Now working in rnds, working around neckline, ch 1, sc over dc just made, ch 6, sl st in first ch of last ch-3 of next flower petal, (ch 3, tr in ch-2 sp between flowers, ch 3, sk next ch-3 and 2 dc of flower petal, sl st in first ch of next ch-3) around, join with sl st in 3rd ch of beg ch-3, fasten off.

Rnd 4: Working on opposite side of row 2, turn work upside-down, neckline now facing down, attach yarn with a sc in ch-2 lp below beg tr of last row, (ch 8, sk ch-3 and 2 dc of next petal, sl st in first ch of next ch-3, ch 5, tr in next ch-2 sp between flowers) around to last ch lp, ch 2, join with dc in 4th ch of beg ch-8.

Rnd 5: Ch 6, dc in same st, (ch 3, (dc, ch 3, dc) in 3rd ch of next ch-5 sp) around, join in 3rd ch of beg ch-6. *(48 ch-3 sps)*

Rnd 6: Sl st into next ch-3 sp, ch 1, sc in center ch ch-3 sp, ch 3, (sc in 2nd ch of next ch-3 sp, ch 3) around, join in beg sc.

Rnd 7: Sl st into center ch of ch-3 sp, ch 1, sc in same ch, ch 4, (sc in center ch of next ch-3 sp, ch 4) around, join in beg sc.

Rnd 8: Sl st into ch-4 sp, ch 1, sc in same ch-4 sp, ch 5, (sc in next ch-4 sp, ch 5) around, join in beg sc.

Rnd 9: Sl st into center ch of ch-5 sp, ch 1, sc in same ch as beg ch-1, (ch 5, sc in center ch of next ch-5 sp) around, ending with ch 2, dc in beg sc to position hook in center of last ch sp.

Rnds 10–24: Ch 1, sc in same sp as beg ch-1, (ch 5, sc in center ch of next ch-5 sp) around, ending with ch 2, dc in beg sc to position hook in center of last ch sp.

Rnd 25: Ch 1, sc in same sp as beg ch-1, ch 1, sk next ch, sl st in next ch, (sk next sc, sl st in next ch of next ch-5 sp, ch 1, (sc, ch 3, sc) in 3rd ch of same ch-5 sp, ch 1, sk next ch, sl st in 5th ch of same ch-5 sp) around, ending with sc in same st as beg sc, ch 3, join in beg sc, fasten off. ✂

Evening Elegance Capelet
Continued from page 53

Row 2: Ch 3 *(counts as first dc throughout)*, **cross-st** *(see Special Stitch)* across to last st, dc in last st, turn. *(29 cross-sts, 2 dc)*

Row 3: Ch 1, sc in first st, (ch 5, sc in sp between next 2 cross-sts) across to last st, dc in last st, turn. *(29 ch-5 sps)*

Row 4: Ch 3, 2 dc in next ch-5 sp, (ch 3, 2 dc in next ch-5 sp) across to last st, dc in last st, turn. *(60 dc)*

Row 5: Ch 3, cross-st over next 2 sts, (2 dc in next ch-3 sp, cross-st over next 2 sts) across to last st, dc in last st, turn. *(29 cross-sts, 58 dc)*

Row 6: Ch 1, sc in first st, ch 5, (sk next cross-st, sc in sp before next 2 dc, ch 5, sk next 2 sts, sc in sp before next cross-st, ch 5) across to last st, sc in last st, turn. *(57 ch-5 sps)*

Row 7: Ch 3, 2 dc in each ch-5 sp across, ending with dc in last st, turn. *(116 dc)*

Row 8: Ch 3, (cross-st over next 2 dc) across to last st, dc in last st, turn. *(57 cross-sts, 2 dc)*

Row 9: Ch 1, sc in first st, ch 5, (sc in sp between next 2 cross-sts, ch 5) across, ending with sc in last st, turn. *(57 ch sps)*

Rows 10–27: Rep rows 7–9. At the end of last rep, do not fasten off.

Edging
Ch 1, working in ends of rows, (sc in end of each sc row and 2 sc in end of each dc row) across, working in opposite side of foundation ch of row 1, (sc, ch 2, sc) in 2nd ch and in each ch across, ending with sc in last ch, working down side edge in ends of rows, (sc in end of each sc row and 2 sc in end of each dc row) across, fasten off. ✂

Toddlers to Teens

Crochet some fun for the young ones in your life! This chapter is devoted to projects you can stitch for youngsters from toddlers to teens. Decorate their rooms and complement their outfits with accessories that will carry them through their busy days in fun, fanciful style.

Sweet Dreams Baby Blanket

Design courtesy of Bernat

Pretty pastel shades of silky-soft eyelash yarn create the cloud-soft texture of this heavenly blanket for baby.

INTERMEDIATE

Finished Size
26 x 32½ inches

5 BULKY

Materials
- Bernat Baby Lash Yarn chunky (bulky) weight yarn (1¾ oz/50 yds/50g per ball):
    5 balls #67005 wee white (MC)
    3 balls #67144 baby blues
    2 balls each #67315 little lilac and #67230 gentle green
- Size N/15/10mm crochet hook or size needed to obtain gauge

Gauge
Each motif = 6½ inches square

Pattern Notes
Weave in loose ends as work progresses. Join rounds with a slip stitch unless otherwise stated.

Special Stitches
Cluster (cl): [Yo hook, insert hook in ch sp, yo, draw up a lp, yo, draw through 2 lps on hook] 3 times in next ch sp, yo, draw through all 4 lps on hook.

Beginning cluster (beg cl): Ch 3, (yo hook, insert hook in same ch sp, yo, draw up a lp, yo, draw through 2 lps on hook) twice, yo, draw through all 3 lps on hook.

Motif
Make 5 with wee white as MC, baby blues as first color and little lilac as 2nd color.

Make 5 with wee white as MC, gentle green as first color and baby blues as 2nd color.

Make 5 with wee white as MC, little lilac as first color and baby blues as 2nd color.

Make 5 with wee white as MC, baby blues as first color and gentle green as 2nd color.

Rnd 1: With first color, ch 4, sl st in first ch to form a ring, ch 3 *(counts as first dc throughout)*, 2 dc in ring, ch 3, (3 dc in ring, ch 3) 3 times, join in 3rd ch of beg ch-3, fasten off. *(12 dc, 4 ch-3 corner sps)*

Rnd 2: Attach 2nd color with sl st in any ch-3 sp, **beg cl** *(see Special Stitches)* in same ch sp, ch 3, **cl** *(see Special Stitches)* in same

ch sp, *ch 1, 3 dc in center dc of next dc group, ch 1**, (cl, ch 3, cl) in next ch-3 sp, rep from * around, ending last rep at **, join with sl st in top of beg cl, fasten off.

Rnd 3: Attach MC with sl st in and ch-3 corner sp, ch 3, (2 dc, ch 3, 3 dc) in same ch sp, *sc in next ch-1 sp, ch 5, sc in next ch-1 sp**, (3 dc, ch 3, 3 dc) in next ch-3 sp, rep from * around, ending last rep at **, join in 3rd ch of beg ch-3, fasten off.

With RS tog, sc motifs tog, making 5 rows of 4 motifs. ✂

Lemon Squares Blanket

Design by Amy Venditti

This sweet yellow blanket with pretty scalloped edges and berry-colored stripes will wrap your little one in warm, sunny softness.

Finished Size
38 x 44 inches

Materials
- Lion Brand Homespun Baby bulky (chunky) weight yarn (3 oz/93 yds/85g per skein):
    - 5 skeins #157 sunshine (MC)
    - 4 skeins #104 sweet pea (CC)
- Size K/10½/6.5mm crochet hook or size needed to obtain gauge

Gauge
Rnds 1–5 = 6½ x 9 inches

Pattern Notes
Weave in loose ends as work progresses.
Join rounds with a slip stitch unless otherwise stated.
Begininning of foundation chain is worked with 2 strands of CC held together, remainder is worked with 1 strand of yarn.

Special Stitch
Picot: Ch 2, sl st in 2nd ch from hook.

Blanket
Rnd 1 (RS): With 2 strands CC held tog, ch 9, fasten off, attach 1 strand MC, ch 4, 2 dc in first ch of beg ch-4, ch 1, sk 2 chs, (3 dc in next ch, ch 1, sk next 2 chs) twice, ({3 dc, ch 1} twice, 3 dc) in last ch, working on opposite side of foundation ch, (ch 1, sk next 2 chs, 3 dc in next ch) twice, ch 1, (3 dc, ch 1) twice in same ch as beg 3-dc, sl st in 4th ch of beg ch-4, fasten off. *(10 dc groups)*

Rnd 2: Attach CC in any corner ch-1 sp, ch 1, *(sc, ch 3, sc) in corner ch-1 sp, ch 3, (sc in next ch-1 sp, ch 3) across to next corner ch-1 sp, rep from * around, join in beg sc, fasten off. *(14 ch-3 sps)*

Rnd 3: Attach MC in any corner ch-3 sp, ch 3 *(counts as first dc)*, (2 dc, ch 1, 3 dc) in corner ch-3 sp, ch 1, (3 dc in next ch-3 sp, ch 1) across to next corner ch-3 sp, *(3 dc, ch 1) twice in next corner ch-3 sp, (3 dc in next ch-3 sp, ch 1) across to next corner ch-3 sp, rep from * around, join in 3rd ch of beg ch-3, fasten off. *(18 dc groups)*

Rnds 4–21: Rep rnds 2 and 3.

Rnd 22: Rep rnd 2, do not fasten off. *(94 ch-3 sps)*

Rnd 23: Sl st into next ch-3 sp, rep rnd 3, do not fasten off. *(98 dc groups)*

Rnd 24: Sl st to corner ch-1 sp, ch 1, *(sc, ch 3, sc) in corner ch-1 sp, ch 3, (sc in next ch-1 sp, ch 3) across to next corner ch-1 sp, rep from * around, join in beg sc, fasten off. *(102 ch-3 sps)*

Rnd 25: Rep rnd 3, fasten off. *(106 dc groups)*

Rnd 26: Rep rnd 2, do not fasten off. *(110 ch-3 sps)*

Rnd 27: Rep rnd 23, do not fasten off. *(114 dc groups)*

Rnd 28: Rep rnd 24, fasten off. *(118 ch-3 sps)*

Rnds 29–32: Rep rnds 3 and 2. *(134 ch-3 sps)*

Rnds 33 & 34: With CC, sl st in first ch-3 sp, ch 1, (sc, ch 3) twice in same sp, (sc in next ch-3 sp, ch 3) across to next corner ch-3 sp, *(sc, ch 3) twice in corner ch-3 sp, (sc in next ch-3 sp, ch 3) across to next corner, rep from * around, join in beg sc, fasten off.

Rnd 35: With MC, working long side of Blanket first, (ch 3, 2 dc, **picot** *(see Special Stitch)*, 3 dc) in corner ch-3 sp, sc in next ch-3 sp, *(3 dc, picot, 3 dc) in next ch-3 sp, sc in next ch-3 sp*, rep from * to * 16 times, (3 dc, picot, 3 dc) in next ch-3 sp, **sc dec** *(see Stitch Guide)* in next 2 ch-3 sps tog, (3 dc, picot, 3 dc) in corner ch-3 sp, sc in next ch-3 sp, rep from * to * across short side of Blanket to next corner ch-3 sp, (3 dc, picot, 3 dc) in corner ch-3 sp, sc dec next 2 ch-3 sps tog, rep from * to * across long side of Blanket to next corner ch-3 sp, (3 dc, picot, 3 dc) in corner ch-3 sp, sc in next ch-3 sp, rep from * to * across short side of Blanket, sl st in 3rd ch of beg ch-3, fasten off. ✂

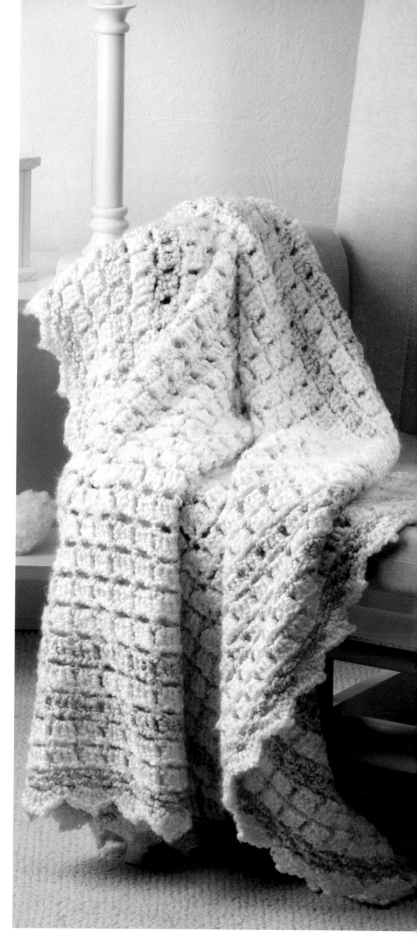

Rainbow Travel Set

Designs by Lori Zeller

Just the thing for an overnight trip to Grandma's; this crayon-bright blanket, matching bag and sunny-face pillow will make it even more fun!

INTERMEDIATE

4 MEDIUM

Finished Size
Tote: 9½ x 10 inches
Pillow: 8½ inches
in diameter,
excluding rays

Materials
• Medium (worsted) weight yarn (3 oz/170 yds/85g per skein):
  1 skein each gold, black, dark violet, royal blue, green, orange and burgundy
• Size F/5/3.75mm crochet hook or size needed to obtain gauge
• Fiberfill
• Straight pins .

Tote & Pillow

Gauge
13 sts = 3 inches; 12 rows = 3 inches

Pattern Notes
Weave in loose ends as work progresses. Join rounds with a slip stitch unless otherwise stated.

Tote Body
Make 2.

Row 1: With dark violet, ch 42, sc in 2nd ch from hook, sc in next ch, (ch 1, sk next ch, sc in each of next 2 chs) across, turn. *(28 sc, 13 ch-1 sps)*

Row 2: Ch 1, sc in each of first 2 sc, (ch 1, sk next ch-1 sp, sc in each of next 2 sc) across, turn.

Row 3: Rep row 2, fasten off.

Row 4: With royal blue, rep row 2.

Row 5: Rep row 2.

Row 6: Rep row 2, fasten off.

Rows 7–9: With green, rep rows 4–6.

Rows 10–12: With gold, rep rows 4–6.

Rows 13–15: With orange, rep rows 4–6.

Rows 16–18: With burgundy, rep rows 4–6.

Rows 19–21: With dark violet, rep rows 4–6.

Rows 22–24: With royal blue, rep rows 4–6.

Rows 25–27: With green, rep rows 4–6.

Rows 28–30: With gold, rep rows 4–6.

Rows 31–33: With orange, rep rows 4–6.

Rows 34–36: With burgundy, rep rows 4–6.

Rnd 37: Now working in rnds, attach black with sc in last sc made, work another sc in same st, working around entire piece, sc in each st around, working 2 sc in each corner st, join in beg sc, fasten off.

Gusset

Row 1: With black, ch 12, sc in 2nd ch from hook, sc in next ch, (ch 1, sk next ch, sc in each of next 2 chs) across, turn. *(8 sc, 3 ch-1 sps)*

Row 2: Ch 1, sc in each of next 2 sc, (ch 1, sk next ch sp, sc in each of next 2 sc) across, turn.

Rows 3–41: Rep row 2.

Row 42: Ch 1, working in **back lp** *(see Stitch Guide)* of each st, sc in each of next 2 sts, (ch 1, sk next ch sp, sc in each of next 2 sts) across, turn.

Rows 43–87: Rep row 2.

Row 88: Rep row 42.

Rows 89–127: Rep row 2.

Row 128: Rep row 2, fasten off.

Pocket

Make 4.

Row 1: With black, ch 12, sc in 2nd ch from hook, sc in next ch, (ch 1, sk next ch, sc in each of next 2 chs) across, turn.

Rows 2–12: Ch 1, sc in each of next 2 sc, (ch 1, sk next ch sp, sc in each of next 2 sc) across, turn. At the end of row 12, fasten off.

Handle

Make 2.

With black, ch 2, sc in 2nd ch from hook, (ch 1, turn, sc in sc) 63 times, turn, sl st in each sc back to beg, fasten off.

Assembly

With black, sl st 2 Pockets to the WS of each Tote Body, leaving opening at top of each Pocket.

Working through sts on 1 side of Gusset and 1 Tote Body at the same time, sc Gusset to sides and bottom of Tote Body leaving top edge open *(dark violet)*. Attach 2nd Tote Body to opposite side of Gusset, working through both thicknesses, sc around sides and bottom, do not fasten off.

Pin each Handle to top of Tote 1½ inches in from side edge of top opening, sc around top of Tote, securing each end of each Handle with at least 2 sc, join in beg sc, fasten off.

Travel Pillow

Pillow Back

Rnd 1: With gold, ch 2, 7 sc in 2nd ch from hook, join in beg sc. *(7 sc)*

Rnd 2: Ch 1, 2 sc in each sc around, join in beg sc. *(14 sc)*

Rnd 3: Ch 1, (sc in next sc, 2 sc in next sc) around, join in beg sc. *(21 sc)*

Rnd 4: Ch 1, (sc in each of next 2 sc, 2 sc in next sc) around. *(28 sc)*

Rnd 5: Ch 1, (sc in each of next 3 sc, 2 sc in next sc) around, join in beg sc. *(35 sc)*

Rnd 6: Ch 1, (sc in each of next 4 sc, 2 sc in next sc) around. *(42 sc)*

Rnd 7: Ch 1, (sc in each of next 5 sc, 2 sc in next sc) around, join in beg sc. *(49 sc)*

Rnd 8: Ch 1, (sc in each of next 6 sc, 2 sc in next sc) around, join in beg sc. *(56 sc)*

Rnd 9: Ch 1, (sc in each of next 7 sc, 2 sc in next sc) around, join in beg sc. *(63 sc)*

Rnd 10: Ch 1, (sc in each of next 8 sc, 2 sc in next sc) around, join in beg sc. *(70 sc)*

Rnd 11: Ch 1, (sc in each of next 9 sc, 2 sc in next sc) around, join in beg sc. *(77 sc)*

Rnd 12: Ch 1, (sc in each of next 10 sc, 2 sc in next sc) around, join in beg sc. *(84 sc)*

Rnd 13: Ch 1, (sc in each of next 11 sc, 2 sc in next sc) around, join in beg sc. *(91 sc)*

Rnd 14: Ch 1, (sc in each of next 12 sc, 2 sc in next sc) around, join in beg sc. *(98 sc)*

Rnd 15: Ch 1, (sc in each of next 13 sc, 2 sc in next sc) around, join in beg sc. *(105 sc)*

Rnd 16: Ch 1, (sc in each of next 14 sc, 2 sc in next sc) around, join in beg sc. *(112 sc)*

Rnd 17: Ch 1, sc in each sc around, join in beg sc.

Rnd 18: Ch 1, sc in each sc around, join in beg sc, fasten off.

Pillow Front

Rnds 1–17: Rep rnds 1–17 of Pillow Back.
Rnd 18: Ch 1, sc in each sc around, join in beg sc, draw up a lp, remove hook.

Eye
Make 2.
With black, ch 3, 2 sc in 2nd ch from hook, 4 sc in next ch, working on opposite side of foundation ch, 2 sc in next ch, join in beg sc, fasten off. *(8 sc)*
Sl st Eyes to Pillow Front 2½ inches apart.

Mouth
With black, centered below Eyes, working between rnds 6 and 7, work 12 ch sts, fasten off.

Assembly
Holding Pillow Front and Back tog, pick up dropped lp of rnd 18 of Pillow Front, working in the back lps of each section through both thicknesses, sl st in each st around, stuffing with fiberfill before closing, do not fasten off.

Sun Rays
Rnd 1: Ch 1, working in rem free lps of both Front and Back of Pillow of rnd 18, sc in first st, *dc in next st, tr in next st, (tr, ch 1, sl st in last tr made, tr) in next st, dc in next st**, sc in each of next 2 sts, rep from * around, ending last rep at **, sc in last st, join in beg sc, fasten off. *(16 Sun Rays)*

Blanket

Gauge
8 sts = 2 inches; 7 rows = 2 inches

Pattern Notes
Weave in loose ends as work progresses.
Join rounds with slip stitch unless otherwise stated.
Blanket strips are joined as work progresses.

INTERMEDIATE

MEDIUM 4

Finished Size
35 x 45 (45 x 50) inches
Pattern is written for smaller size with changes for larger size in brackets.

Materials
- Medium (worsted) weight yarn (3 oz/170 yds/85g per skein):
    2 skeins each dark violet, royal blue, green, gold, orange and burgundy
    1 skein black
- Size J/10/6mm crochet hook or size needed to obtain gauge

First Strip
Row 1: With dark violet, ch 22 (26), sc in 2nd ch from hook, (ch 1, sk next ch, sc in next ch) across, turn. *(11 (13) sc)*
Row 2: Ch 1, sc in first sc, sc in first ch-1 sp, (ch 1, sc in next ch-1 sp) 9 (11) times, sc in last sc, turn.
Row 3: Ch 1, sc in first sc, (ch 1, sk next sc, sc in next ch-1 sp) 9 (11) times, ch 1, sc in last sc, turn.
Row 4: Rep row 2.
Row 5: Rep row 3, fasten off, turn.
Row 6: With royal blue, rep row 2.
Row 7: Rep row 3.
Row 8: Rep row 2.
Row 9: Rep row 3.
Row 10: Rep row 2.
Row 11: With green, rep row 3.
Row 12: Rep row 2.
Row 13: Rep row 3.
Row 14: Rep row 2.
Row 15: Rep row 3.
Row 16: With gold, rep row 2.
Row 17: Rep row 3.
Row 18: Rep row 2.
Row 19: Rep row 3.
Row 20: Rep row 2.
Row 21: With orange, rep row 3.

Row 22: Rep row 2.
Row 23: Rep row 3.
Row 24: Rep row 2.
Row 25: Rep row 3.
Row 26: With burgundy, rep row 2.
Row 27: Rep row 3.
Row 28: Rep row 2.
Row 29: Rep row 3.
Row 30: Rep row 2.
Row 31: With dark violet, rep row 3.
Rows 32–121 (32–151): (Rep rows 2–31) 3 (4) times.
Rows 122–149 (152–179): Rep rows 2–29.
Row 150 (180): Ch 1, sc in first sc, sc in first ch-1 sp, (ch 1, sc in next ch-1 sp) 9 (11) times, sc in last sc, fasten off.

2nd Strip

Row 1: Attach burgundy in 21st ch of beg ch on previous strip, ch 22 (26), sc in 2nd ch from hook, (ch 1, sk next ch, sc in next ch) across, sl st in end st of first row on previous strip, sl st in end st of next row above, turn.
Row 2: Ch 1, sc first sc, sc in first ch-1 sp, (ch 1, sc in next ch-1 sp) 9 (11) times, sc in last sc, turn.
Row 3: Ch 1, sc in first sc, (ch 1, sk next sc, sc in next ch-1 sp) 9 (11) times, ch 1, sc in last sc, sl st in end of next 2 rows on previous strip, turn.
Row 4: Rep row 2.
Row 5: Ch 1, sc in first sc, (ch 1, sk next sc, sc in next ch-1 sp) 9 (11) times, ch 1, sc in last sc, **change color** (see Stitch Guide) to dark violet, sl st in end of next 2 rows on previous strip, turn.
Row 6: Rep row 2.
Row 7: Rep row 3.
Row 8: Rep row 2.
Row 9: Rep row 3.
Row 10: Ch 1, sc in first sc, sc in first ch-1 sp, (ch 1, sc in next ch-1 sp) 9 (11) times, sc in last sc, change color to royal blue, turn.
Row 11: Rep row 3.

Row 12: Rep row 2.
Row 13: Rep row 3.
Row 14: Rep row 2.
Row 15: Rep row 5, change color to green, sl st in end of next 2 rows on previous strip, turn.
Row 16: Rep row 2.
Row 17: Rep row 3.
Row 18: Rep row 2.
Row 19: Rep row 3.
Row 20: Rep row 10, change color to gold in last sc, turn.
Row 21: Rep row 3.
Row 22: Rep row 2.
Row 23: Rep row 3.
Row 24: Rep row 2.
Row 25: Rep row 5, change color to orange, sl st in end of next 2 rows on previous strip, turn.
Row 26: Rep row 2.
Row 27: Rep row 3.
Row 28: Rep row 2.
Row 29: Rep row 3.
Row 30: Rep row 10, change color to burgundy in last sc, turn.
Row 31: Rep row 3.
Rows 32–121 (32–151): (Rep rows 2–31) 3 (4) times.
Rows 122–149 (152–179): Rep rows 2–29.
Row 150 (180): Ch 1, sc in first sc, sc in first ch-1 sp, (ch 1, sc in next ch-1 sp) 9 (11) times, sc in last sc, fasten off.

3rd Strip

Note: *Color sequence for 3rd strip: orange, burgundy, dark violet, royal blue, green and gold.*
Rows 1–150 (1–180): Rep rows 1–150 (1–180) of 2nd Strip.

4th Strip

Note: *Color sequence for 4th strip: gold, orange, burgundy, dark violet, royal blue and green.*
Rows 1–150 (1–180): Rep rows 1–150 (1–180) of 2nd Strip.

5th Strip

Note: *Color sequence for 5th strip: green, gold, orange, burgundy, dark violet and royal blue.*
Rows 1-150 (1-180): Rep rows 1–150 (1–180) of 2nd Strip.

6th Strip

Note: *Color sequence for 6th strip: royal blue, green, gold, orange burgundy and dark violet.*
Rows 1-150 (1-180): Rep rows 1–150 (1–180) of 2nd Strip.

Edging

Rnd 1: Working across top edge of Blanket, attach black in end sc, ch 1, sc in same sc as beg ch-1 , *(ch 1, sk next sc, sc in next ch sp) across to joining of strips, ch 1, sc in each of next 2 sc, rep from * 4 times, (ch 1, sk next sc, sc in next ch sp) across last strip, ending with ch 1, sc in last sc, ch 2, sc in end st of next row down (corner), (ch 1, sk next row, sc in end of next row) across edge, ch 2, working on opposite side of foundation ch, sc in first ch (corner), **(sc in next ch sp, ch 1, sk next st) across to joining of strips, sc in next ch sp, ch 2, sk next 2 sts, rep from ** 4 times, (sc in next ch sp, ch 1, sk next st) across last strip, sc in next ch sp, sc in last st, ch 2, sc in end st of next row (corner), (ch 1, sk next row, sc in end of next row) across ends of rows, ending with ch 2 (corner), join in beg sc.

Rnd 2: Sl st into first ch-1 sp, ch 1, sc in same sp, *(ch 1, sk next sc, sc in next ch-1 sp) across to next 2-sc group, ch 2, sk next 2 sc, sc in next ch-1 sp, rep from * 4 times, (ch 1, sk next sc, sc in next ch-1 sp) across to next ch-2 corner sp, ch 1, (sc, ch 2, sc) in ch-2 corner sp, (ch 1, sk next sc, sc in next ch-1 sp) across to next ch-2 corner sp, ch 1, (sc, ch 2, sc) in corner ch-2 sp, sc in next sc, **(ch 1, sk next sc, sc in next ch-1 sp) across to next ch-2 sp, ch 1, 2 sc in ch-2 sp, rep from ** 4 times, (ch 1, sk next sc, sc in next ch-1

sp) across to next corner ch-2 sp, ch 1, (sc, ch 2, sc) in corner ch-2 sp, (ch 1, sk next sc, sc in next ch-1 sp) across to next corner, ch 1, (sc, ch 2, sc) in corner ch-2 sp, ch 1, join in beg sc, fasten off.

Rnd 3: Attach dark violet in last ch-2 corner sp, ch 1, (sc, ch 2, sc) in corner ch-2 sp, *(ch 1, sk next sc, sc in next ch-1 sp) across to next ch-2 sp, ch 1, 2 sc in ch-2 sp, rep from * 4 times, (ch 1, sk next sc, sc in next ch-1 sp) across to next corner ch-2 sp, ch 1, (sc, ch 2, sc) in corner ch-2 sp, (ch 1, sk next sc, sc in next ch-1 sp) across to next corner ch-2 sp ch 1, (sc, ch 2, sc) in corner ch-2 sp, sc in next sc, **(ch 1, sk next sc, sc in next ch-1 sp) across to next 2-sc group, ch 2, sk next 2 sc, sc in next ch-1 sp, rep from ** 4 times, (ch 1, sk next sc, sc in next ch-1 sp) across to corner, sc in next sc, (sc, ch 2, sc) in corner sc, (ch 1, sk next sc, sc in next ch-1 sp) across, ending with ch 1, join in beg sc, fasten off.

Rnd 4: Attach royal blue in last corner ch-2 sp, ch 1, (sc, ch 2, sc) in corner ch-2 sp, *(ch 1, sk next sc, sc in next ch-1 sp) across to next 2 sc, ch 2, sk next 2 sc, sc in next ch-1 sp, rep from * 4 times, (ch 1, sk next sc, sc in next ch-1 sp) across to corner, ch 1, (sc, ch 2, sc) in corner ch-2 sp, (ch 1, sk next sc, sc in next ch-1 sp) across to next corner, ch 1, (sc, ch 2, sc) in corner ch-2 sp, sc in next sc, **(ch 1, sk next sc, sc in next ch-1 sp) across to next ch-2 sp, ch 1, 2 sc in ch-2 sp, rep from ** 4 times, (ch 1, sk next sc, sc in next ch-1 sp) across, sc in sc before corner, (sc, ch 2, sc) in corner ch-2 sp, (ch 1, sk next sc, sc in next ch-1 sp) across, ch 1, join in beg sc, fasten off.

Rnd 5: Attach green, rep rnd 3.
Rnd 6: Attach gold, rep rnd 4.
Rnd 7: Attach orange, rep rnd 3.
Rnd 8: Attach burgundy, rep rnd 4.
Rnd 9: Attach black, rep rnd 3, do not fasten off.
Rnd 10: Sl st into corner ch-2 sp, rep rnd 4. ✀

Charm-ing Bag & Belt

Designs by Sandy Abbate

Your little girl will love this rainbow-striped bag and belt set with interchangeable charms for a variety of fun looks.

EASY

4 MEDIUM

Finished Size

Bag: 7 x 12 inches,
  excluding Straps
Belt: 1½ inches wide

Materials

- Medium (worsted) weight yarn (3 oz/170 yds/85g per ball):
  3 balls green
  1 ball print (light green, peach, pink, lilac and yellow)
  10 yds each lilac, pink, peach, light green and yellow
- Sizes G/6/4mm and J/10/6mm crochet hooks or sizes needed to obtain gauge
- 4 x 10-inch plastic canvas
- Straight pins
- Craft glue
- Stitch marker

Gauge

Size J hook: 7 sc = 2½ inches; 3 sc rnds = 1 inch
Size G hook: 4 sc = 1 inch; 4 rows = 1 inch

Pattern Notes

Weave in loose ends as work progresses. Join rounds with a slip stitch unless otherwise stated.

Handbag

Outer Bottom

Rnd 1 (RS): With size J hook and 2 strands of green, ch 16, sc in 2nd ch from hook, sc in next 13 chs, 5 sc in last ch, working on opposite side of foundation ch, sc in each of next 13 chs, 4 sc in last ch, join in beg sc. *(36 sc)*

Rnd 2: Ch 1, sc in same st as beg ch-1 , sc in each of next 14 sts, 2 sc in each of next 3 sts, sc in each of next 15 sts, 2 sc in each of next 3 sts, join in beg sc. *(42 sc)*

Rnd 3: Ch 1, sc in same st as beg ch-1 , sc in each of next 15 sts, 2 sc in each of next 4 sts, sc in each of next 17 sts, 2 sc in each of next 4 sts, sc in last st, join in beg sc. *(50 sc)*

Rnd 4: Ch 1, sc in same st as beg ch-1 , sc in each of next 17 sts, 2 sc in each of next 4 sts, sc in each of next 21 sts, 2 sc in each of next 4 sts, sc in next 3 sts, join in beg sc. *(58 sc)*

Rnd 5: Ch 1, sc in same st as beg ch-1 , sc in each of next 19 sts, 2 sc in each of next 4 sts, sc in each of next 25 sts, 2 sc in each of next 4 sts, sc in each of next 5 sts, join in beg sc, do not fasten off, draw up a lp, remove hook. *(66 sc)*

Inner Bottom
Rnds 1–5: With 2 strands of print, rep rnds 1–5 of Outer Bottom. At the end of rnd 5, fasten off. Using Inner Bottom as a pattern cut a piece of plastic canvas ½ inch smaller than Inner Bottom.
Rnd 6: Holding WS of print and green tog with plastic canvas sandwiched between layers with green facing and working through both thicknesses, ch 1, sc in each st around, join in **back lp** *(see Stitch Guide)* of beg sc, do not fasten off. *(66 sc)*

Body
Rnd 1: Ch 1, working in back lp, sc in same st as beg ch-1 , sc in each st around, join in beg sc.
Rnd 2: Ch 1, hdc in same st as beg ch-1 , hdc in each rem st around, join in top of first hdc.
Rnd 3: Ch 1, sc in same st as beg ch-1 , sc in each st around, join in beg sc.
Rnds 4–9: Rep rnds 2 and 3.
Rnd 10: Rep rnd 2.
Rnd 11: Ch 1, sc in same st as beg ch-1 , sc in each of next 26 sts, **sc dec** *(see Stitch Guide)* in next 2 sts, sc in each of next 31 sts, sc dec over next 2 sts, sc in each of next 4 sts, join in beg sc. *(64 sc)*
Rnd 12: Ch 1, hdc in same st as beg ch-1 , hdc in each of next 26 sts, **hdc dec** *(see Stitch Guide)* over next 2 sts, hdc in each of next 30 sts, hdc dec over next 2 sts, hdc in next 3 sts, join in beg hdc. *(62 hdc)*
Rnd 13: Ch 1, sc in same st as beg ch-1 , sc in each of next 25 sts, sc dec over next 2 sts, sc in each of next 29 sts, sc dec over next 2 sts, sc in last 3 sts, join in beg sc. *(60 sc)*
Rnd 14: Ch 1, hdc in same st as beg ch-1 , hdc in each of next 24 sts, hdc dec over next 2 sts, hdc in each of next 28 sts, hdc dec over next 2 sts, hdc in next 3 sts, join in beg hdc. *(58 hdc)*

Rnd 15: Ch 1, sc in same st as beg ch-1 , sc in each of next 23 sts, sc dec over next 2 sts, sc in each of next 27 sts, sc dec over next 2 sts, sc in each rem st, join in beg sc. *(56 sc)*
Rnd 16: Ch 1, hdc in same st as beg ch-1 , hdc in each of next 22 sts, hdc dec over next 2 sts, hdc in each of next 26 sts, hdc dec over next 2 sts, hdc in each rem st around, join in beg hdc. *(54 hdc)*
Rnd 17: Ch 1, sc in same st as beg ch-1 , sc in each of next 3 sts, ch 3, sk next 4 sts *(eyelet)*, sc in each of next 11 sts, ch 3, sk next 4 sts, sc in each of next 8 sts, ch 3, sk each of next 4 sts, sc in each of next 11 sts, ch 3, sk next 4 sts, sc in each of next 4 sts, join in beg sc. *(38 sc, 4 ch-3 eyelet sps)*
Rnd 18: Ch 1, hdc in same st as beg ch-1 , hdc in each of next 3 sts, 4 hdc in ch-3 sp, hdc in each of next 11 sts, 4 hdc in next ch-3 sp, hdc in each of next 8 sts, 4 hdc in next ch-3 sp, hdc in each of next 11 sts, 4 hdc

in next ch-3 sp, hdc in next 4 sts, join in beg hdc, fasten off. *(54 hdc)*

Inner Pocket
Row 1: With size G hook and 1 strand of print, ch 17, dc in 4th ch from hook, dc in each rem ch across, turn. *(15 dc)*
Rows 2–9: Ch 3 *(counts as first dc throughout)*, dc in each dc across, turn.
Rnd 10: Now working in rnds, ch 1, sc in each sc around outer edge, with 3 sc in each corner, join in beg sc.
Position pocket inside Handbag, pin in place with straight pins, catching 1 strand of inner Handbag, sl st pocket into place on sides and bottom of pocket, fasten off.

Strap
Make 2.
Row 1 (WS): With size G hook and 1 strand of print, ch 136, sc in 2nd ch from hook, sc in each rem ch across, turn. *(135 sc)*
Row 2: Ch 1, sc in each st across, fasten off.
Row 3: With RS facing, attach green in first st, ch 1, sc in same st as beg ch-1 , sc in each rem st across, fasten off.
Row 4: With RS facing, working in opposite side of foundation ch of row 1, attach green, ch 1, sc in same ch as beg ch-1 , sc in each ch across, fasten off.
Weave first Strap ends from inside to outside through eyelets on front, passing ends to center bottom of Bag. Weave 2nd Strap ends from inside to outside through eyelets on back, passing ends to center bottom of Bag. With size G hook and green, sl st Strap ends tog at center bottom.

Button
Rnd 1 (WS): With size G hook and print, ch 3, sl st to join in first ch to form a ring, ch 1, 6 sc in ring, join in beg sc. *(6 sc)*
Rnd 2: Ch 1, working over sts of rnd 1 and into beg ring, work 12 sc over rnd 1, join in beg sc. *(12 sc)*

Rnd 3: Ch 1, sc in same st as beg ch-1 , sk next st, (sc in next st, sk next st) around, join in beg sc, leaving a length of yarn, fasten off. With size G hook, sl st Button to center front over rnd 17.

Fastener
With size G hook, attach print to rnd 18 at center inside of back, ch 18, sl st in same st fasten off.
Leaving lp large enough to fit over Button, tie a knot in Fastener.

Charms

Flower

Rnd 1: With size G hook and peach, ch 3, sl st to join in first ch to form a ring, ch 1, (sc in ring, ch 3) 5 times, join in beg sc. *(5 ch-3 sps)*
Rnd 2: Sl st into ch-3 sp, (sc, ch 1, dc, tr, dc, ch 1, sc) in each ch-3 sp around, join in beg sc, fasten off. *(5 petals)*

Hanging Loop
Attach peach at back around any st near center, make 1½-inch lp, secure yarn around same sc, fasten off.

Star
Rnd 1: With size G hook and yellow, ch 4, sl st to join in first ch to form a ring, ch 1, 10 sc in ring, join in beg sc. *(10 sc)*
Rnd 2: (Ch 4, sc in 2nd ch from hook, hdc in next ch, dc in next ch, sk next sc of rnd 1, sl st in next sc of rnd 1) 5 times, fasten off.
With yellow, rep Flower Hanging Loop.

Heart
Rnd 1: With size G hook and pink, ch 3, sl st to join in first ch to form a ring, ch 1, 6 sc in ring, join in beg sc. *(6 sc)*

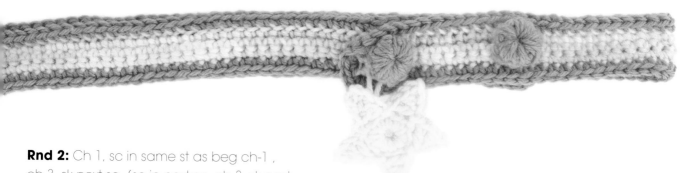

Rnd 2: Ch 1, sc in same st as beg ch-1 , ch 3, sk next sc, (sc in next sc, ch 3, sk next sc) twice, join in beg sc. *(3 ch-3 sps)*

Rnd 3: Sl st in ch-3 sp, ch 1, (sc, ch 1, dc, 4 tr) in same ch-3 sp, ch 3, sl st in next sc, ch 3, (4 tr, dc, ch 1, sc) in next ch-3 sp, sc in next sc, sc, ch 2 in last ch-3 sp, (yo, insert hook in same ch-3 sp, yo, draw up a lp, yo, draw through 2 lps on hook) 5 times, yo, draw through all 6 lps on hook, ch 2, sc in same ch-3 sp, sc in next sc, join in beg sc, fasten off. With pink, rep Flower Hanging Loop.

Bow
First Side
Row 1: With size G hook and lilac, ch 4, 4 dc in 4th ch from hook, turn. *(5 dc)*

Row 2: Ch 3, dc in same st as beg ch-3, 2 dc in each rem dc across, fasten off. *(10 dc)*

2nd Side
Row 1: Attach lilac in opposite side of foundation ch, ch 3, 4 dc in same ch, turn. *(5 dc)*

Row 2: Rep row 2 of First Side.
Wrap lilac yarn around center of Bow 10 times, knot ends to secure, form 1½-inch Hanging Loop, secure ends, fasten off.

Shamrock
Rnd 1: With size G hook and light green, ch 3, sl st to join in first ch to form a ring, ch 1, (sc in ring, ch 3) 3 times, join in beg sc. *(3 ch-3 sps)*

Rnd 2: *Sl st in next ch-3 sp, (ch 3, 2 dc, sc, 2 dc, ch 3, sl st) in ch-3 sp, rep from * twice, sl st in beg ring, ch 5, sc in 2nd ch from hook, sc in each of next 3 chs, sl st in ring, fasten off. With light green, rep Flower Hanging Loop.

Belt
Note: *Measure waistline with print and make a ch this length, place st marker, ch 16 for buttonhole placket.*

Row 1 (RS): With size G hook and print, sc in 2nd ch from hook, sc in each rem ch across, turn.

Row 2: Ch 1, sc in each st across to st marker, ch 2, sk 2 sts, sc in each of next 9 sts, ch 2, sk next 2 sts, sc in each of next 2 sts, turn. *(2 buttonholes)*

Row 3: Ch 1, sc in each of next 2 sc, 2 sc in next ch-2 sp, sc in each of next 9 sc, 2 sc in next ch-2 sp, sc in each rem sc across, fasten off.

Rnd 4: Now working in rnds, with RS facing, attach green with sc in first st, sc across to last st, 3 sc in last st, working across ends of rows, work 3 sc in side edge of row 2, working across opposite side of foundation ch work 3 sc in first ch, sc in each ch across to last ch, 3 sc in last ch, 3 sc in end of row 2, 2 sc in same sc as beg sc, join in beg sc, fasten off.

Button
Make 2.
Rnds 1–3: With size G hook and green, work Handbag Button rnds 1–3.
With size G hook, sl st Buttons to center of Belt in line with buttonholes. ✂

Furry Photo Frame

Design by Donna Collinsworth

Youngsters will get a kick out of this fun and funky faux fur photo frame. Match the yarn to their rooms for a color-coordinated accessory.

INTERMEDIATE

Finished Size
5 x 7-inch picture frame

5 BULKY

6 SUPER BULKY

Materials
- Lion Brand Fun Fur bulky (chunky) weight yarn (1¾ oz/60 yds/50g per ball):
  - 1 ball #105 light blue
- Size F/5/3.75mm crochet hook or size needed to obtain gauge
- Craft glue
- 5 x 7-inch wooden frame

Gauge
6 hdc = 1½ inches; 3 hdc rows = 1 inch

Pattern Notes
Weave in loose ends as work progresses. Join rounds with a slip stitch unless otherwise stated.

Picture Frame
First Short Side
Row 1: With light blue, ch 7, hdc in 2nd ch from hook, hdc in each rem ch across, turn. (6 hdc)
Row 2: Ch 1, hdc in each hdc across, turn.
Rows 3–15: Rep row 2. At end of row 15, fasten off.

Continued on page 87

Bare Necessities Necklace Purse

Design by Rose Pirrone

Perfectly sized for lunch money or notes from boys, this great little purse will always be within reach for those important little things.

EASY

Finished Size
3 x 3 inches, excluding neckline strap

Materials
- DMC Pearl Cotton size 5 thread (27 yds per skein):
    2 skeins #943 jade
- DMC Metallic Thread (43 yds per spool):
    1 spool silver
- Size B/1/2.25mm crochet hook or size needed to obtain gauge
- 2 D-rings1-inch

Gauge
7 sts = 1 inch; 6 rows = 1 inch

Pattern Notes
Weave in loose ends as work progresses. Join rounds with a slip stitch unless otherwise stated.

Special Stitch
Picot: Ch 4, sc in first ch of ch-4.

Continued on page 87

Girly-Girl Pillow

Design by Darla Sims

Pearl-accented flowers and dimensional bands of raised shell stitches give this soft and sassy bolster pillow a fanciful, feminine look.

Finished Size
14 inches long

Materials
- Bernat Satin medium (worsted) weight yarn (3½ oz/163 yds/100g per skein):
    - 2 skeins #04007 silk
    - 1 skein each #04610 sunrise and #04605 sunset
- Size H/8/5mm crochet hook or size needed to obtain gauge
- 5 x 14-inch bolster pillow form
- 7 pearl 10mm beads
- Stitch marker

Gauge
7 dc = 2 inches; 2 dc rows = 2 inches

Pattern Notes
Weave in loose ends as work progresses. Join rounds with a slip stitch unless otherwise stated.

Special Stitch
Shell: (Sc, {ch 1, dc} 3 times, ch 1, sc, ch 1) around front of post (*see Stitch Guide*) of indicated st.

Pillow
Row 1: With silk, ch 74, dc in 4th ch from hook, dc in each rem ch across, turn. *(72 dc)*
Rows 2–24: Ch 3 *(counts as first dc)*, dc in each dc across, turn. At the end of row 24, fasten off.

Shell Trim
Row 1: Working over sts of row 2, sk first dc, attach sunrise around post of next dc, (working from bottom to top of dc post work **shell** *(see Special Stitch)* over dc post, turn, working from top to bottom of next dc work shell over dc post) across to last dc, leaving last dc unworked, fasten off.
Row 2: Sk rows 3 and 4 of Pillow, sk first dc of row 5, attach sunset, rep row 1 of Shell Trim.
Row 3: Sk rows 6–19 of Pillow, sk first dc of row 20, attach sunset, rep row 1 of Shell Trim.
Row 4: Sk rows 21 and 22 of Pillow, sk first dc of row 23, attach sunrise, rep row 1 of Shell Trim.

Flower
Make 7.
Rnd 1: With sunset, ch 2, 12 sc in 2nd ch from hook, join in beg sc, draw up a lp of sunrise, fasten off sunset. *(12 sc)*
Rnd 2: Sl st in top of first sc, (ch 10, sl st in same sc, sl st in next sc) around, fasten off. *(12 petals)*

Thread a length of sunset through center of pearl bead, knot pearl bead to center of Flower.

Position 5 Flowers evenly sp across center of Pillow, sl st Flowers to Pillow.

Pillow End

Make 2.

Rnd 1: With silk, ch 2, 8 sc in 2nd ch from hook, do not join, use stitch marker. *(8 sc)*

Rnd 2: 2 sc in each sc around. *(16 sc)*

Rnd 3: (Sc in next sc, 2 sc in next sc) around. *(24 sc)*

Rnd 4: (Sc in each of next 2 sc, 2 sc in next sc) around. *(32 sc)*

Rnd 5: (Sc in each of next 3 sc, 2 sc in next sc) around. *(40 sc)*

Rnd 6: (Sc in each of next 4 sc, 2 sc in next sc) around. *(48 sc)*

Rnd 7: Sc in each sc around.

Rnd 8: (Sc in each of next 5 sc, 2 sc in next sc) around. *(56 sc)*

Rnd 9: (Sc in each of next 6 sc, 2 sc in next sc) around. *(64 sc)*

Rnd 10: (Sc in each of next 7 sc, 2 sc in next sc) around. *(72 sc)*

Rnd 11: Rep rnd 7, sl st in next st, fasten off. Position a Flower at center of Pillow End and sl st in place over center.

Finishing

Attach silk in end of row 1 of Pillow, holding beg and end of rows tog and working through both thicknesses, sl st across ends of rows, draw up a lp, remove hook, do not fasten off.

Place crocheted Pillow over pillow form. Pick up dropped lp, holding Pillow End over end of Pillow, working through both thicknesses, sl st in each st around, fasten off.

Attach silk at opposite end of Pillow, holding Pillow End over end of Pitlow, working through both thicknesses, sl st around, fasten off. ✂

Funky Fringe Poncho

Design courtesy of Coats & Clark

Three rows of vibrant jewel-toned tape-yarn fringe create a striking contrast on this textured black poncho.

INTERMEDIATE

6
SUPER BULKY

Finished Size
One size fits most

Gauge
9 sts = 4 inches; 5 rows = 4 inches

Pattern Notes
Weave in loose ends as work progresses. Join rounds with a slip stitch unless otherwise stated.

Poncho Body
Row 1: With black, ch 27, hdc in 3rd ch from hook, hdc in each rem ch across, turn. *(25 hdc)*

Materials
- Red Heart Grandé super bulky (super chunky) weight yarn (6 oz/143 yds/170g per skein):
    - 2 skeins #2112 black
- Moda Dea Ticker Tape (1¾ oz/67 yds/50g per ball):
    - 2 balls #9507 festival
- Size M/13/9mm crochet hook or size needed to obtain gauge

Row 2: Ch 2 *(does not count as a hdc)*, hdc in each hdc across, turn.

Rows 3–68: Rep row 2.

Row 69: With RS facing, holding opposite side of foundation ch to row 68, sl st in each st across, fasten off.

Top Edging
Rnd 1: Working in ends of rows, attach festival in seam, ch 1, work 68 sc evenly sp around, join in beg sc. *(68 sc)*

Rnd 2: Ch 1, sc in each sc around, join in beg sc.

Rnd 3: Rep rnd 2.

Rnd 4: Ch 1, (sc in each of next 2 sc, **sc dec** *(see Stitch Guide)* in next 2 sc) 17 times, join in beg sc. *(51 sc)*

Rnds 5–7: Rep rnd 2.

Rnd 8: Ch 1, **reverse sc** *(see Stitch Guide)* in each sc around, join in beg sc, fasten off.

Fringe
Cut 12-inch lengths of festival. Holding 2 strands tog, fold in half forming a lp, insert hook in indicated st, draw strands through at fold, draw cut ends through lp on hook and pull ends to secure. Attach fringe in every other row of Poncho Body around top, center and bottom *(first, 13th and 25th hdc sts)*. Trim ends. ✂

Daisy Chain Throw

Design by Rena Stevens

Remember the fun of making daisy chains as a child? Here's a whole new way of re-inventing this fanciful creation with yarn and hook!

INTERMEDIATE

MEDIUM

Finished Size

46 x 68 inches, excluding fringe

Materials

- Red Heart Super Saver medium (worsted) weight yarn (7 oz/364 yds/198g per skein):
    5 skeins #316 soft white
- Red Heart Classic medium (worsted) weight yarn (3½ oz/190 yds/99g per skein):
    2 skeins #848 skipper blue
    5 oz/272 yds/142g each #230 yellow, #245 orange and #912 cherry red
- Sizes I/9/5.5mm and J/10/6mm crochet hooks or size needed to obtain gauge
- Stitch marker

Gauge

Size J hook: 13 sts = 4 inches

Pattern Notes

Weave in loose ends as work progresses. Afghan is crocheted vertically.

Special Stitches

Attach: Yo, insert hook to attach motif as instructed, yo, draw yarn through, yo, finish dc as usual.

Full petal: Ch 3, (dc, ch 2, sl st) in 3rd ch from hook.

Partial petal: Ch 3, dc in 3rd ch from hook.

Flower Strip

Make 4 each yellow, orange & cherry red.

With size I hook, work 2 **full petals** (see Special Stitches), mark last petal made as RS bottom half of flowers, *work 1 **partial petal** (see Special Stitches), ch 1 (leaving this extra ch-1 unworked), work 1 partial petal, work 1 full petal, rep from * until 30 half flowers are completed, work 3 full petals on 30th half flower, working back along half flowers, sk next 4 petals, (sl st in top of next dc, ch 2, sl st in same ch at base of same dc, sl st in next ch-1 sp, sl st in top of next dc, ch 2, sl st in same ch at base of same dc, work 2 full

Continued on page 86

Techno Door Curtain

Design by Jennifer Hansen

Your favorite computer whiz kid or music lover will appreciate this one-of-a-kind door curtain adorned with shiny CDs and glittering beads.

INTERMEDIATE

4
MEDIUM

Finished Size

29¾ x 83 inches to fit over molding of standard-size doorway

Materials

- Lion Brand Glitterspun medium (worsted) weight yarn (1¾ oz/115 yds/50g per skein):
    3 skeins #150 silver
- Size G/6/4mm crochet hook or size needed to obtain gauge
- 60 CDs
- Beads of various sizes
- 36-inch #6-32 treaded rods *(optional)*: 2
- #6-32 cap nuts *(optional)*: 4
- Dremel tool or hacksaw to trim threaded rod
- Zip-top bags
- Stitch markers

Gauge

29 sc = 8 inches

Sc Over Rod

Pattern Notes

Weave in loose ends as work progresses. Optional threaded rod and cap nuts provide structure to the finished curtain and prevent the top of the curtain from sagging when hung. These materials are inexpensive and readily available at any home improvement or hardware store. If you choose to omit the treaded rod, you will need to create several more attachments points to secure the curtain to the door.

Hold 2 strands of yarn together throughout. It is easy to work with 2 strands of yarn from the same skein of yarn, simply pull a strand from center of the skein and 1 strand from the outside of the skein and work with both strands at the same time.

To keep the work manageable as CDs are added, keep CD strings in zip-top bags to prevent tangling. Decreasing 3 stitches at 1 time will create a hole in the fabric. Attach beads or other ornaments from these holes to achieve a decorative look.

To attach the curtain to door, simply nail 3 finishing nails just above the molding at the top of the door and hang the curtain on them. They will poke through between stitches just under the upper threaded rod and hold the divider securely above the door. As gauge indicates, stitches are worked tightly to create a stiff fabric.

Creating a larger curtain to span a wider doorway, hall or even an entire room is easy. Simply add additional triangular panels; add 36 chains to your base chain for each additional triangular panel desired (*approximately 10-inch length*). You will need 24 more CDs for every additional triangular panel added.

Upper Panel

Row 1 (RS): With 2 strands held tog, ch 109, sc in 2nd ch from hook, sc in each rem ch across, turn. *(108 sc)*

Row 2: Ch 1, sc in each st across, turn.

Row 3: Ch 4 *(counts as first tr)*, tr in each st across, turn.

Row 4: Rep row 2.

First Triangular Panel

Note: *Mark the 36th and 72nd sts from hook.*

Row 5: Work over rod *(see illustration)*, ch 1, sc in each st across to marker, sc in marked st, leaving rem sts unworked, turn. *(36 sc)*

Rows 6-13: Ch 1, **sc dec** *(see Stitch Guide)* over next 3 sts, sc in each st across with sc dec over last 3 sts, turn. *(4 sc)*

Row 14: Ch 1, (sc dec over next 2 sts) twice, turn. *(2 sc)*

Row 15: Ch 1, sc dec over next 2 sts, turn. *(1 sc)*

CD String

Ch 3, (draw up a lp on hook so that a CD fits snugly between hook and bottom of lp, yo, draw through lp, ch 3, draw up lp on hook so that upper half of CD fits snugly between hook and bottom of lp, yo, draw through lp, ch 8) 11 times, draw up lp on hook so that CD fits snugly between hook and bottom of the lp, yo, draw through lp, ch 3, sl st in 3rd ch from hook, fasten off.

Second Triangular Panel

Row 1: Working over rod, attach with a sl st to last st worked in *(marked st)*, sc in next st and in each st to next marker, sc in marked st leaving rem sts unworked, turn.

Rows 2–11: Rep rows 6–15 of First Triangular Panel.
Rep CD String.

Third Triangular Panel

Row 1: Working over rod, attach with a sl st to last st worked in *(marked st)*, sc in next st and in each st across, turn.

Rows 2–11: Rep rows 6–15 of First Triangular Panel.
Rep CD String.

Remaining CD String
Make 2.

In valley created between Triangular Panels, join with sl st, rep CD String.

Finishing

1. With RS facing, working in starting ch on opposite side of row 1 around rem rod, join with sl st in first st on left, working from left to right, **reverse sc** *(see Stitch Guide)* in each ch across, fasten off.

2. Attach beads in 1 or more of the sps created by dec sts.

3. With dremel tool or hacksaw, trim ends of rod to length and screw on cap nuts over each end. ✂

Daisy Chain Throw
Continued from page 82

petals) across, ending with sl st in beg ch of flower strip, fasten off. *(30 flowers)*

Afghan

Row 1 (RS): With size J hook and soft white, ch 215 slightly loosely, dc in 4th ch from hook, dc in each rem ch across, fasten off, turn. *(213 dc)*

Row 2: Working in **back lp** *(see Stitch Guide)* of each st across, attach skipper blue, ch 3, dc in each st across, fasten off, turn.

Row 3: With white, rep row 2.

Rows 4–7: Rep rows 2 and 3, do not fasten off white at the end of row 7.

Rows 8 & 9: With white, rep row 2, do not fasten off.

Row 10 (WS): Work in back lp only of background dc sts, ch 3, with WS of yellow Flower Strip against RS of background and with bottom half of strip overlapping previous background row, **attach** *(see Special Stitches)* in next background dc and through any 2 WS lps at tip of first flower's side petal, *working in front of Flower Strip, dc in next 6 dc, attach by inserting hook in next background dc and under entire occupied ch-1 between flower just passed and next flower*, rep from * to * across, untwist Flower Strip if necessary, tack down last flower by attaching in next to last background dc and through any 2 WS lps at tip of last side petal, dc in last dc, turn.

Rows 11 & 12: Rep row 8.

Row 13 (RS): Work in **front lp** *(see Stitch Guide)* only of background dc sts, ch 3, holding WS of orange flowers against RS of background as described in row 10, attach through any 2 WS lps at tip of first flower's side petal and in next background dc, *working behind Flower Strip, dc in next 6 dc, attach by inserting hook under entire occupied ch-1 between flower just passed and next flower and in next background dc*, rep from * to * across tacking down last flower by attaching through any 2 WS lps at tip of last side petal and in next to last background dc, dc in last st, turn.

Rows 14 & 15: Rep row 8.

Row 16: Attaching red Flower Strip, rep row 10.

Rows 17–19: Rep row 8.
Rows 20–73: Rep rows 2–19.
Rows 74–79: Rep rows 2–7.

Fringe

Use 8 strands each 14 inches long for each fringe. Across each end of afghan, attach 1 matching fringe at each Flower Strip and at each skipper blue stripe, 1 white fringe on background between all skipper blue stripes and Flower Strips and 1 white fringe at each corner.

Fold 8 strands in half, insert hook in indicated st, draw strands through at fold to form a lp on hook, draw cut ends through lp on hook. Trim ends even. ✄

Furry Photo Frame
Continued from page 76

First Long Side
Row 1: Count over 6 rows from end of First Short Side, attach light blue, ch 1, hdc in side edge of same row, hdc in each of next 5 rows, turn. *(6 hdc)*
Rows 2–24: Rep row 2 of First Short Side. At the end of row 24, fasten off.

2nd Long Side
Row 1: Working on opposite end of First Short Side, attach light blue, ch 1, hdc in each of next 6 sts, turn.
Rows 2–24: Rep row 2 of First Short Side. At end of row 24, fasten off.

2nd Short Side
Row 1: Attach light blue in side edge of Long Side, ch 1, hdc in same st as beg ch-1 , hdc in each of next 5 hdc, turn.
Rows 2–15: Rep row 2 of First Short Side.
Row 16: Holding last row to side edge of sts and working through both thicknesses, sl st across next 6 sts, fasten off.

Finishing
Apply craft glue on outer edge and front of Picture Frame, press crocheted frame to Picture Frame. Glue Fun Fur edges down around frame edges. ✄

Bare Necessities Necklace Purse
Continued from page 77

Purse
Make 2.
Row 1: Attach 1 strand each jade and silver to D-ring, ch 1, work 20 sc over flat edge of D-ring, turn. *(20 sc)*
Row 2: Ch 1, sc in first st, dc in next st, (sc in next st, dc in next st) across, turn. *(20 sts)*
Row 3: Ch 1, (sc in dc, dc in sc) across, turn,
Rows 4–15: Rep row 3.

Joining
Row 1: Holding both pieces of Purse tog, attach 1 strand each jade and silver metallic in side edge of row 4 and working through both thicknesses, sc in side edge of row 4, **picot** *(see Special Stitch)*, (sc in next st, picot, sc in next st) around to opposite side of row 4 of Purse, sl st in same st as last st in row 4, do not fasten off.

Neckline Strap
Make ch 28 inches in length or to desired length, sl st in same st at beg of row 4 on opposite side of Purse *(same row as joining was started)*, fasten off. ✄

Haven-ly Home Accents

Turn your house into a restful, welcoming haven with this colorful collection of home accessories. Brilliant brights energize your decor and muted neutrals create a calm, peaceful atmosphere. Whether you're looking for a rug or a throw, a pillow or a pot holder, you'll find a variety of designs to dress up your home.

Peruvian Print Throw

Design by Katherine Eng

Neon-bright and toasty warm, this luscious throw features a variety of delicious textures and stitches in vibrant colors to brighten any space.

INTERMEDIATE

6 SUPER BULKY

Finished Size

37 x 54 inches

Materials

- Lion Brand Boucle super bulky (super chunky) weight yarn (2½ oz/57 yds/70g per skein):
  - 5 skeins #106 blueberry
  - 4 skeins #112 rose
  - 2 skeins each #133 tangerine and #194 lime
- Lion Brand Incredible ribbon yarn (1¾ oz/110 yds/50g per ball):
  - 4 balls #207 purple party
- Size H/8/5mm crochet hook or size needed to obtain gauge

Gauge

Row 1, 3 sc and 2 ch-1 sps = 2½ inches; first 2 rows = 2 inches at shell point

Pattern Notes

Weave in loose ends as work progresses. Join rounds with a slip stitch unless otherwise stated.

Special Stitch

Shell: 5 dc in indicated st.

Throw

Row 1 (RS): Beg at bottom edge, with blueberry, ch 98, sc in 2nd ch from hook, (ch 1, sk next ch, sc in next ch) across, turn. *(49 sc, 48 ch-1 sps)*

Row 2: Ch 1, sc in first sc, (ch 1, sk next sc, **shell** *(see Special Stitch)* in next sc, ch 1, sk next sc, sc in next sc) across, fasten off, turn. *(12 shells)*

Row 3: Draw up a lp of tangerine in first sc, ch 3 *(counts as first dc)*, dc in same sc, ch 2, sc in center dc of next shell, (ch 2, (dc, ch 1, dc) in next sc, ch 2, sc in center dc of next shell) across, ending with ch 2, 2 dc in last sc, fasten off.

Row 4: Draw up a lp of rose in first dc of previous row, ch 1, sc in same dc, ch 1, sk next dc, sc in next ch-2 sp, ch 1, sc in next sc,

Continued on page 113

North Woods Throw

Design by Katherine Eng

This cozy, earthy throw, stitched in luxurious bulky yarns, features the subtle, serene woodland colors that perfectly complement a rustic decor.

INTERMEDIATE

5 BULKY

Finished Size
41 x 57 inches

Materials
- Lion Brand Homespun bulky (chunky) weight yarn (6 oz/185 yds/ 170g per skein):
  - 3 skeins #309 deco
  - 2 skeins #326 ranch
- Lion Brand ChenilleThick and Quick bulky (super chunky) weight yarn (108 yds per skein):
  - 2 skeins each #178 basil and #155 champagne
- Lion Brand Wool-Ease medium (worsted) weight yarn (3 oz/197 yds/85g per skein):
  - 2 skeins each #125 camel, #99 fisherman and #127 mink
- Sizes F/5/3.75mm, G/6/ 4mm and H/8/5mm crochet hooks or size needed to obtain gauge

Gauge
Size F hook: rnds 1 and 2 = 3 inches; completed square = 5¾ inches

Pattern Notes
Weave in loose ends as work progresses. Join rounds with a slip stitch unless otherwise stated.

When joining motifs, alternate Motifs A and B throughout.

Special Stitches
Popcorn (pc): 3 dc in indicated st, drop lp from hook, insert hook front to back through top of first dc, pick up dropped lp, draw lp through st on hook.

Shell: 3 dc in indicated st.

Motifs A and B
Make 32 (31).
Rnd 1: With size F hook and fisherman, ch 4, join in first ch to form a ring, ch 3 *(counts as first dc)* (**pc** *(see Special Stitches)* in ring, ch 3) 8 times, join in top of first pc, fasten off. *(8 pc, 8 ch-3 sps)*

Rnd 2: With size G hook, draw up lp of camel in any ch-3 sp, ch 1, (2 sc, ch 2, 2 sc) in same sp, *(3 dc, ch 2, 3 dc) in next ch-3 sp**, (2 sc, ch 2, 2 sc) in next ch-3 sp, rep from * around, ending last rep at **, join in beg sc, fasten off.

Continued on page 111

Confetti Stars Pillow

Design by Katherine Eng

Add a touch of celebrity chic to your decor with this star-studded pillow. Multicolored tape yarn jazzes up this decorative hot-pink design.

INTERMEDIATE

Finished Size
15 inches square

Materials
- Lion Brand Lion Suede bulky (chunky) weight yarn (3 oz/122 yds/85g per skein):
    - 2 skeins #140 rose
    - 1 skein #177 sage
- Lion Brand Incredible bulky (chunky) weight ribbon yarn (1¾ oz/110 yds/50g per ball):
    - 1 ball each #207 purple party and #205 carnival
- Size H/8/5mm crochet hook or size needed to obtain gauge
- 15-inch gold pillow

Gauge
Rnds 1 and 2 = 3 inches; completed motif = 5 inches

Pattern Notes
Weave in loose ends as work progresses.

Join rounds with a slip stitch unless otherwise stated.

When joining motifs, alternate Motifs A and B throughout.

Motifs A and B
Make 10 (8).
Rnd 1 (RS): With purple party (carnival), ch 4, join in first ch to form a ring, ch 3 (*counts as first dc*), 2 dc in ring, ch 2, (3 dc, ch 2) 3 times in ring, join in 3rd ch of beg ch-3, fasten off. (*12 dc, 4 ch-2 sps*)

Rnd 2: Draw up a lp of sage in center dc of any 3-dc group, ch 1, sc in same dc, *ch 1, sk 1 dc, (sc, ch 3, sc) for corner in next ch-2 sp, ch 1, sk 1 dc**, sc in next dc, rep from * around, ending last rep at **, join in beg sc, fasten off. (*12 sc, 8 ch-1 sps, 4 corner ch-3 sps*)

Rnd 3: Draw up a lp of carnival (purple party) in first ch-1 sp to the left of any corner, ch 1, sc in same ch-1 sp, *ch 2, sk next sc, sc in next ch-1 sp, ch 1, sk next sc, (sc, ch 3, sc) in next corner ch-2 sp, ch 1, sk next sc**, sc in next ch-1 sp, rep from * around, ending last rep at **, join in beg sc, fasten off. (*16 sc, 12 ch sps, 4 corner ch-3 sps*)

Note: *Work rnd 4 around first square Motif A, then join motifs as specified on rnd 4 of rem motifs as work progresses.*

Rnd 4: Draw up a lp of rose in first ch-1 sp to the left of any corner ch sp, ch 1, sc in same ch-1 sp, *(2 hdc, ch 2, 2 hdc) in next ch-2 sp, sc in next ch-1 sp, (2 dc, ch 4, 2 dc) in corner ch-3 sp**, sc in next ch-1 sp, rep from * around, ending last rep at **, join in beg sc, fasten off. *(16 dc, 16 hdc, 6 sc, 4 corner ch-4 sps)*

For each Pillow side arrange Motifs in 3 rows of 3 Motifs *(9 Motifs each side of pillow)*, join in alternate patterns beg with Motif A. Join on 1 or 2 sides as necessary after completing first Motif. Continuing in pattern st, join ch-4 sps by working ch 2, drop lp from hook, draw lp under to over through opposite ch-4 sp, ch 2 and continue. Join ch-2 sps by working ch 1, drop lp from hook, draw lp under to over through opposite ch-2 sp, ch 1 and continue. To join where 4 corners meet, ch 2, drop lp from hook, draw lp under to over through opposite ch-4 sp, ch 1, drop lp from hook, sk next ch-4 sp, draw lp under to over through next ch-4 sp, ch 2 and continue.

Border

Rnd 1: Working around a 9-motif piece, draw up a lp of rose in any corner ch-4 sp, ch 1, *(sc, ch 4, sc) in corner ch-4 sp, (ch 3, (sc, ch 2, sc) in next ch-2 sp, ch 3, (sc, ch 2, sc) in each of next 2 ch-4 sps at seam) twice, ch 3, (sc, ch 2, sc) in next ch-2 sp, ch 3, (sc, ch 2, sc) in next ch-2 sp, ch 3, rep from * around, join in beg sc, sl st into ch-4 sp.

Rnd 2: Ch 1, *(sc, ch 4, sc) in corner ch-4 sp, (ch 1, (sc, ch 2, sc) in next ch-3 sp, ch 1, (sc, ch 2, sc) in next ch-2 sp, ch 1, (sc, ch 2, sc) in next ch-3 sp, ch 1, (sc, ch 2, sc) in each of next 2 ch-4 sps) twice, ch 1, (sc, ch 2, sc) in next ch-3 sp, ch 1, (sc, ch 2, sc) in next ch-2 sp, ch 1, (sc, ch 2, sc) in next ch-3 sp, ch 1, rep from * around, join in beg sc, fasten off. Rep rnds 1 and 2 on 2nd 9-motif piece.

Rnd 3: Holding WS of Pillow sides tog and working through both thicknesses, draw up a lp of purple party in corner ch-4 sps, ch 1, *(sc, ch 2, sc, ch 4, sc, ch 2, sc) in corner ch-4 sp, (ch 2, (sc, ch 2, sc) in next ch-2 sp) 3 times, ch 2, (sc, ch 2, sc) in next ch-2 sp, ch 1, (sc, ch 2, sc) in next ch-2 sp, (ch 2, (sc, ch 2, sc) in next ch-2 sp) 3 times, ch 2, (sc, ch 2, sc) in next ch-2 sp, ch 1, (sc, ch 2, sc) in next ch-2 sp, ch 2, (sc, ch 2, sc) in next ch-2 sp) 3 times, ch 2, rep from * around, join in beg sc, fasten off. ✄

Asian Mosaic Pillow

Design by Margret Willson

Inspired by the reverse-appliqué technique used by the Hmong people of Laos, this striking pillow will add an artistic Asian touch to any decor.

INTERMEDIATE

4 MEDIUM

Finished Size
20 inches square

Materials
- Red Heart Super Saver medium (worsted) weight yarn (5 oz/278 yds/141g per skein):
  3 skeins #318 watercolor
- Red Heart Super Saver medium (worsted) weight yarn (7 oz/364 yds/198g per skein):
  1 skein #312 black
- Sizes G/6/4mm and H/8/5mm crochet hooks or size needed to obtain gauge
- 20-inch square pillow insert

Gauge
Size G hook: 10 rows = 2 inches; 8 sts = 2 inches

Pattern Notes
Weave in loose ends as work progresses. Join rounds with a slip stitch unless otherwise stated.

Special Stitch
Slip stitch surface crochet (sl st surface crochet): With yarn held in back of work and allowing a 6-inch tail to work in later, insert hook in given space between sts, yo and draw lp through to front, *insert hook in next given space, yo and draw through to front and through lp on hook as for a sl st, rep from * as indicated by chart on page 115. When section is complete, leaving a 6-inch length fasten off, draw end of yarn to front. Then insert hook from back and draw tail back through same sp. Weave in ends as each section is completed.

Pillow Side
Make 2.
Row 1: With size G hook and watercolor, ch 79, sc in 2nd ch from hook, sc in each rem ch across, turn. *(78 sc, 77 sps between sts)*
Rows 2–100: Ch 1, sc in each st across, turn. At the end of last rep, fasten off.

Embellishment
With size H hook and black yarn, work **sl st surface crochet** *(see Special Stitch)* according to chart on page 115. Grid lines represent sc sts, grid sps represents sps between sc sts. Center design *(shaded in red)* are worked double, at end of double section, turn and work back into each same sp, fasten off at beg st.

Assembly

Holding Pillow Sides with WS tog, with size G hook and working through both thicknesses, attach black in any corner, ch 1, (3 sc in corner st, sc in each st across edge) around, inserting pillow form at the end of 3rd side, then finish across rem 4th side, join in beg sc, fasten off.

Tassel
Make 4.

Cut 18 watercolor and 8 black strands each 10 inches long. Set aside 2 strands of black. Holding all watercolor and 6 strands of black tog, tie a length of black around center of bundle of yarn. Hold by tie strand and arrange yarn into a tassel. Tie another strand of black around tassel 1 inch below top. With size G hook, draw 1 strand of top tie strand through center corner st of pillow, knot firmly with other end of top tie strand. Use hook to work ends of tie back through several sts. Trim tassel ends even. ✄

Flower Fields Rug

Design by Rena Stevens

Set foot onto your own summer garden with this brightly striped rug strewn with rows of multicolored flowers.

 INTERMEDIATE

 MEDIUM

Finished Size
29 x 40 inches

Materials
- Red Heart Classic medium (worsted) weight yarn (3½ oz/198 yds/99g per skein):
    - 2 skeins each #917 cardinal and #230 yellow
    - 1 skein each #220 cornmeal, #848 skipper blue and #689 forest green
- Red Heart Hokey Pokey medium (worsted) weight yarn (4 oz/222 yds/113g per skein):
    - 1 skein each #7110 spearmint and #7111 blue bonnet
- Red Heart Tweed medium (worsted) weight yarn (4 oz/222 yds/113g per skein):
    - 1 skein #7074 cranberry
- Size I/9/5.5mm crochet hook or size needed to obtain gauge

Gauge
7 dc = 2 inches; 2 dc rows = 1¼ inches

Pattern Note
Weave in loose ends as work progresses.

Special Stitches
Leaves: (Sc, ch 10, sc, ch 9, sc, ch 10, sc) in indicated st.

Catch loop (catch lp): Yo, insert hook in indicated dc and under next ch-10 lp, yo, draw up a lp, (yo, draw through 2 lps on hook) twice.

Popcorn (pc): Work 6 dc in indicated st, drop lp from hook, insert hook from front to back in first dc of 6-dc group, pick up dropped lp, draw through st on hook, ch 1.

Rug
Row 1 (RS): With cardinal, ch 106, dc in 4th ch from hook, dc in each rem ch across, turn. *(103 dc)*

Row 2: Ch 3 *(counts as first dc throughout)*, working in **front lp** *(see Stitch Guide)* of each st, dc in each st across, draw up a lp, remove hook, drop yarn, do not fasten off, turn.

Row 3: Attach blue bonnet in first dc, ch 1, sc in same st as beg ch-1, sc in each of next 5 dc, *work **leaves** *(see Special Stitches)* in next dc, ch 1**, sc in each of next 9 dc, rep from * across, ending last rep at **, sc in each of next 6 dc, fasten off, do not turn. *(10 leaf groups)*

Row 4: Working in **back lp** *(see Stitch Guide)* of each st across, pick up dropped lp of cardinal, ch 3, dc in each of next 5 sc, *working behind leaves, ch 1, sk next leaf group and ch-1 sp**, dc in each of next 9 sc, rep from * across, ending last rep at **, dc in each of next 6 sc, turn.

Row 5: Working in front lps of dc sts, ch 3, dc in each of next 2 dc, *catch lp *(see Special Stitches)* in next ch-10 lp, dc in each of next 5 sts, sk center ch-9 lp, catch lp in next ch-10 lp, dc in each of next 3 dc, rep from * across, turn.

Row 6: Working in front lps only, ch 1, sc in same st as beg ch-1, sc in each of next 5 sts, ch 1, sk next dc, (sc in each of next 9 dc, ch 1, sk next dc) across, ending with dc in each of last 6 dc, draw up a lp, remove hook, drop yarn, do not fasten off, do not turn.

Row 7: Work current row sl sts loosely in back lps only, join tweed color *(same color as previous leaves color)* in first st, sl st in each of next 6 sts, *working in front of current row *(folding current row back)*, work **pc** *(see Special Stitches)* by inserting hook in back *(top)* lp of 5th ch of next ch-9 lp and in both lps of next free dc 1 row below, on current row, sk next ch-1**, sl st in next 9 sts, rep from * across, ending last rep at **, fasten off tweed, turn.

Row 8: Working in back lps only of previous background row to hide tweed sl sts, pick up dropped lp, ch 1, sc in same st as beg ch-1, sc in each of next 5 sts, *ch 1, sk next pc and the ch-1 under**, sc in each of next 9 sc, rep from * across, ending last rep at **, sc in each of next 6 sc, turn.

Row 9: Ch 3, working in front lps only, dc in each st across, turn.

Row 10: Rep row 2.

Row 11: Join yellow in first dc, ch 1, sc in same st as beg ch-1, sc in each of next 10 dc, *work leaves in next dc, ch 1**, sc in each of next 9 dc, rep from * across, ending last rep at **, sc in each of next 11 sts, fasten off, do not turn. *(9 leaf groups)*

Row 12: Working in back lps only, pick up dropped lp, ch 3, dc in each of next 10 sts, *working behind leaves, ch 1, sk next leaf group and ch-1**, dc in each of next 9 sts, rep from * across, ending last rep at **, dc in last 11 sts, turn.

Row 13: Working in front lps only, ch 7, dc in each of next 7 dc, *catch lp in next ch-10 lp, dc in each of next 5 sts, sk center ch-9 lp, catch lp in next ch-10 lp**, dc in each of next 3 dc, rep from * across, ending last rep at **, dc in each of next 8 sts, turn.

Row 14: Working in front lps only, ch 1, sc in same st as beg ch-1, sc in each of next 10 sts, (ch 1, sk next dc, sc in each of next 9 sts) across, ending with sc in each of last 11 sts, draw up a lp, drop lp, do not fasten off, do not turn.

Continued on page 114

Pretty Blossoms Pot Holders

Designs by Diane Stone

Treat yourself to these pretty pot holders with lacy edgings and bold, dimensional flowers, or make them as special gifts for family or friends.

Aster

EASY

4 MEDIUM

Finished Size
7½ inches in diameter

Materials
- Lily Sugar'n Cream medium (worsted) weight cotton yarn (2½ oz/120 yds/70g per ball):
    1 ball #00001 white
- Size 10 crochet cotton:
    50 yds light green
    30 yds lilac
    5 yds yellow
- Sizes D/3/3.25mm and F/5/3.75mm crochet hooks or size needed to obtain gauge
- Size 7/1.65mm steel crochet hook

Gauge
Size F hook: rnds 1 and 2 = 2½ inches

Pattern Notes
Weave in loose ends as work progresses.

Join rounds with a slip stitch unless otherwise stated.

Special Stitches
Beginning popcorn (beg pc): Ch 4, 4 tr in same st as beg ch-4, drop lp from hook, insert hook in top of beg ch-4, pick up dropped lp, draw through st on hook.

Popcorn (pc): 5 tr in indicated st, drop lp from hook, insert hook in first tr of 5-tr group, pick up dropped lp, draw through st on hook.

Shell: (2 dc, ch 2, 2 dc) in indicated st.

Pot Holder

Front
Rnd 1: With size F hook and white, leaving a length of yarn, form a ring with yarn, ch 3 *(counts as first dc throughout)*, 13 dc in ring, join in 3rd ch of beg ch-3. Pull rem beg length to close beg opening, secure end. *(14 dc)*

Rnd 2: Ch 3, dc in same st as beg ch-3, 2 dc in each dc around, join in 3rd ch of beg ch-3. *(28 dc)*

Rnd 3: Ch 3, dc in same st as beg ch-3, dc in next st, (2 dc in next st, dc in next st) around, join in 3rd ch of beg ch-3. *(42 dc)*

Rnd 4: Ch 3, dc in same st as beg ch-3, dc in each of next 2 sts, (2 dc in next st, dc in each of next 2 sts) around, join in 3rd ch of beg ch-3. *(56 dc)*

Rnd 5: Ch 3, (dc, ch 2, 2 dc) in same st as beg ch-3, sk next 3 dc, *shell *(see Special Stitches)* in next dc, sk next 3 dc, rep from * around, join in top of beg ch-3, fasten off. *(14 shells)*

Back
Rnds 1–5: Rep rnds 1–5 of Front.

Joining
Rnd 6: Holding Front and Back tog with WS facing, with size D hook and 2 strands of light green held tog and working through both thicknesses, attach in ch-2 sp, ch 3, 7 dc in same ch-2 sp, (sl st, ch 3, sl st) in sp between shells, (7 dc in ch-2 sp of next shell, (sl st, ch 3, sl st) in sp between shells) around, join in top of beg ch-3, fasten off.

Rnd 7: With size 7 steel hook, attach lilac in any ch-3 sp, ch 1, *(sc, ch 3, sc) in ch-3 sp, ch 1, (sc in next dc, ch 3) 7 times, sc in next dc, ch 1, rep from * around, join in beg sc.

Hanging Loop
Rnd 8: With size D hook and 2 strands of lilac, sl st into next ch-3 sp, ch 9, sl st in same ch-3 sp, ch 1, (sc, 14 hdc, sc) in ch-9 lp, fasten off.

Flower

Center
Rnd 1: With size D hook and 2 strands of yellow, ch 2, 6 sc in 2nd ch from hook, join in beg sc. *(6 sc)*

Rnd 2: Ch 1, 2 sc in each sc around, join in beg sc. *(12 sc)*

Rnds 3–5: Ch 1, sc in each sc around, join in beg sc. At the end of rnd 5, fasten off.

Petal
Rnd 1: With size D hook, attach 2 strands of lilac in any sc, (**beg pc**—*see Special Stitches*, ch 1, **pc**—*see Special Stitches*, ch 1) in same sc, ((pc, ch 1) twice in next sc) around, join in 4th ch of beg ch-4, fasten off. *(24 Petals)*

Leaves
Rnd 2: With size D hook, attach 2 strands of light green in any ch-1 sp of rnd 1 with a sl st, *ch 3, sl st in next ch-1 sp, ch 4, sl st in 2nd ch from hook, sc in next ch, dc in last ch, sl st in next ch-1 sp, rep from * around, fasten off. *(12 Leaves)*

With size 7 steel hook, sl st Flower to center front of Pot Holder, do not sl st Leaves to Pot Holder.

Continued on page 112

Sunflowers Pot Holder & Towel Topper

Designs by Diane Stone

Cheery sunflowers on a field of sky blue bring fresh outdoor appeal to your kitchen no matter what the season.

EASY

Finished Size

Pot holder: 6 inches in diameter

Towel topper: 9 inches long

Gauge

Size 4 steel hook: rnds 1–3 = 1¼ inches; 6 sc = 1 inch

Materials

- Size 10 crochet cotton:
  260 yds light blue
  100 yds dark yellow
  60 yds white
  40 yds light green
- Embroidery floss (8.7 yds per skein):
  3 skeins brown
- Sizes 6/1.80mm and 4/2.00mm steel crochet hooks or size needed to obtain gauge
- 2-inch plastic ring
- 1-inch plastic ring
- ⅝-inch white button
- Terry kitchen towel

Pattern Notes

Weave in loose ends as work progresses. Join rounds with a slip stitch unless otherwise stated.

Special Stitches

Popcorn (pc): 3 dc in indicated st, drop lp from hook, insert hook front to back through top of first dc, pick up dropped lp, draw lp through st on hook.

Pot Holder

Front

Rnd 1: With size 4 steel hook and 2 strands of light blue, ch 5, sl st to join to form a ring, ch 3 (*counts as first dc*), 15 dc in ring, join in 3rd ch of beg ch-3. (*16 dc*)

Rnd 2: Ch 3, dc in same st as beg ch-3, 2 dc in each dc around, join in 3rd ch of beg ch-3. (*32 dc*)

Rnd 3: Ch 3, 2 dc in next dc, (dc in next dc, 2 dc in next dc) around, join in 3rd ch of beg ch-3. (*48 dc*)

Rnd 4: Ch 3, dc in next dc, 2 dc in next dc, (dc in each of next 2 dc, 2 dc in next dc) around, join in 3rd ch of beg ch-3. *(64 dc)*

Rnd 5: Ch 3, dc in each of next 2 dc, 2 dc in next dc, (dc in each of next 3 dc, 2 dc in next dc) around, join in 3rd ch of beg ch-3. *(80 dc)*

Rnd 6: Ch 3, dc in each of next 3 dc, 2 dc in next dc, (dc in each of next 4 dc, 2 dc in next dc) around, join in 3rd ch of beg ch-3, fasten off. *(96 dc)*

Back

Rnds 1–6: Rep rnds 1–6 of Front.

Joining

Rnd 1: Holding WS of Front and Back tog and working through both thicknesses, with size 4 steel hook, attach 2 strands of white, ch 6 *(counts as first dc, ch 3),* dc in st before beg ch-6 *(beg cross-st),* (sk next st, dc in next st, ch 3, dc in sk st *(cross-st))* around, join in 3rd ch of beg ch-3, fasten off. *(48 cross-sts)*

Hanger

Rnd 1: With size 4 steel hook, attach 2 strands light blue to 1-inch plastic ring, ch 1, work 24 sc around plastic ring, join in beg sc, turn. *(24 sc)*

Row 2: Now working in rows, ch 1, sc in each of next 6 sc, turn.

Rows 3–8: Ch 1, sc in each of next 6 sc, turn. At the end of row 8, fasten off.

Rnd 9: Now working in rnds, attach 2 strands of white in last sc of row 8, ch 1, sc in same st as beg ch-1, sc in each st across, working

2 sc in corner st, sc evenly sp up side edge, around 18 sc sts of rnd 1 and down opposite side edge, ending with sc in same st as beg ch-1, turn.

Row 10: Now working in rows, holding 8 sts of bottom edge of Hanger to Back of Pot Holder and working through sts of rnd 6, sl st Hanger to Back, fasten off.

Flower Center

Rnd 1: With size 6 steel hook and brown embroidery floss, ch 3, sl st in first ch to form a ring, ch 1, 9 sc in ring, join in beg sc. *(9 sc)*

Rnd 2: Ch 1, 2 sc in each sc around, join in beg sc, fasten off. *(18 sc)*

Continued on page 110

Summer Breeze Throw

Design by Diane Stone

Puffy white daisies with a hint of shimmer stand out on a pretty pastel background in this gorgeous throw that's as light as a summer breeze.

INTERMEDIATE

4 MEDIUM

Finished Size
48½ x 61½ inches

Gauge
Daisy = 3½ inches in diameter; strip width = 7¾ inches

Materials
- Red Heart Baby Sport Econo medium (worsted) weight yarn (6 oz/480 yds/170g per skein):
    - 2 skeins #1001 white pompadour
    - 1 skein #1224 baby yellow pompadour
- Red Heart Super Saver medium (worsted) weight yarn (7 oz/364 yds/198g per skein):
    - 3 skeins #774 light raspberry
    - 2 skeins #661 frosty green
- Size H/8/5mm crochet hook or size needed to obtain gauge

Pattern Notes
Weave in loose ends as work progresses.
Join rounds with a slip stitch unless otherwise stated.
Center of Daisy will cup and this produces the necessary puffiness.

Special Stitches
Shell: (3 dc, ch 2, 3 dc) in indicated st.
Beginning shell (beg shell): Ch 3, (2 dc, ch 2, 3 dc) in same st as beg ch-3.

Daisy
Make 72.
Center
Rnd 1: With baby yellow leaving a slight length at beg, ch 2, 8 sc in 2nd ch from hook, join in beg sc, pull rem beg end to close opening. *(8 sc)*
Rnds 2 & 3: Ch 1, sc in each sc around, join in beg sc. At the end of rnd 3, fasten off. *(8 sc)*

Petals
Rnd 4: Attach white in any sc of rnd 3, ch 4 *(counts as first tr)*, (3 tr, ch 3, 4 tr) in same sc as beg ch-4, ch 3, (4 tr, ch 3) twice in each

Continued on page 108

Butterfly Lace Throw

Design by Rena Stevens

Rows of dainty butterflies take flight in the lacy, openwork pattern of this light, airy throw that will add a touch of sunshine to any room.

INTERMEDIATE

MEDIUM

Materials
- Lion Brand Wool-Ease medium (worsted) weight yarn (3 oz/197 yds/85g per skein):
    4 skeins #158 buttercup yellow
    3 skeins #100 white
- Size J/10/6mm crochet hook or size needed to obtain gauge

Finished Size
37 x 47 inches, excluding fringe

Gauge
Rows 2–7 = 4 inches; 15 hdc = 4 inches

Pattern Notes
Weave in loose ends as work progresses.
Join rounds with a slip stitch unless otherwise stated.
Throw is crocheted vertically.
Leave a 7-inch length of yarn at beg and end of a row when joining or fastening off yarn colors.

Special Stitch
2-tr cluster (2-tr cl): *Yo hook twice, insert hook in indicated st, yo, draw up a lp, (yo, draw through 2 lps on hook) twice, rep from * once in same st, yo, draw through all 3 lps on hook.

Throw
Row 1 (WS): With white, loosely ch 171, hdc in 4th ch from hook, hdc in each rem ch across, fasten off, turn. *(169 hdc)*

Row 2: Working in **back lp** *(see Stitch Guide)* of each st, draw up a lp of buttercup, ch 4, sk next hdc, dc in next hdc, (ch 1, sk next hdc, dc in next hdc) across, fasten off, turn.

Row 3: Draw up a lp of white in top of dc, ch 2, hdc in next ch sp, (sk next dc, 2 hdc in next ch sp) across, ending with hdc in 3rd ch of beg ch-4 of previous row, fasten off, turn.

Rows 4–7: Rep rows 2 and 3.

Row 8: Working in back lps only, attach buttercup in hdc, ch 1, sc in same hdc, *ch 7, sk next 5 hdc, sc in next hdc, ch 4, **2-tr cl** *(see Special Stitch)* in same st as last sc, sk next 5 hdc, 2-tr cl in next hdc, ch 4, sc in same place as last 2-tr cl, rep from * across, turn.

Row 9: Ch 6, *(2-tr cl, ch 4, sc, ch 4, 2-tr cl) in top junction of next tr cl group, ch 3, sc in

next ch-7 sp, ch 3, rep from * across, dtr in sc at base of last ch-7, fasten off, turn.

Row 10: Draw up a lp of white in top of dtr, ch 1, sc in same st as beg ch-1, (ch 5 loosely, sc in top of next 2-tr cl) across, turn. *(28 ch-5 sps)*

Row 11: Working in top lps only, ch 2, sk first sc, hdc in each rem st across, fasten off, turn.

Row 12: Working in back lps only, attach buttercup, ch 1, sc in same hdc, *ch 4, 2-tr cl in same st as last sc, sk next 5 hdc, 2-tr cl in next hdc, ch 4, sc in same place as last 2-tr cl, ch 7, sk next 5 hdc, sc in next hdc, rep from * across, turn.

Row 13: Ch 8, sc in first ch-7 sp, ch 3, *(2-tr cl, ch 4, sc, ch 4, 2-tr cl) in top junction of next tr cl group**, ch 3, sc in next ch-7 sp, ch 3, rep from * across, ending last rep at **, dtr in sc of last petal of previous row, fasten off, turn.

Row 14: Draw up a lp of white in top of end cl, ch 1, sc in same st as beg ch-1, (ch 5 loosely, sc in top of next cl) across, ending with ch 5, sc in 4th ch of beg ch-8, turn.

Row 15: Rep row 11.

Rows 16–57: (Rep rows 2–15) 3 times.

Rows 58–63: Rep rows 2–7. At the end of last rep, fasten off.

Fringe

Use 14-inch lengths of up to 6 strands per fringe, depending on the number of yarn ends incorporated. Use a mixture of white and buttercup including nearby yarn ends in each fringe. Place a fringe at each hdc row and at each butterfly motif across each end of Throw.

Fold strands in half, insert hook in end of row, draw strands at fold through to form a lp on hook, including rem strands of yarn, draw cut ends through lp on hook, pull gently to secure. Trim ends even. ✄

Summer Breeze Throw
Continued from page 104

Continued from page 104

rem sc around, join in 4th ch of beg ch-4, fasten off. *(16 tr Petals)*

Leaf Trim
Make 6 strips of 12 daisies in each row.

First Daisy
Attach frosty green in any ch-3 sp of rnd 4 of Petals, ch 1, sc in same ch-3 sp, ch 5, *sc in next ch-3 sp, ch 1, sc in next ch-3 sp, ch 5, sc in next ch-3 sp, ch 5, sl st in 2nd ch from hook, hdc in next ch, dc in each of next 2 chs**, sc in next ch-3 sp, ch 5, rep from * around, ending last rep at **, join in beg sc, fasten off.

2nd Daisy
Attach frosty green in any ch-3 sp of rnd 4 of Petals, ch 1, sc in same ch-3 sp, ch 5, *sc in next ch-3 sp, ch 1, sc in next ch-3 sp, ch 5, sc in next ch-3 sp, ch 5, with WS facing, sl st in tip of leaf on previous Daisy, sl st in 2nd ch from hook, hdc in next ch, dc in each of next 2 chs, sc in next ch-3 sp of working Daisy, ch 2, sc in next ch-5 sp on previous Daisy, ch 2, sc in next ch-3 sp on working Daisy, ch 1, sc in next ch-3 sp on working Daisy, ch 2, sc in next ch-5 sp on previous Daisy, ch 2, sc in next ch-3 sp on working Daisy, ch 5, sl st in tip of next leaf on previous Daisy, *sl st in 2nd ch from hook, hdc in next ch, dc in each of last 2 chs**, sc in next ch-3 sp on working Daisy, ch 5, sc in next ch-3 sp, ch 1, sc in next ch-3 sp, ch 5, sc in next ch-3 sp, ch 5, rep from * around, ending last rep at ** join in beg sc, fasten off.

Join rem 10 daisies in same manner as 2nd Daisy.

Edging

First Strip

Rnd 1: Attach light raspberry with sl st in first ch-5 sp to the left of corner leaf in right upper corner and working across long edge, **beg shell** (see Special Stitches) in same ch-5 sp, **shell** (see Special Stitches) in next ch-5 sp, ch 7, (shell in each of next 2 ch-5 sps, ch 7) around, join in 3rd ch of beg ch-3.

Rnd 2: Sl st into ch-2 sp of beg shell, beg shell in same ch-2 sp, shell in ch-2 sp of next shell, *ch 1, working over ch-7 of previous row and between leaves, work 2 dc, ch 1, (shell in next shell, ch 1) twice, rep from * around, working at each of the 4 corner leaves, ch 1, working into 4th ch of ch-7 and tip of corner leaf, shell in tip of leaf, ch 1, ending with join in 3rd ch of beg ch-3, fasten off.

2nd Strip

Rnd 1: Rep rnd 1 of First Strip.

Rnd 2: Sl st into ch-2 sp of shell, ch 3, 2 dc in same ch sp, ch 1, holding previous strip next to working strip, sl st in ch-2 sp of adjacent shell, ch 1, 3 dc in same ch-2 sp as beg ch-3, ch 1, 3 dc in ch-2 sp of next shell, ch 1, sl st in adjacent ch-2 sp on previous strip, ch 1, 3 dc in same ch-2 sp on working strip, *ch 1, working over ch-7 sp and into sp between leaves, work 2 dc, (ch 1, 3 dc in ch-2 sp of next shell, ch 1, sl st in adjacent ch-2 sp on previous strip, ch 1, 3 dc in same ch-2 sp of shell on working strip) twice, rep from * across edge, ch 1, working over ch-7 of previous row and between leaves, work 2 dc, ch 1, (shell in next shell, ch 1) twice, rep from * around, working at each of the 4 corner leaves, ch 1, working into 4th ch of ch-7 and tip of corner leaf, shell in tip of leaf, ending with join in 3rd ch of beg ch-3, fasten off.

Join rem strips in the same manner as 2nd strip was joined to First Strip joining adjacent side in last rnd.

Edging

Rnd 1: Working across top of throw, attach light raspberry in upper right corner ch-2 of shell (ch-2 sp of shell to left above corner leaf), beg shell in same ch-2 sp, *((ch 1, sc, ch 1) in sp between shells, shell in next shell) 3 times, ch 1, sc in next ch-1 sp, sl st in each of next 3 dc of shell, sc in ch-2 sp of shell, ch 3, sc in ch-2 sp of next shell on next strip, sl st in each of next 3 dc of shell, sc in next ch-1 sp, ch 1, shell in ch-2 sp of next shell, rep from * 4 times, (ch 1, sc in next ch-1 sp between shells, ch 1, shell in next shell) 5 times, (ch 1, sc in next ch-1 sp, ch 3, sk next 2 dc, sc in next ch-1 sp, shell in ch-2 sp of next shell, (ch 1, sc, ch 1) in next ch-1 sp between shells, shell in next shell) 11 times, (ch 1, sc, ch 1) in next ch-1 sp between shells, shell in next shell, rep from * around, join in top of beg ch-3.

Rnd 2: Sl st into corner ch-2 sp of shell, ch 4 (counts as first dc, ch 1), ({dc, ch 1} 4 times, dc) in corner ch-2 sp above a corner leaf, *(ch 1, sc in next ch-1 sp, sk next sc, sc in next ch-1 sp, (ch 1, dc) 6 times in ch-2 sp of next shell) 3 times, ch 1, sc in next ch-1 sp, ch 1, 2 dc in next ch-3 sp, ch 1, sc in next ch-1 sp, (ch 1, dc) 6 times in ch-2 sp of next shell, rep from * 4 times, (ch 1, sc in next ch-1 sp, sk next sc, sc in next ch-1 sp, (ch 1, dc) 6 times in ch-2 sp of next shell) 5 times, (ch 1, 2 dc in next ch-3 sp, (ch 1, dc) 6 times in ch-2 sp of next shell, ch 1, sc in next ch-1 sp, sk next sc, sc in next ch-1 sp, (ch 1, dc) 6 times in ch-2 sp of next shell) 11 times, ch 1, sc in next ch-1 sp, sk next sc, sc in next ch-1 sp**, (ch 1, dc) 6 times in corner ch-2 sp above a corner leaf, rep from * around, ending last rep at **, join in 3rd ch of beg ch-4, fasten off. ✂

Sunflowers Pot Holder & Towel Topper

Continued from page 103

Front Petals

Rnd 3: With size 6 hook, attach dark yellow in any sc of rnd 2, ((ch 3, dc, ch 1, sl st in top of last dc, dc, ch 3, sl st) in sc, sk next sc) 9 times, do not fasten off.

Back Petals

Rnd 4: Ch 2, working behind Front Petals in sk sts of rnd 2, sl st in next sk st, (ch 4, tr, ch 1, sl st in top of tr, tr, ch 4, sl st) in same st, ((ch 4, tr, ch 1, sl st in top of tr, tr, ch 4, sl st) in next sk st) around, fasten off.

Leaf Ring

With size 6 steel hook and light green, (ch 7, sl st in 2nd ch from hook, sc in next ch, hdc in next ch, dc in each of next 3 chs) 9 times, join in base of beg ch, fasten off.

With size 6 steel hook, sl st Leaf Ring to center front of Pot Holder. Sl st Flower centered over Leaf Ring.

Towel Topper

Ring

Rnd 1: With size 4 steel hook, attach 2 strands light blue to 2-inch plastic ring, ch 1, work 40 sc around plastic ring, join in beg sc. *(40 sc)*

Row 2: Now working in rows, ch 1, sc in each of next 7 sc, turn.

Row 3: Ch 1, sc in each sc across, turn.

Rows 4–45: Rep row 3.

Row 46: Ch 1, sc in each of next 2 sc, ch 3, sk next 3 sc *(buttonhole)*, sc in each of next 2 sc, turn.

Row 47: Ch 1, sc in each of next 2 sc, work 3 sc in ch-3 sp, sc in each of next 2 sc, turn.

Row 48: Rep row 3.

Row 49: Ch 1, **sc dec** *(see Stitch Guide)* in next 2 sc, sc in each of next 3 sc, sc dec over next 2 sc, turn. *(5 sc)*

Row 50: Ch 1, sc dec in next 2 sc, sc in next sc, sc dec over next 2 sc, turn. *(3 sc)*

Row 51: Ch 1, draw up a lp in each of next 3 sc, yo, draw through all 4 lps on hook, fasten off.

Rnd 52: Attach 2 strands of white in any sc on Ring, ch 1, working around entire piece, sc evenly sp around, working 3 sc in point of row 51, join in beg sc, fasten off.

With size 6 hook and a length of white cotton, attach button to row 29 of Towel Topper.

Flower Center

Rnd 1: With size 4 steel hook, holding 2 strands of brown tog, ch 4, sl st in first ch to form a ring, ch 1, 10 sc in ring, join in beg sc. *(10 sc)*

Rnd 2: Ch 1, (sc in next sc, 2 sc in next sc) 5 times, join in beg sc. *(15 sc)*

Rnd 3: Ch 1, (sc in each of next 2 sc, 2 sc in next sc) 5 times, join in beg sc. *(20 sc)*

Rnd 4: Ch 1, (sc in next sc, 2 sc in next sc) 10 times, join in beg sc, fasten off. *(30 sc)*

Front Petals

Rnd 5: Attach dark yellow with sl st in any sc of rnd 4, (ch 3, tr, ch 1, sl st in top of tr, tr, ch 3, sl st) in same st, sk next st, ((ch 3, tr, ch 1, sl st in top of tr, tr, ch 3, sl st) in next st, sk next st) around. *(15 petals)*

Back Petals

Rnd 6: Ch 2, working behind Front Petals, sl st in first sk st of rnd 4, (ch 4, dtr, ch 1, sl st in top of dtr, dtr, ch 4, sl st) in same st, ((ch 4, dtr, ch 1, sl st in top of dtr, dtr, ch 4, sl st) in next sk st) around, join, fasten off.

Leaf Spray

With size 4 steel hook and 2 strands of light green, (ch 8, sl st in 2nd ch from hook, sc in next ch, dc in each of next 2 chs, tr in each of next 3 chs) 12 times, join in base of beg ch-8, fasten off.

Finishing

Place Towel Topper on a flat surface, with button fastened into buttonhole and button facing, glue Leaf Spray centered between strap and plastic ring. With size 6 steel hook, sl st Flower centered over Leaf Spray.

Pass terry towel through plastic ring. ✀

North Woods Throw
Continued from page 92

Continued from page 92

Rnd 3: With size G hook, draw up lp of mink in any corner ch-2 sp, ch 1, sc in same sp, *ch 1, (3 dc, ch 2, 3 dc) in next ch-2 sp, ch 1**, sc in next ch-2 sp, rep from * around, ending last rep at **, join in beg sc, fasten off.

Rnd 4: With size H hook, draw up a lp of basil (champagne) in any st, ch 1, sc in each st and in each ch-1 sp around working (sc, ch 2, sc) in each corner ch-2 sp, join in beg sc, fasten off. *(44 sc, 4 ch-2 sps)*

Note: *Work rnd 5 around first square of Motif A, then join motifs as specified on rnd 5 of remaining motifs as work progresses.*

Rnd 5: With size H hook, draw up a lp of ranch (deco) in 2nd sc to the left of any corner ch-2 sp, ch 1, (sc, ch 2, sc) in same sc, (sk 1 sc, (sc, ch 2, sc) in next sc) around, working at each corner (sc, ch 4, sc) in corner ch-2 sps, join in beg sc, fasten off. *(20 ch-2 sps, 4 ch-4 sps)*

Joining motifs: Alternating Motifs A and B and working rnd 5, join in 7 rows of 9 motifs. To join corner sps where 2 corners meet, continuing in pattern st, ch 2, drop lp, draw lp under to over through opposite ch-4 sp, ch 2 and continue. To join ch-2 sps, ch 1, drop lp, draw lp under to over through opposite ch-2 sp, ch 1 and continue. To join where 4 corners meet, ch 2, drop lp, draw lp under to over through opposite ch-4 sp, ch 1, drop lp, sk next ch-4 sp, draw lp under to over through next ch-4 sp, ch 2 and continue.

Border

Rnd 1 (RS): With size H hook, draw up a lp of deco in first ch-2 sp to the left of any corner ch-4 sp, ch 1, sc in same sp, *ch 2, sc in next ch-2 sp *(or ch-4 sp of corners at joining seams)*, rep from * around, working ch 2, (sc, ch 4, sc) in each corner ch-4 sp, join last ch 2 to beg sc, sl st into next ch-2 sp.

Rnd 2: Ch 1, (sc, ch 2, sc) in each ch-2 sp, ({sc, ch 2} 3 times, sc) in each corner ch-4 sp, join in beg sc, fasten off.

Rnd 3: Draw up a lp of camel in any ch-2 sp, ch 1, (sc, ch 2, sc) in each ch-2 sp around, join in beg sc, fasten off, turn.

Rnd 4: Draw up a lp of champagne in any ch-2 sp *(not in a corner)*, ch 1, sc in same sp, (ch 1, sc in next ch-2 sp) around, working at each corner, ch 1, (sc, ch 3, sc) in each corner ch-2 sp, join in beg sc, fasten off, turn.

Rnd 5: Draw up a lp of mink in any sc, ch 1, (sc, ch 2, sc) in each sc and (sc, ch 3, sc) in each corner ch-3 sp, join in beg sc, fasten off, turn.

Rnd 6: Draw up a lp of basil in any sc, rep rnd 4.

Rnd 7: Draw up a lp of ranch in first ch sp to the left of any corner ch-3 sp, ch 1, sc in same sp, (**shell** *(see Special Stitches)* in next ch sp, sc in next ch sp) around, working 5 dc in each corner ch-3 sp, join in beg sc.

Rnd 8: With size G hook, *ch 2, (sc, ch 2, sc) in center dc of next shell, ch 2, sl st in next sc, rep from * around, working at each corner, ch 2, sk 1 dc, (sc, ch 2, sc) in next dc, (sc, ch 3, sc) in next dc, (sc, ch 2, sc) in next dc, ch 2, sk last dc, sl st in next sc, ending with sl st in same st as beg ch-2, fasten off. ✀

Pretty Blossoms Pot Holders

Continued from page 101

Rose

EASY

Finished Size

7 inches in diameter

Materials

- Size 10 crochet cotton:
  150 yds white
  75 yds red
  2 yds light green
- Sizes 6/1.80mm and 4/2.00mm steel crochet hooks or size needed to obtain gauge
- 5/16-inch-wide red sheer satin ribbon: 24 inches

Gauge

Size 4 steel hook: 6 dc = 1 inch; 2 dc rnds = 1 inch

Pattern Notes

Weave in loose ends as work progresses. Join rounds with a slip stitch unless otherwise stated.

Pot Holder

Front

Rnd 1: With size 4 steel hook, holding 2 strands of white tog, ch 4, sl st to join in first ch to form a ring, ch 3 *(counts as first dc)*, 15 dc in ring, join in 3rd ch of beg ch-3. *(16 dc)*

Rnd 2: Ch 3, dc in same st as beg ch-3, 2 dc in each st around, join in 3rd ch of beg ch-3. *(32 dc)*

Rnd 3: Ch 3, 2 dc in next st, (dc in next st, 2 dc in next st) around, join in 3rd ch of beg ch-3. *(48 dc)*

Rnd 4: Ch 3, dc in next st, 2 dc in next st, (dc in each of next 2 sts, 2 dc in next st) around, join in 3rd ch of beg ch-3. *(64 dc)*

Rnd 5: Ch 3, dc in each of next 2 sts, 2 dc in next st, (dc in each of next 3 sts, 2 dc in next st) around, join in 3rd ch of beg ch-3. *(80 dc)*

Rnd 6: Ch 3, dc in each of next 3 sts, 2 dc in next st, (dc in each of next 4 sts, 2 dc in next st) around, join in 3rd ch of beg ch-3, fasten off. *(96 dc)*

Back

Rnds 1–6: Rep rnds 1–6 of Front.

Heart Edging

Rnd 1: With size steel 4 hook, holding Front and Back with WS tog, working in **back lp** *(see Stitch Guide)* of each st around, attach 2 strands of red in rnd 6, (ch 3, 2 dc, ch 2, 3 dc) in same st, (sk next 4 sts, (3 dc, ch 3, 3 dc) in next dc) 18 times, join in 3rd ch of beg ch-3.

Rnd 2: *(Dc, 2 tr, ch 4, sl st, ch 4, 2 tr, dc) in ch-2 sp, sk next 2 dc, sl st in each of next 2 dc, rep from * around, fasten off.

Rose

Rnd 1: With size 6 steel hook and 1 strand of red, ch 3, join in first ch to form ring, ch 3 *(counts as first dc)*, 9 dc in ring, join in 3rd ch of beg ch-3. *(10 dc)*

Rnd 2: Ch 1, sc in same st as beg ch-1, ch 3, (sk next st, sc in next st, ch 3) around, join in beg sc. *(5 ch-3 lps)*

Rnd 3: Sl st into first ch-3 sp, (ch 2, 4 dc, ch 2, sl st) in same ch-3 sp, (sl st in next ch-3 sp, (ch 2, 4 dc, ch 2, sl st) in same ch-3 sp) around, do not join. *(5 petals)*

Rnd 4: Ch 1, working behind petals of previous rnd, sc in first sk dc of rnd 1, ch 4, (sc in next sk dc of rnd 1, ch 4) around, join in beg sc. *(5 ch-4 lps)*

Rnd 5: Sl st into ch-4 sp, (ch 2, 6 dc, ch 2, sl st) in same ch-4 sp, ((sl st, ch 2, 6 dc, ch 2, sl st) in next ch-4 sp) around, do not join. *(5 petals)*

Rnd 6: Ch 2, working over ch-4 lps of rnd 4, insert hook from back to front, work 1 sc over ch-4 lp between 3rd and 4th dc of first petal, ch 6, (sc over ch-4 lp between 3rd and 4th dc of next petal, ch 6) around, join in beg sc. *(5 ch lps)*

Rnd 7: Sl st into first ch sp, (ch 2, 8 dc, ch 2, sl st) in same ch-6 sp, (sl st in next ch-6 sp, (ch 2, 8 dc, ch 2, sl st) in same ch sp) around, ending with sl st in same sp as beg sl st, fasten off.

Leaf Spray

With size 4 steel hook and 2 strands of light green held tog, (ch 5, sc in 2nd ch from hook, hdc in next ch, dc in each of next 2 chs) twice, fasten off.

Finishing

With size 4 steel hook, sl st Leaf Spray to back of Rose and sl st Rose to center front of Pot Holder.

Weave ribbon through sts of rnd 6 of Front, weaving over 2 sts, under 2 sts around, fasten off ribbon, with size 4 steel hook, sl st ends of ribbon to underside of front.

Cut an 8-inch length of ribbon for hanging lp, tie ends tog in a knot and lp between hearts. Tie rem length of ribbon into a bow and center below hanging lp. ✂

Peruvian Print Throw
Continued from page 90

Continued from page 90

(ch 1, sc in next ch-2 sp, ch 1, sc in next ch-1 sp, ch 1, sc in next ch-2 sp, ch 1, sc in next sc) across, ending with ch 1, sc in next ch-2 sp, ch 1, sk next dc, sc in last dc, turn.

Row 5: Rep row 2.

Row 6: With lime, rep row 3.

Row 7: With WS facing, draw up a lp of purple party in first dc, rep row 4, turn.

Row 8: Ch 1, sc in first sc, (ch 1, sk next ch-1 sp, sc in next sc) across, fasten off.

Row 9: With RS facing, draw up a lp of blueberry in first sc, ch 1, sc in first sc, (ch 1, sk next ch-1 sp, sc in next sc) across, turn.

Rows 10–81: (Rep rows 2–9) 9 times.

Rows 82–86: Rep rows 2–6 consecutively.

Border

Rnd 1 (WS): Draw up a lp of purple party in first dc, ch 1, sc in same dc, ch 1, sk next dc, sc in next ch-2 sp, ch 1, sc in next sc, (ch 1, sc in next ch-2 sp, ch 1, sc in next ch-1 sp, ch 1, sc in next ch-2 sp, ch 1, sc in next sc) across ending with ch 1, sk next dc, (sc, ch 2, sc) in corner dc, working down left edge of Throw, *(ch 1, sc in next sc) twice, ch 1, sc over post of next dc, (ch 1, sc in next sc) twice**, ch 1, sk next sc, sc in next sc, ch 1, sc over post of next dc, rep from * across, ending last rep at **, ch 1, (sc, ch 2, sc) in corner ch, working across bottom opposite side of foundation ch, (ch 1, sk next ch, sc in next ch) across, ending with ch 1, sk next ch, (sc, ch 2, sc) in last ch, working up right edge, (ch 1, sc in next sc) twice, ch 1, sc over post of next dc, (ch 1, sc in next sc) twice, ch 1, sc over post of next dc, (ch 1, sc in next sc, ch 1, sk next sc, sc in next sc, {ch 1, sc in next sc} twice, ch 1, sc over post of next dc, {ch 1, sc in next sc} twice, ch 1, sc over post of next dc) across, ending with ch 1, (sc, ch 2) in same dc as beg sc, join in beg sc, turn.

Rnd 2: Ch 1, (sc, ch 2, sc) in corner ch-2 sp, (ch 1, sk next sc, sc in next ch-1 sp) around, working at each corner, ch 1, sk next sc, (sc, ch 2, sc) in corner ch-2 sp, ending with ch 1, sk last sc, join in beg sc, turn. *(50 sc top* *and bottom, 78 sc each side)*

Rnd 3: Ch 1, beg with sc in next ch-1 sp, rep rnd 2, join in beg sc, fasten off, turn.

Rnd 4: Draw up a lp of tangerine in ch-1 sp near center of any side, ch 1, rep rnd 2, join in beg sc, fasten off.

Rnd 5: Draw up a lp of purple party in ch-1 sp near center of any side, ch 1, rep rnd 2, join in beg sc, fasten off.

Rnd 6: With lime, rep rnd 5, turn.

Rnd 7: Rep rnd 5, turn.

Rnd 8: With blueberry, rep rnd 5, do not fasten off, sl st into next ch-1 sp.

Rnd 9: (Ch 2, sk next sc, sl st in next ch-1 sp) around, working at each corner, ch 2, sk next sc, (sl st, ch 3, sl st) in corner ch-2 sp, ending with ch 2, sk last sc, sl st in same ch-1 sp as beg sl st, fasten off. ✂

Flower Fields Rug
Continued from page 99

Row 15: Work current row, sl st loosely in back lps only, join matching tweed color of leaves in first st, sl st in each of next 11 sts, *working in front of current row, work pc by inserting hook in back lp only of 5th ch of next ch-9 lp and in both lps of next free dc 1 row below on current row, sk next ch-1**, sl st in each of next 9 sts, rep from * across, ending last rep at **, sl st in next 11 sts, fasten off, turn.

Row 16: Working in back lps only of previous background row, pick up dropped lp, ch 1, sc in same st as beg ch-1, sc in each of next 10 sts, *ch 1, sk next pc and the ch-1 under**, sc in each of next 9 sc, rep from * across, ending last rep at **, sc in each of next 11 sc, turn.

Row 17: Rep row 9.

Row 18: Ch 3, dc in front lp of each st across, fasten off.

Row 19: Attach spearmint in first dc, ch 1, sc in each st across, turn.

Row 20: Ch 2 *(counts as first hdc)*, hdc in next sc, (ch 1, sk next sc, hdc in each of next 2 sc) 33 times, ch 1, sk next sc, hdc in last st, turn.

Row 21: Ch 1, sc in same st as beg ch-1, (sc in next ch-1 sp, sc in each of next 2 hdc) across, fasten off, do not turn. *(103 sc)*

Row 22: Attach cornmeal, ch 3, dc in each sc across, turn.

Rows 23–42: Rep rows 2–21, continuing to use cornmeal for background and using cranberry for first flower motif, spearmint for 2nd flower motif and blue bonnet for color break between backgrounds *(rows 19–21)*.

Row 43: With forest green, rep row 22.

Rows 44–63: Rep rows 2–21, continuing to use forest green for background and yellow for first flower motif, blue bonnet for 2nd flower motif and cranberry for color break between backgrounds *(rows 19–21)*.

Row 64: With skipper blue, rep row 22.

Rows 65–84: Rep rows 2–21, continuing to use skipper blue for background and using spearmint for first flower motif, cranberry for 2nd flower motif and yellow for color break between backgrounds *(rows 19–21)*.

Row 85: With cardinal, rep row 22.

Rows 86–102: Rep rows 2–18.

Fringe

Cut 5 strands cardinal each 9 inches in length for each fringe. (Fold 5 strands in half, insert hook in st, draw strands through at fold to form a lp on hook, draw cut ends through lp on hook, pull ends gently to secure strands) 33 times on each end of Rug.

Add backing if firmer Rug is desired. ✂

Asian Mosaic Pillow

Continued from page 97

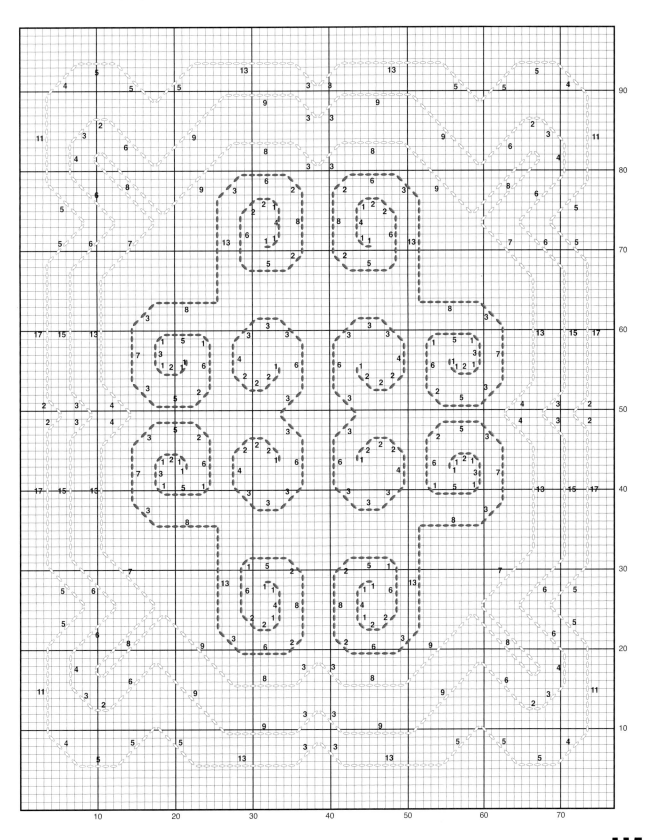

Treasures in Thread

The beautiful thread treasures you create in crochet are not only projects to bring beauty to your home, they are memories to be shared. Whether you crochet a bonnet and booties for a baby's christening, a pretty bookmark for a special friend or delicate doilies for a housewarming, each becomes a treasured keepsake.

Flower-Fresh Bookmarks

Designs by Diane Stone

Two pretty patterns with different flower variations equal a bouquet of bookmarks for all the book lovers on your list.

EASY

Finished Size
2½ x 8¼ inches

Materials
- Size 10 crochet cotton (350 yds per ball):
    - 30 yds each light yellow and white
    - 8 yds dark yellow
    - 60 yds white
    - 3 yds lilac
    - 2 yds light green
- Size 6/1.80mm steel crochet hook or size needed to obtain gauge
- 3 pearl 3mm beads
- 12 inches ⅝-inch-wide white satin ribbon
- 10 inches ³⁄₁₆-inch-wide picot edged white ribbon
- Washable fabric glue
- White craft glue
- Paper towel
- Waxed paper

Violets Bookmark

Gauge
1 sc and 7 tr = 1¼ inches

Pattern Notes
Weave in loose ends as work progresses. Join rounds with a slip stitch unless otherwise stated.

Special Stitch
Shell: 7 tr in indicated st.

Bookmark
Row 1: With light yellow, ch 72, sc in 2nd ch from hook, (sk next 4 chs, **shell** *(see Special Stitch)* in next ch, sk next 4 chs, sc in next ch) 7 times, fasten off. *(7 shells)*

Row 2: With light yellow, ch 72, sc in 2nd ch from hook, holding row 1 next to row 2 matching tr sts of shells, (sk next 4 chs, 4 tr in next ch, sl st 4th tr of shell of row 1, 3 tr in same ch on row 2 as previous 4 tr, sk next 4 chs, sc in next ch) 7 times, fasten off.

Row 3: Working on opposite side of foundation ch of row 1, attach white in same ch as first sc, ch 1, sc in same ch as beg ch-1, (sk

next 4 chs, shell in same ch as shell of row 1, sk next 4 chs, sc in next ch) 7 times, fasten off.

Row 4: Working on opposite side of foundation ch of row 2, attach white in same ch as first sc, ch 1, sc in same ch as beg ch-1, (sk next 4 chs, shell in same ch as shell of row 2, sk next 4 chs, sc in next ch) 7 times, fasten off.

Rnd 5: Now working in rnds, attach dark yellow in first sc of row 4, ch 1, sc in same sc as beg ch-1, *(ch 1, sc in next tr) 7 times, ch 1, sl st in next sc, rep from * 5 times, (ch 1, sc in next tr) 7 times, ch 1, sc in last sc, (ch 1, sc in next tr) twice across light yellow section, ch 3, sc in 6th tr of next light yellow section, ch 1, sc in next tr, ch 1**, sc in next sc, rep from * around, ending last rep at **, join in beg sc, fasten off.

Flower
Make 3.
Leaving a slight length at beg, with lilac form a ring, *(ch 2, 2 dc, ch 2, sl st) 5 times in ring, fasten off. Draw beg rem length to close opening, secure end with a drop of glue, fasten off rem length. *(5 petals)*

Leaf
Make 3.
With light green, (ch 5, sl st in 2nd ch from hook, hdc in next ch, dc in last ch) twice, fasten off.

Finishing
For starch, stir tog well 2 tablespoons of white craft glue and 3 tablespoons of water. Saturate Bookmark only with starch, with paper towel, blot excess starch from Bookmark. Place Bookmark on waxed paper and allow to dry.

Weave ⅝-inch ribbon through Bookmark over and under shells at center, glue ends on WS of marker.

Continued on page 145

Pretty Pineapples

Designs by Judy Teague Treece

Dainty pineapple doilies in a trio of spring pastels bring a breath of fresh air to any tabletop.

Finished Size

Yellow doily: 10 inches in
   diameter

Aqua doily: 11½ inches in
   diameter

Lavender doily: 11 inches
   in diameter

Materials

• DMC Cebelia size 10
   crochet cotton (284
   yds per ball):
      1 ball #745 banana
         yellow

• Aunt Lydia's size 10
   crochet cotton (350
   yds per ball):
      1 ball each #450
         aqua and #495
         wood violet

• Size 7/1.65mm
   steel crochet hook
   or size needed to
   obtain gauge

Gauge

3 tr rnds = 1 inch

Pattern Notes

Weave in loose ends as work progresses.
Join rounds with a slip stitch unless otherwise stated.

Special Stitches

Shell: (2 tr, ch 2, 2 tr) in indicated st.

Beginning shell (beg shell): Sl st into ch sp, ch 4, (tr, ch 2, 2 tr) in same ch sp as beg ch-4.

3-treble crochet cluster (3-tr cl): *Yo hook twice, insert hook in indicated st, yo, draw up a lp, (yo, draw through 2 lps on hook) twice, rep from * twice, yo, draw through all 4 lps on hook.

Yellow Doily

Rnd 1: With banana yellow, ch 6, sl st in first ch to form a ring, ch 4 (*counts as first tr*), tr in ring, ch 2, (2 tr, ch 2) 7 times in ring, join in 3rd ch of beg ch-4. (*16 tr, 8 ch-2 sps*)

Rnd 2: Ch 4, tr in next tr, ch 4, (tr in each of next 2 tr, ch 4) 7 times, join in 4th ch of beg ch-4.

Rnd 3: Ch 4, tr in next tr, *ch 3, sc in next ch-4 sp, ch 3**, tr in each of next 2 tr, rep from * around, ending last rep at **, join in 4th ch of beg ch-4.

Rnd 4: Ch 4, tr in next tr, *ch 3, sc in next ch-3 sp, ch 2, sc in next ch-3 sp, ch 3**, tr in each of next 2 tr, rep from * around, ending last rep at **, join in 4th ch of beg ch-4.

Rnd 5: Ch 4, tr in next tr, *ch 3, sc in next ch-3 sp, ch 2, (tr, ch 2, tr) in next ch-2 sp, ch 2, sc in next ch-3 sp, ch 3**, tr in each of next 2 tr, rep from * around, ending last rep at **, join in 4th ch of beg ch-4.

Rnd 6: Ch 4, tr in same st as beg ch-3, ch 1, 2 tr in next tr, *ch 3, sc in next ch-3 sp, ch 2, sk next ch-2 sp (sc, ch 7, sc) in ch-2 sp between tr sts, ch 2, sk next ch-2 sp, sc in next ch-3 sp, ch 3**, 2 tr in next tr, ch 1, 2 tr in next tr, rep from * around, ending last rep at **, join in 4th ch of beg ch-4. *(8 pineapple bases)*

Rnd 7: Sl st into ch-1 sp, ch 5 *(counts as first tr, ch 1)*, tr in same ch-1 sp, *ch 3, sc in next ch-3 sp, ch 2, 7 tr in next ch-7 sp, ch 2, sc in next ch-3 sp, ch 3**, (tr, ch 1, tr) in next ch-1 sp, rep from * around, ending last rep at **, join in 4th ch of beg ch-5.

Rnd 8: Sl st into ch-1 sp, ch 1, *(sc, ch 5, sc) in ch-1 sp, ch 3, sc in next ch-3 sp, ch 3, sc in next tr, (ch 2, sc in next tr) 6 times, ch 3, sc in next ch-3 sp, ch 3, rep from * around, join in beg sc.

Rnd 9: Sl st into ch-5 sp, ch 4, 6 tr in same ch-5 sp, *ch 3, sc in next ch-3 sp, ch 4, sc in next ch-2 sp, (ch 2, sc in next ch-2 sp) 5 times, ch 4, sk next sp, sc in next ch sp, ch 3**, 7 tr in next ch-5 sp, rep from * around, ending last rep at **, join in 4th ch of beg ch-4.

Rnd 10: Ch 4, (ch 1, tr in next tr) 6 times, *ch 3, sc in next ch-3 sp, ch 4, sc in next ch-2 sp, (ch 2, sc in next ch-2 sp) 4 times, ch 4, sc in next ch-3 sp, ch 3**, tr in next tr, (ch 1, tr in next tr) 6 times, rep from * around, ending last rep at **, join in 4th ch of beg ch-4.

Rnd 11: Sl st into ch-1 sp, ch 4, *(ch 2, tr in next ch-1 sp) 5 times, ch 4, sc in next ch-3 sp, ch 4, sc in next ch-2 sp, (ch 2, sc in next ch-2 sp) 3 times, ch 4, sc in next ch-3 sp, ch 4**, tr in next ch-1 sp, rep from * around, ending last rep at **, join in 4th ch of beg ch-4.

Rnd 12: Sl st into ch-2 sp, ch 5, tr in same ch-2 sp, *(ch 1, (tr, ch 1, tr) in next ch-2 sp) 4 times, ch 4, sc in next ch-4 sp, ch 5, sk next ch-4 sp, sc in next ch-2 sp, (ch 2, sc in next ch-2 sp) twice, ch 5, sk next ch-4 sp, sc in next ch-4 sp, ch 4**, (tr, ch 1, tr) in next ch-2 sp, rep from * around, ending last rep at **, join in 4th ch of beg ch-5.

Rnd 13: Sl st into ch-1 sp, ch 5, tr in same ch-1 sp, *(ch 1, (tr, ch 1, tr) in next ch-1 sp) 8 times, ch 4, sc in next ch-4 sp, ch 6, sc in next ch-2 sp, ch 2, sc in next ch-2 sp, ch 6, sc in next ch-4 sp, ch 4**, (tr, ch 1, tr) in next ch-1 sp, rep from * around, ending last rep at **, join in 4th ch of beg ch-5.

Rnd 14: Sl st into ch-1 sp, ch 5, tr in same ch-1 sp, *(ch 1, sk next ch-1 sp, (tr, ch 1, tr) in next ch-1 sp) 8 times, ch 4, sc in next ch-4 sp, ch 2, sk next ch-6 sp, next ch-2 sp and next ch-6 sp, sc in next ch-4 sp ch 4**, (tr, ch 1, tr) in next ch-1 sp, rep from * around, ending last rep at **, join in 4th ch of beg ch-5.

Rnd 15: Sl st into ch-1 sp, ch 1, *((sc, ch 3, sc) in ch-1 sp, 2 sc in next ch-1 sp) 8 times, (sc, ch 3, sc) in next ch-1 sp, 2 sc in each of next 2 ch-4 sps, rep from * around, join in beg sc, fasten off.

Aqua Doily

Rnd 1: With aqua, ch 6, sl st in first ch to form a ring, ch 4 *(counts as first tr)*, 20 tr in ring, join in 3rd ch of beg ch-3. *(21 tr)*

Rnd 2: Ch 5 *(counts as first tr, ch-1)*, tr in same st as beg ch-5, sk next 2 sts, (ch 4, (tr, ch 1, tr) in next tr, sk next 2 tr) around, join in 4th ch of beg ch-5. *(7 ch-1 sps, 7 ch-4 sps)*

Rnd 3: Sl st into ch-1 sp, **beg shell** *(see Special Stitches)* in same ch-1 sp, *ch 4, sc in next ch-4 sp, ch 4**, **shell** *(see Special Stitches)* in next ch-1 sp, rep from * around, ending last rep at **, join in 4th ch of beg ch-4. *(7 shells)*

Rnd 4: Sl st into ch-2 sp, beg shell in same ch-2 sp, *ch 4, sc in next ch-4 sp, ch 2, sc in next ch-4 sp, ch 4**, shell in next ch-2 sp of next shell, rep from * around, ending last rep at **, join in 4th ch of beg ch-4.

Rnd 5: Sl st into ch-2 sp, ch 1, *(sc, ch 7, sc) in ch-2 sp, ch 4, (tr, ch 1, tr) in next ch-2 sp, ch 4, rep from * around, join in beg sc.

Rnd 6: Sl st into ch-7 sp, ch 4, 8 tr in same ch-7 sp, *ch 4, sc in next ch-4 sp, ch 3, (tr, ch 1, tr) in next ch-1 sp, ch 3, sc in next ch-4 sp, ch 4**, 9 tr in next ch-7 sp, rep from * around, ending last rep at **, join in 4th ch of beg ch-4. *(7 pineapple bases)*

Rnd 7: Ch 1, *sc in first tr, (ch 2, sc in next tr) 8 times, ch 3, (tr, ch 2, tr) in next ch-1 sp, ch 3, rep from * around, join in beg sc.

Rnd 8: Sl st into ch-2 sp, ch 1, *sc in ch-2 sp, (ch 2, sc in next ch-2 sp) 7 times, ch 3, ({tr, ch 1} twice, tr) in next ch-2 sp, ch 3, rep from * around, join in beg sc.

Rnd 9: Sl st into ch-2 sp, ch 1, *sc in ch-2 sp, (ch 2, sc in next ch-2 sp) 6 times, ch 3, (tr, ch 1, tr) in next ch-1 sp, ch 1, (tr, ch 1, tr) in next ch-1 sp, ch 3, rep from * around, join in beg sc.

Rnd 10: Sl st into ch-2 sp, ch 1, *sc in ch-2 sp, (ch 2, sc in next ch-2 sp) 5 times, ch 4, (**3-tr cl** —*see Special Stitches*, ch 2, 3-tr cl) next ch-1 sp, ch 3, sk next ch-1 sp, (3-tr cl, ch 2, 3-tr cl) in next ch-1 sp, ch 4, rep from * around, join in beg sc.

Rnd 11: Sl st into ch-2 sp, ch 1, *sc in ch-2 sp, (ch 2, sc in next ch-2 sp) 4 times, ch 5, (3-tr cl, ch 2, 3-tr cl) in next ch-2 sp, ch 2, 3-tr cl in next ch-3 sp, ch 2, (3-tr cl, ch 2, 3-tr cl) in next ch-2 sp, ch 5, rep from * around, join in beg sc.

Rnd 12: Sl st into ch-2 sp, ch 1, *sc in ch-2 sp, (ch 2, sc in next ch-2 sp) 3 times, ch 6, (3-tr cl, ch 2, 3-tr cl) in next ch-2 sp, (ch 2, 3-tr cl in next ch-2 sp) twice, ch 2, (3-tr cl, ch 2, 3-tr cl) in next ch-2 sp, ch 6, rep from * around, join in beg sc.

Rnd 13: Sl st into ch-2 sp, ch 1, *sc in ch-2 sp, (ch 2, sc in next ch-2 sp) twice, ch 7, (3-tr cl, ch 2, 3-tr cl) in next ch-2 sp, (ch 3, 3-tr cl in next ch-2 sp) 3 times, ch 3, (3-tr cl, ch 2, 3-tr cl) in next ch-2 sp, ch 7, rep from * around, join in beg sc.

Rnd 14: Sl st into ch-2 sp, ch 1, *sc in ch-2 sp, ch 2, sc in next ch-2 sp, ch 9, (3-tr cl, ch 2, 3-tr cl) in next ch-2 sp, (ch 4, 3-tr cl in next ch-3 sp) 4 times, ch 4, (3-tr cl, ch 2, 3-tr cl) in next ch-2 sp, ch 9, rep from * around, join in beg sc.

Rnd 15: Sl st into ch-2 sp, ch 1, *sc in ch-2 sp, ch 9, (3-tr cl, ch 2, 3-tr cl) in next ch-2 sp, (ch 4, 3-tr cl in next ch-4 sp) 5 times, ch 4, (3-tr cl, ch 2, 3-tr cl) in next ch-2 sp, ch 9, rep from * around, join in beg sc.

Rnd 16: Sl st in each of next 9 chs, sl st in next ch-2 sp, ch 3, (yo hook twice, insert hook in indicated st, yo, draw up a lp, {yo, draw through 2 lps on hook} twice) twice, yo, draw through all 3 lps on hook *(beg 3-tr cl)*, ch 2, 3-tr cl in same ch-2 sp, *(ch 4, 3-tr cl in next ch-4 sp) 6 times, ch 4, (3-tr cl, ch 2, 3-tr cl) in next ch-2 sp, ch 2**, (3-tr cl, ch 2, 3-tr cl) in next ch-2 sp, rep from * around, ending last rep at **, join in top of beg 3-tr cl.

Rnd 17: Sl st into next ch sp, ch 1, (2 sc, ch 3, 2 sc) in each ch sp around, join in beg sc, fasten off.

Lavender Doily

Rnd 1: With wood violet, ch 6, sl st in first ch to form a ring, ch 4 *(counts as first tr)*, 19 tr in ring, join in 4th ch of beg ch-4. *(20 tr)*

Rnd 2: Ch 6 *(counts as first tr, ch 2)*, (tr in next tr, ch 2) around, join in 4th ch of beg ch-6. *(20 tr, 20 ch-2 sps)*

Rnd 3: Sl st into ch-2 sp, ch 5, tr in same ch-2 sp, ch 2, *(tr, ch 1, tr) in next ch-2 sp, ch 2, rep from * around, join in 4th ch of beg ch-5.

Rnd 4: Sl st into ch-1 sp, ch 5, tr in same sp as beg ch-5, ch 3, *(tr, ch 1, tr) in next ch-1 sp, ch 3, rep from * around, join in 4th ch of beg ch-5.

Rnd 5: Sl st into ch-1 sp, ch 1, *(sc, ch 7, sc) in ch-1 sp, ch 4, sc in next ch-1 sp, ch 4, rep from * around, join in beg sc. *(10 ch-7 sps)*

Rnd 6: Sl st into ch-7 sp, ch 4, 6 tr in same ch-7 sp, *ch 2, ((tr, ch 1, tr) in next ch-4 sp) twice, ch 2**, 7 tr in next ch-7 sp, rep from * around, ending last rep at **, join in 4th ch of beg ch-4. *(10 pineapple bases)*

Continued on page 144

Heirloom Lace Bonnet & Booties

Designs by Sandy Abbate

Snowy white lace and organza ribbon make a picture-perfect set to dress up Baby on her special day.

INTERMEDIATE

Finished Size

Newborn

Materials
- Size 10 crochet cotton (350 yds per ball): 1 ball white
- Size 6/1.80mm steel crochet hook or size needed to obtain gauge
- 2 yds white sheer ⅜-inch-wide ribbon with satin edges
- Spray starch

Bonnet

Gauge
5 dc rows = 1 inch; 10 dc = 1 inch

Pattern Notes
Weave in loose ends as work progresses. Join rounds with a slip stitch unless otherwise stated.

Back
Rnd 1: Ch 4, 11 dc in 4th ch from hook, join in 4th ch of beg ch-4. (12 dc)

Rnd 2: Ch 3 (counts as first dc throughout), dc in same st as beg ch-3, 2 dc in each dc around, join in 3rd ch of beg ch-3. (24 dc)

Rnd 3: Ch 3, 2 dc in next dc, (dc in next dc, 2 dc in next dc) around, join in 3rd ch of beg ch-3. (36 dc)

Rnd 4: Ch 3, dc in next dc, 2 dc in next dc, (dc in each of next 2 dc, 2 dc in next dc) around, join in 3rd ch of beg ch-3. *(48 dc)*

Rnd 5: Ch 3, dc in each of next 2 dc, 2 dc in next dc, (dc in each of next 3 dc, 2 dc in next dc) around, join in 3rd ch of beg ch-3. *(60 dc)*

Rnd 6: Ch 3, dc in each of next 3 dc, 2 dc in next dc, (dc in each of next 4 dc, 2 dc in next dc) around, join in 3rd ch of beg ch-3. *(72 dc)*

Rnd 7: Ch 3, dc in each of next 4 dc, 2 dc in next dc, (dc in each of next 5 dc, 2 dc in next dc) around, join in 3rd ch of beg ch-3. *(84 dc)*

Rnd 8: Ch 3, dc in each of next 5 dc, 2 dc in next dc, (dc in each of next 6 dc, 2 dc in next dc) around, join in 3rd ch of beg ch-3. *(96 dc)*

Rnd 9: Ch 3, dc in each of next 6 dc, 2 dc in next dc, (dc in each of next 7 dc, 2 dc in next dc) around, join in 3rd ch of beg ch-3. *(108 dc)*

Rnd 10: Ch 3, dc in each of next 7 dc, 2 dc in next dc, (dc in each of next 8 dc, 2 dc in next dc) around, join in 3rd ch of beg ch-3.

Row 11: Now working in rows, ch 3, dc in each of next 104 dc, turn. *(105 dc)*

Row 12: Ch 3, dc in each of next 104 dc, fasten off. *(105 dc)*

Crown & Sides

Row 1 (RS): Ch 17, dc in 4th ch from hook, dc in each rem ch across, turn. *(15 dc)*

Row 2: Ch 3, dc in each of next 4 dc, ch 5, sk next 2 dc, sc in next dc, ch 5, sk next 2 dc, dc in each of next 5 dc, turn.

Row 3: Ch 3, dc in each of next 2 dc, ch 5, (sc in next ch-5 sp, ch 5) twice, sk next 2 dc, dc in each of last 3 dc, turn.

Row 4: Ch 3, dc in each of next 2 dc, 2 dc in next ch-5 sp, ch 5, sc in next ch-5 sp, ch 5, 2 dc in next ch-5 sp, dc in each of last 3 dc, turn.

Row 5: Ch 3, dc in each of next 4 dc, 2 dc in next ch-5 sp, **dc dec** *(see Stitch Guide)* in same ch-5 sp and next ch-5 sp, 2 dc in same ch-5 sp, dc in each of next 5 dc, turn. *(15 dc)*

Rows 6 & 7: Ch 3, dc in each dc across, turn.

Rows 8–43: Rep rows 2–7.

Rows 44–47: Rep rows 2–5. At the end of row 47, do not turn.

Front Edging

Row 1 (RS): Ch 1, working in sides of rows, work 5 sc across side edge of first 2 rows, *ch 5, sk next row, work 9 sc across next 5 rows, rep from * 6 times, ch 5, sk next row, work 5 sc across side edge of last 2 rows, turn.

Row 2: Ch 1, sc in each of next 4 sc, ch 4, sc in next ch-5 sp, ch 4, *sk next sc, sc in each of next 7 sc, ch 4, sc in next ch-5 sp, ch 4, rep from * across to last 5 sc, sk next sc, sc in each of last 4 sc, turn.

Row 3: Ch 1, sc in each of first 3 sc, ch 4, (sc in next ch-4 sp, ch 4) twice, *sk next sc, sc in each of next 5 sc, ch 4, (sc in next ch-4 sp, ch 4) twice, rep from * across to last 4 sc, sk next sc, sc in each of last 3 sc, turn.

Row 4: Ch 1, sc in each of first 2 sc, ch 4, (sc in next ch-4 sp, ch 4) 3 times, *sk next sc, sc in each of next 3 sc, ch 4, (sc in next ch-4 sp, ch 4) 3 times, rep from * to last 3 sc, sk next sc, sc in each of last 2 sc, turn.

Row 5: Ch 1, sc in first sc, *ch 4, (sc in next ch-4 sp, ch 4) 4 times, sk next sc, sc in next sc, rep from * across, fasten off.

Back Edging

Row 1: With RS of Crown and Sides facing, working in ends of rows, attach white with sc in side of first row, work 104 sc evenly sp across edge, turn. *(105 sc)*

Row 2: Ch 5 *(counts as first tr, ch-1)*, sk next sc, tr in next sc, (ch 1, sk next sc, tr in next sc) across, turn.

Row 3: Holding Crown and Sides and Back tog with WS facing and working through both thicknesses of all sts, ch 1, sc in each of next 105 sts evenly sp across, turn.

Row 4: Ch 1, sc in first sc, (ch 3, sk 1 sc, sc in next sc) across, turn.

Row 5: Ch 1, (sc, ch 3, sc) in each ch-3 sp across, fasten off.

Neck Edging

Row 1: With RS facing, attach white with sc at neck edge, work 60 sc evenly sp across edge, turn. *(61 sc)*

Row 2: Ch 5, sk 1 sc, tr in next sc, (ch 1, sk 1 sc, tr in next sc) across, turn.

Row 3: Ch 1, sc in first tr, (ch 3, sc in 3rd ch from hook *(for picot)*, sc in next tr) across, fasten off.

Finishing

Spray Crown and Sides lightly with spray starch and press with iron. Weave 1 yd ribbon through ch-1 sps of row 2 of Neck Edging. Tie ends tog to form a bow.

Booties

Make 2.

Instep

Row 1: Ch 13, dc in 4th ch from hook, dc in each rem ch across, turn. *(11 dc)*

Rows 2 & 3: Ch 3, dc in same st as beg ch-3, dc in each st across to last st, 2 dc in last st, turn. *(15 dc)*

Rows 4–9: Rep rows 2–7 of Crown and Sides of Bonnet. At the end of row 9, do not turn.

Rnd 10: Now working in rnds, working in ends of rows, ch 1, 18 sc evenly sp across first side of Instep, 11 sc across opposite side of foundation ch, 18 sc across 2nd side of Instep, ch 30, join in **back lp** *(see Stitch Guide)* of first sc of rnd. *(47 sc)*

Sides

Rnd 1: Working in back lps only, ch 3, dc in each sc and in each ch around, join in 3rd ch of beg ch-3. *(77 dc)*

Rnds 2 & 3: Ch 3, dc in each dc around, join in 3rd ch of beg ch-3.

Sole

Rnd 1: Ch 3, dc in each of next 18 dc, (dc dec in next 2 sts) twice, dc in next dc, (dc dec in next 2 sts) twice, dc in each of next 30 dc, (dc dec in next 2 sts) 4 times, dc in each of last 11 dc, join in 3rd ch of beg ch-3. *(69 dc)*

Rnd 2: Ch 3, dc in each of next 16 dc, (dc dec in next 2 sts) twice, dc in next dc, (dc dec in next 2 sts) twice, dc in each of next 26 dc, (dc dec in next 2 sts) 4 times, dc in each of last 9 dc, join in 3rd ch of beg ch-3. *(61 dc)*

Rnd 3: Ch 3, dc in each of next 14 dc, (dc dec in next 2 sts) twice, dc in next dc, (dc dec in next 2 sts) twice, dc in each of next 22 sts, (dc dec in next 2 dc) 4 times, dc in each of next 7 dc, join in 3rd ch of beg ch-3. *(53 dc)*

Rnd 4: Ch 3, dc in each of next 8 dc, (dc dec in next 2 sts) 4 times, dc in next dc, (dc dec in next 2 sts) 4 times, dc in each of next 10 dc, (dc dec in next 2 sts) 8 times, dc in next dc, join in 3rd ch of beg ch-3, fasten off. *(37 dc)* With RS tog, fold rnd 4 to form Sole, attach white, working through both thicknesses, sl st across opening, fasten off.

Cuff

Rnd 1: Working in opposite side of foundation ch of ch-30 and sts around Instep, with RS facing, attach white with sc at back of bootie, work 49 sc around, join in beg sc. *(50 sc)*

Rnd 2: Ch 5 *(counts as first tr, ch-1)*, sk next sc, (tr in next sc, ch 1, sk next sc) around, join in 4th ch of beg ch-5. *(25 tr)*

Rnd 3: Ch 1, sc in same st as beg ch-1, sc in next ch-1 sp, (sc in next tr, sc in next ch-1 sp) around, join in beg sc. *(50 sc)*

Rnd 4: Ch 1, sc in same sc as beg ch-1, sc in each of next 3 sc, ch 5, sk next 3 sc, (sc in each of next 7 sc, ch 5, sk next 3 sc) 4 times, sc in each of next 3 sc, join in beg sc.

Rnd 5: Ch 1, sc in same st as beg ch-1, sc in each of next 2 sc, ch 4, sc in next ch-5 sp, ch 4, sk next sc, (sc in each of next 5 sc, ch 4, sc in next ch-5 sp, ch 4, sk next sc) 4 times, sc in each of next 2 sc, join in beg sc.

Rnd 6: Ch 1, sc in same st as beg ch-1, sc in next sc, ch 4, (sc in next ch-4 sp, ch 4) twice, sk next sc, *sc in each of next 3 sc, ch 4, (sc in next ch-4 sp, ch 4) twice, sk next sc, rep from * 3 times, sc in next sc, join in beg sc.

Rnd 7: Ch 1, sc in same sc as beg ch-1, ch 4, (sc in next ch-4 sp, ch 4) 3 times, sk next sc, *sc in next sc, ch 4, (sc in next ch-4 sp, ch 4) 3 times, sk next sc, rep from * 3 times, join in beg sc, fasten off.

Finishing

Spray Cuff lightly with starch and iron. Beg at center front of Cuff; weave 18 inches of ribbon through ch-1 sps of rnd 2 of Cuff. Tie ends in a bow at center front. ✄

Daisy Valance

Design by Diane Stone

Petite yellow daisies grace the edge of a pretty lace valance to add a spring-fresh touch to any room.

INTERMEDIATE

Finished Size

14 x 45 inches

Materials

- Size 10 crochet cotton (350 yds per ball):
    2 balls white
    1 ball each light yellow, dark yellow and light green
- Size 6/1.80mm steel crochet hook or size needed to obtain gauge

Gauge

Flower = 1 inch in diameter; 3 dc rows = 1 inch

Pattern Notes

Weave in loose ends as work progresses. Join rounds with a slip stitch unless otherwise stated.

Special Stitches

Triple treble crochet (trtr): Yo hook 4 times, insert hook in indicated st, yo, draw up a lp, (yo, draw through 2 lps on hook) 5 times.

Shell: (2 dc, ch 2, 2 dc) in place indicated.

Flower

Make 32.

Rnd 1: With dark yellow, form a ring, leaving beg tail free, ch 1, 12 sc in ring, join in beg sc, fasten off. Draw beg tail tightly to close ring and secure. *(12 sc)*

Rnd 2: Attach light yellow with sl st in any sc of rnd 1, ch 3 *(counts as first dc)*, (2 dc, ch 3, sl st) in same st as beg ch-3, sk next sc, *(sl st, ch 3, 2 dc, ch 3, sl st) in next sc, sk next sc, rep from * around, do not join, fasten off. *(6 petals)*

Leaf Group

Make 32.

Row 1: With light green, (ch 6, sl st in 2nd ch from hook, sc in next ch, hdc in next ch, dc in each of next 2 chs) twice, fasten off.

Curtain Top Band

Row 1: Ch 19, dc in 4th ch from hook, dc in each of next 3 chs, ch 7, sk next 7 chs, dc in each of next 5 chs, turn. *(5 dc, ch 7, 5 dc)*

Row 2: Ch 3 *(counts as first dc)*, dc in each of next 4 dc, dc in each of next 7 chs, dc in each of next 5 dc, turn. *(17 dc)*

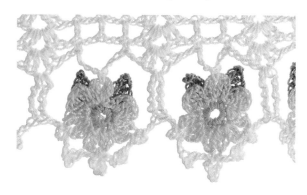

Row 3: Ch 3, dc in each dc across, turn.

Row 4: Rep row 3.

Row 5: Ch 3, dc in each of next 4 dc, ch 7, sk next 7 dc, dc in each of next 5 dc, turn.

Row 6: Ch 3, dc in each of next 4 dc, ch 7, sk next ch-7 sp, dc in each of next 5 dc, turn.

Rows 7–126: Rep rows 2–6.

Rows 127–130: Rep rows 2–5. At the end of last rep, do not fasten off.

Curtain

Row 1: Working in ends of Curtain Top Band rows, sl st over center of last row, ch 1, sc over same dc row, (ch 4, sc over next dc row) 128 times, turn. *(129 ch-4 sps)*

Row 2: Sl st into ch-4 sp, ch 3, 3 dc in same ch-4 sp, ch 1, dc in next ch-4 sp, (ch 2, dc in next ch-4 sp) twice, ch 1, *****shell *(see Special Stitches)* in next ch-4 sp, ch 1, (dc in next ch-4 sp, ch 2) twice, dc in next ch-4 sp, ch 1, rep from * across, ending with 4 dc in last ch-4 sp, turn. *(31 shells)*

Row 3: Ch 3, dc in each of next 3 dc, ch 1, dc in next dc, (ch 2, dc in next dc) twice, ch 1, *****shell in next ch-2 sp of next shell, ch 1, dc in next dc, (ch 2, dc in next dc) twice, ch 1, rep from * across, ending with dc in each of last 4 dc, turn.

Rows 4–28: Rep row 3.

Row 29: Sl st in next dc, ch 3, (dc, ch 2, 2 dc) in same st as beg ch-3 *(beg shell)*, ch 2, sc in next dc, ch 4, pick up a flower, sc between center 2 dc sts of any petal, ch 4, sk next dc, sc in next dc, ch 2, *****shell in next shell, ch 2, sk next ch-1 sp, sc in next dc, ch 4, pick up next flower, sc between center 2 dc sts of any petal, ch 4, sk next dc, sc in next dc, ch 2, rep from * across, ending with sk first dc of 4-dc group, shell in next dc, fasten off, do not turn.

Continued on page 146

Dainty Lace Pot Holders

Designs by Judy Teague Treece

Accent your tea-time table with a collection of delicate hot pads stitched in a variety of patterns and colors.

EASY

Finished Size

Shades of yellow: 6¼ inches square

Shades of ocean: 6¾ inches in diameter

Shades of green: 7¼ inches in diameter

Pink hearts: 6½ inches in diameter

Materials

- Aunt Lydia's size 10 crochet cotton (350 yds per ball):
    1 ball each #421 goldenrod, #995 ocean, #450 aqua, #15 shaded pinks
- Caron Grandma's Best size 10 crochet cotton (300 yds per ball):
    1 ball each #166 sunset ombre and #164 mint green ombre
- DMC Cebelia size 10 crochet cotton (284 yds per ball):
    1 ball each #955 Nile green and #3326 wild rose
- Size 7/1.65mm steel crochet hook or size needed to obtain gauge

Gauge

4 dc rnds = 1 inch; 9 dc = 1 inch

Pattern Notes

Weave in loose ends as work progresses. Join rounds with a slip stitch unless otherwise stated.

Special Stitch

3-double crochet cluster (3-dc cl): (Yo, insert hook in indicated sp, yo, draw up a lp, yo, draw through 2 lps on hook) 3 times in same sp, yo, draw through all 4 lps on hook.

Shades of Yellow

Front

Rnd 1: With sunset ombre, ch 5, sl st in first ch to form a ring, ch 1, 12 sc in ring, join in beg sc. (12 sc)

Rnd 2: Ch 3 (counts as first dc), dc in same st as beg ch-3, 2 dc in each of next 2 sc, ch 3, (2 dc in each of next 3 sc, ch 3) around, join in 3rd ch of beg ch-3. (24 dc, 4 ch-3 sps)

Rnd 3: Ch 4 (counts as first dc, ch-1), (sk next dc, dc in next dc, ch 1) twice, *(dc, ch 2, dc) in corner ch-3 sp, ch 1**, (dc in next dc,

ch 1, sk next dc) 3 times, rep from * around, ending last rep at **, join in 3rd ch of beg ch-5. *(20 dc, 16 ch-1 sps, 4 ch-2 corner sps)*

Rnds 4 & 5: Sl st in next ch sp, ch 4, *(dc in next ch sp, ch 1) across to next corner ch sp, (dc, ch 3, dc) in corner ch sp, ch 1, rep from * around, join in 3rd ch of beg ch-4.

Rnds 6–8: Sl st in next ch sp, ch 5 *(counts as first dc, ch-2)*, *(dc in next ch sp, ch 2) across to next corner ch sp, (dc, ch 3, dc) in corner

ch sp, ch 2, rep from * around, join in 3rd ch of beg ch-5. *(40 dc around)*

Rnds 9–13: Sl st in next ch sp, ch 6 *(counts as first dc, ch-3)*, *(dc in next ch sp, ch 3) across to next corner ch sp, (2 dc, ch 3, 2 dc) in corner ch sp, ch 3, rep from * around, join in 3rd ch of beg ch-6, fasten off. *(52 dc, 4 corner shells)*

Rnd 14: Attach sunset ombre in corner ch-3 sp, ch 1, *3 sc in corner ch-3 sp, sc in each of next 2 dc, (2 sc in next ch-3 sp, sc in next dc, 3 sc in next ch-3 sp, sc in next dc) 7 times, sc in next dc, rep from * 3 times, join in beg sc, fasten off.

Back
Rnds 1 & 2: With goldenrod, rep rnds 1 and 2 of Front. *(24 dc, 4 ch-3 sps)*
Rnds 3-12: Ch 3, dc in each dc around, working (2 dc, ch 3, 2 dc) in each corner ch sp, join in 3rd ch of beg ch-3.

Joining
Rnd 1: Holding WS of Front and Back tog, working through both thicknesses, attach sunset ombre in any center corner st, ch 15, sl st in same st, 24 sc over ch-15 lp *(hanging lp)*, sc in each st around outer edge of pot holder, join in beg sc.
Rnd 2: Sk sts of hanging lp, (ch 6, sk 2 sts, sc in next st) around, join in beg sc, fasten off.

Shades of Ocean

Front
Rnd 1: With ocean, ch 6, sl st to join in first ch to form a ring, ch 3, 15 dc in ring, join in 3rd ch of beg ch-3. *(16 dc)*
Rnd 2: Ch 3, dc in same st as beg ch-3, 2 dc in each dc around, join in 3rd ch of beg ch-3. *(32 dc)*
Rnd 3: Ch 3, dc in same st, *sk next st, ch 2, sc in next st, ch 2, sk next st**, 2 dc in next st, rep from * around, ending last rep at **, join in 3rd ch of beg ch-3. *(16 dc, 8 sc, 16 ch-2 sps)*
Rnd 4: Ch 3, dc in next dc, *ch 3, sc in next ch-2 sp, ch 1, sc in next ch-2 sp, ch 3**, dc in each of next 2 dc, rep from * around, ending last rep at **, join in 3rd ch of beg ch-3.
Rnd 5: Ch 3, dc in next dc, *ch 3, sc in next ch-3 sp, ch 2, sc in next ch-3 sp, ch 3**, dc in each of next 2 dc, rep from * around, ending last rep at **, join in 3rd ch of beg ch-3.
Rnd 6: Ch 3, dc in next dc, *ch 3, sc in next ch-3 sp, ch 3, sc in next ch-3 sp, ch 3**, dc in each of next 2 dc, rep from * around, ending last rep at **, join in 3rd ch of beg ch-3.
Rnd 7: Ch 3, dc in next dc, *ch 3, sc in next ch-3 sp, ch 4, sk center ch-3 sp, sc in next ch-3 sp, ch 4**, dc in each of next 2 dc, rep from * around, ending last rep at **, join in 3rd ch of beg ch-3.
Rnd 8: Ch 3, dc in next dc, *ch 3, sc in next ch-3 sp, ch 5, sc in next ch-3 sp, ch 3**, dc in each of next 2 dc, rep from * around, ending last rep at **, join in 3rd ch of beg ch-3.
Rnd 9: Ch 3, dc in next dc, *ch 3, sc in next ch-3 sp, ch 8, sc in next ch-3 sp, ch 3**, dc in each of next 2 dc, rep from * around, ending last rep at **, join in 3rd ch of beg ch-3.
Rnd 10: Ch 3, dc in next dc, *ch 3, sc in next ch-3 sp, ch 9, sc in next ch-3 sp, ch 3**, dc in each of next 2 dc, rep from * around, ending last rep at **, join in 3rd ch of beg ch-3.
Rnd 11: Ch 3, dc in next dc, *ch 3, sc in next ch-3 sp, ch 10, sc in next ch-3 sp, ch 3**, dc in each of next 2 dc, rep from * around, ending last rep at **, join in 3rd ch of beg ch-3.
Rnd 12: Ch 3, dc in next dc, *ch 3, sc in next ch-3 sp, ch 11, sc in next ch-3 sp, ch 3**, dc in each of next 2 dc, rep from * around, ending last rep at **, join in 3rd ch of beg ch-3.
Rnd 13: Ch 3, dc in next dc, *ch 3, sc in next ch-3 sp, ch 12, sc in next ch-3 sp, ch 3**, dc in each of next 2 dc, rep from * around, ending last rep at **, join in 3rd ch of beg ch-3.
Rnd 14: Ch 3, dc in next dc, *ch 3, sc in next ch-3 sp, ch 14, sc in next ch-3 sp, ch 3**, dc in each of next 2 dc, rep from * around, ending last rep at **, join in 3rd ch of beg ch-3, fasten off.

Back
Rnds 1 & 2: With aqua, rep rnds 1 and 2 of Front. *(32 dc)*
Rnd 3: Ch 3, 2 dc in next dc, (dc in next dc, 2 dc in next dc) around, join in 3rd ch of beg ch-3. *(48 dc)*

Rnd 4: Ch 3, dc in each dc around, join in 3rd ch of beg ch-3.

Rnd 5: Rep rnd 4.

Rnds 6 & 7: Rep rnd 3. *(108 dc)*

Rnds 8 & 9: Rep rnd 4.

Rnd 10: Rep rnd 3. *(162 dc)*

Rnds 11-13: Rep rnd 4. At the end of last rep, turn.

Joining

Rnd 14: Holding WS of Front and Back tog, with Front facing, ch 1, *working in each st of Back and catching **back lp** *(see Stitch Guide)* of each of next 14 chs of Front, sc in each of next 14 sts, working on Back only, sc in each of next 6 sc, rep from * around, join in beg sc.

Rnd 15: Ch 1, sc in each of next 15 sc, *ch 2, sk next sc, dc in each of next 2 sc, ch 2, sk next sc**, sc in each of next 16 sc, rep from * around, ending last rep at **, sc in next sc, join in beg sc.

Rnd 16: Ch 1, *sc in sc, ch 2, sk next 2 sts, ({dc, ch 1} twice, dc) in next sc, ch 2, sk next sc, sc in next sc, ch 2, sk next 2 sc, ({dc, ch 1} twice, dc) in next sc, ch 2, sk next 2 sc, sc in next sc, ch 2, sk next sc, ({dc, ch 1} twice, dc) in next sc, ch 2, sk next sc, sc in next sc, ch 2, (dc, ch 1, dc) in next dc, ch 1, (dc, ch 1, dc) in next dc, ch 2, rep from * around, join in beg sc.

Row 17: Now working in rows, ch 20, sl st in same st *(hanging lp)*, ch 1, 20 sc over ch-20 lp, join in first sc, fasten off.

Shades of Green

Front

Rnd 1: With mint green ombre, ch 6, sl st in first ch to form a ring, ch 1, 12 sc in ring, join in beg sc. *(12 sc)*

Rnd 2: Ch 3, dc in same st as beg ch-3, ch 2, sk next sc, (2 dc in next sc, ch 2, sk next sc) around, join in 3rd ch of beg ch-3. *(12 dc, 6 ch-2 sps)*

Rnd 3: Ch 3, dc in next dc, ch 5, (dc in each of next 2 dc, ch 5) around, join in 3rd ch of beg ch-3.

Rnd 4: Ch 3, dc in next dc, *ch 4, sc in next ch-5 sp, ch 4**, dc in each of next 2 dc, rep from * around, ending last rep at **, join in 3rd ch of beg ch-3.

Rnd 5: Ch 3, dc in next dc, *ch 4, sc in next ch-4 sp, ch 3, sc in next ch-4 sp, ch 4**, dc in each of next 2 dc, rep from * around, ending last rep at **, join in 3rd ch of beg ch-3.

Rnd 6: Ch 3, dc in next dc, *ch 4, sc in next ch-4 sp, ch 3, **3-dc cl** *(see Special Stitch)* in next ch-3 sp, ch 3, sc in next ch-4 sp, ch 4**, dc in next 2 dc, rep from * around, ending last rep at **, join in 3rd ch of beg ch-3.

Rnd 7: Ch 3, dc in next dc, *ch 4, sc in next ch-4 sp, ch 3, 3-dc cl in next ch sp, ch 2, 3-dc cl in next ch sp, ch 3, sc in next ch-4 sp, ch 4**, dc in each of next 2 dc, rep from * around, ending last rep at **, join in 3rd ch of beg ch-3.

Rnd 8: Ch 3, dc in next dc, *ch 4, sc in next ch-4 sp, ch 3, (3-dc cl in next ch sp, ch 2) twice, 3-dc cl in next ch sp, ch 3, sc in next ch-4 sp, ch 4**, dc in each of next 2 dc, rep from * around, ending last rep at **, join in 3rd ch of beg ch-3.

Rnd 9: Ch 3, dc in next dc, *ch 4, sc in next ch-4 sp, ch 3, (3-dc cl in next ch sp, ch 2) 3 times, 3-dc cl in next ch sp, ch 3, sc in next ch-4 sp, ch 4**, dc in each of next 2 dc, rep from * around, ending last rep at **, join in 3rd ch of beg ch-3.

Rnd 10: Ch 3, dc in next dc, *ch 4, sc in next ch-4 sp, ch 4, sk next ch sp, (3-dc cl in next ch sp, ch 2) twice, 3-dc cl in next ch sp, ch 4, sk next ch sp, sc in next ch-4 sp, ch 4**, dc in each of next 2 dc, rep from * around, ending last rep at **, join in 3rd ch of beg ch-3.

Rnd 11: Ch 3, dc in next dc, *ch 4, sc in next ch-4 sp, ch 5, sk next ch sp, 3-dc cl in next ch sp, ch 2, 3-dc cl in next ch sp, ch 5, sk next ch sp, sc in next ch-4 sp, ch 4**, dc in each of next 2 dc, rep from * around, ending last rep at **, join in 3rd ch of beg ch-3.

Rnd 12: Ch 3, 2 dc in same dc as beg ch-3, ch 1, 3 dc in next dc, *ch 4, sc in next ch-4 sp, ch 3, sc in next ch sp, ch 3, 3-dc cl in next ch-2 sp, ch 3, sc in next ch sp, ch 3, sc in next ch-4 sp, ch 4**, 3 dc in next dc, ch 1, 3 dc in next dc, rep from * around, ending last rep at **, join in 3rd ch of beg ch-3.

Rnd 13: Ch 4 (counts as first dc, ch 1), dc in next dc, (ch 1, dc in next dc) 4 times, *ch 3, sk next ch sp, ((dc, ch 1, dc) in next ch sp, ch 3) 4 times ch 3**, dc in first dc of 6-dc group, (ch 1, dc in next dc) 5 times, rep from * around, ending last rep at **, join in 3rd ch of beg ch-4.

Rnd 14: Ch 3, *(dc in next ch-1 sp, dc in next dc) 5 times, ch 3, (sc in next dc, sc in next ch-1 sp, sc in next dc, 2 sc in next ch-3 sp) 3 times, sc in next dc, sc in next ch-1 sp, sc in next dc, ch 3**, dc in next dc, rep from * around, ending last rep at **, join in top of beg ch-3, fasten off.

Back

Rnd 1: With Nile green, ch 6, sl st to join in first ch to form a ring, ch 1, 12 sc in ring, join in beg sc. (12 sc)

Rnd 2: Ch 3, dc in same st as beg ch-3, dc in next dc, (2 dc in next dc, dc in next dc) around, join in 3rd ch of beg ch-3. (18 dc)

Rnd 3: Ch 3, dc in same st as beg ch-3, 2 dc in each dc around, join in 3rd ch of beg ch-3. (36 dc)

Rnds 4–6: Ch 3, dc in same st as beg ch-3, dc in each of next 2 dc, (2 dc in next dc, dc in each of next 2 dc) around, join in 3rd ch of beg ch-4. (85 dc)

Rnd 7: Ch 3, dc in each of next 2 dc, 2 dc in next dc, (dc in each of next 3 dc, 2 dc in next dc) around, join in 3rd ch of beg ch-3. (106 dc)

Rnds 8 & 9: Ch 3, dc in each dc around, join in 3rd ch of beg ch-3.

Rnd 10: Rep rnd 4. (141 dc)

Rnd 11: Rep rnd 8.

Rnd 12: Ch 3, dc around inc 45 dc evenly sp around, join in 3rd ch of beg ch-3, turn. (186 dc)

Rnd 13: Holding Front and Back tog with Front facing, (working through both thicknesses of sc sts of Front and dc sts of Back, ch 1, sc in each of next 18 sc of Front and 18 dc of Back, working on sts of Back only, sc in each of next 13 dc) 6 times, join in beg sc, fasten off Nile green.

Rnd 14: Attach mint green ombre in 2nd dc of any 11-dc group, ch 1, *((sc, ch 3, sc) in 2nd dc, ch 1, sk next dc) 5 times, (sc, ch 3, sc) in next ch-3 sp, ch 2, sk 1 sc, ((sc, ch 3, sc) in next sc, ch 2, sk next 2 sc) 5 times, (sc, ch 3, sc) in next sc, ch 2, sk next sc, (sc, ch 3, sc) in next ch-3 sp, sk next dc, rep from * around, join in beg sc, fasten off.

Hanging Loop

Attach Nile green at Back in any st of rnd 13 between dc scallops, ch 20, sl st in same st, ch 1, work 24 sc over lp, fasten off.

Pink Hearts

Front

Rnd 1: With shaded pinks, ch 6, sl st in first ch to form a ring, ch 3, 23 dc in ring, join in 3rd ch of beg ch-3. (24 dc)

Rnd 2: Ch 3, dc in each dc around, join in 3rd ch of beg ch-3.

Rnd 3: Ch 3, dc in same st as beg ch-3, 2 dc in each rem dc around, join in 3rd ch of beg ch-3. (48 dc)

Rnds 4 & 5: Ch 3, dc in each of next 2 dc, ch 3, sk next st, (dc in each of next 3 sts, ch 3, sk next dc) around, join in 3rd ch of beg ch-3. (30 dc)

Rnd 6: Ch 3, 2 dc in next dc, dc in next dc, ch 4, (dc in next dc, 2 dc in next dc, dc in next dc, ch 4) around, join in 3rd ch of beg ch-3. (40 dc)

Rnd 7: Ch 3, 2 dc in next dc, dc in each of next 2 dc, ch 4, (dc in next dc, 2 dc in next dc, dc in each of next 2 dc, ch 4) around, join in 3rd ch of beg ch-3. *(50 dc)*

Rnd 8: Ch 3, dc in next dc, 2 dc in next dc, dc in each of next 2 dc, ch 4, (dc in each of next 2 dc, 2 dc in next dc, dc in each of next 2 dc, ch 4) around, join in 3rd ch of beg ch-3. *(60 dc)*

Rnd 9: Ch 3, dc in each of next 2 dc, 2 dc in next dc, dc in each of next 2 dc, ch 4, (dc in each of next 3 dc, 2 dc in next dc, dc in each of next 2 dc, ch 4) around, join in 3rd ch of beg ch-3. *(70 dc)*

Rnd 10: Ch 3, dc in each of next 3 dc, 2 dc in next dc, dc in each of next 2 dc, ch 4, (dc in each of next 4 dc, 2 dc in next dc, dc in each of next 2 dc, ch 4) around, join in 3rd ch of beg ch-3. *(80 dc)*

Rnd 11: Ch 3, dc in each of next 3 dc, 2 dc in next dc, dc in each of next 3 dc, ch 4, (dc in each of next 4 dc, 2 dc in next dc, dc in each of next 3 dc, ch 4) around, join in 3rd ch of beg ch-3. *(90 dc)*

Rnd 12: Ch 3, dc in each of next 3 dc, 2 dc in next dc, dc in each of next 4 dc, ch 4, (dc in each of next 4 dc, 2 dc in next dc, dc in each of next 4 dc, ch 4) around, join in 3rd ch of beg ch-3. *(100 dc)*

Rnd 13: Ch 1, sc in same dc as beg ch-1, ch 3, *tr in each of next 3 dc, sc in each of next 2 sc, tr in each of next 3 dc, ch 3, sc in next dc, 4 sc in ch-4 sp**, sc in next dc, ch 3, rep from * around, ending last rep at **, join in beg sc, fasten off.

Back

Rnd 1: With wild rose, ch 6, sl st in first ch to form a ring, ch 3, 19 dc in ring, join in 3rd ch of beg ch-3. *(20 dc)*

Rnd 2: Ch 3, dc in each dc around, join in 3rd ch of beg ch-3.

Rnd 3: Ch 3, dc in same st as beg ch-3, 2 dc in each dc around, join in 3rd ch of beg ch-3. *(40 dc)*

Rnd 4: Ch 3, 2 dc in next dc, (dc in next dc, 2 dc in next dc) around, join in 3rd ch of beg ch-3. *(60 dc)*

Rnd 5: Ch 3, dc in next dc, (2 dc in next dc, dc in each of next 2 dc) around, join in 3rd ch of beg ch-3. *(80 dc)*

Rnd 6: Ch 3, dc in each dc around, join in 3rd ch of beg ch-3.

Rnd 7: Ch 3, dc in each of next 3 dc, (2 dc in next dc, dc in each of next 3 dc) around, join in 3rd ch of beg ch-3. *(100 dc)*

Rnd 8: Ch 3, dc in each of next 3 dc, 2 dc in next dc, (dc in each of next 4 dc, 2 dc in next dc) around, join in 3rd ch of beg ch-3. *(120 dc)*

Rnd 9: Rep rnd 6.

Rnd 10: Ch 3, dc in each of next 4 dc, 2 dc in next dc, (dc in each of next 5 dc, 2 dc in next dc) around, join in 3rd ch of beg ch-3. *(140 dc)*

Rnd 11: Rep rnd 6, fasten off, turn.

Rnd 12: Attach shaded pinks in a dc, ch 1, sc in each dc around, join in beg sc. *(140 dc)*

Joining

Rnd 13: With WS of Front and Back tog, position Front to work in next 4 sc of rnd 13 of Front, ch 1, *working through both thicknesses, sc in each of next 4 sc, working on Front only, sc in next sc, ch 3, dc in each of next 3 tr, sc in each of next 2 sc, dc in each of next 3 tr, ch 3, sc in next sc, rep from * around, join in beg sc.

Hanging Loop

Ch 15, sl st in same st as first ch of ch-15, ch 1, work 24 sc over ch-15 lp, sl st in beg st, fasten off. ✄

Flower Webs Table Topper

Design by Josie Rabier

Beautiful blooms captured in a web of lace create the exquisite design in this one-of-kind table topper.

INTERMEDIATE

Finished Size
19½ x 25 inches

Gauge
Motif = 5 inches square

Pattern Notes
Weave in loose ends as work progresses.
Join rounds with a slip stitch unless otherwise stated.
Use motif diagram as a guide for placement.

Special Stitches
6-treble crochet cluster (6-tr cl): *Yo hook twice, insert hook in next st, yo, draw up a lp, (yo, draw through 2 lps on hook) twice, rep from * twice in same st (*4 lps on hook*), **yo hook twice, insert hook in next st, yo, draw up a lp, (yo, draw through 2 lps on hook) twice, rep from ** twice in same st (*7 lps on hook*),

Materials
- Caron Grandma's Best size 10 crochet cotton (400 yds per ball):
    2 balls #160 ecru
- Size 7/1.65mm steel crochet hook or size needed to obtain gauge

yo, draw through all 7 lps on hook, ch 1.

Beginning 6-treble crochet cluster (beg 6-tr cl): Ch 3 (*counts as first tr of cl*), *yo hook twice, insert hook in same st as beg ch-3, (yo, draw through 2 lps on hook) twice, rep from * once (*3 lps on hook*), **yo hook twice, insert hook in next st, yo, draw up a lp, (yo, draw through 2 lps on hook) twice, rep from ** twice in same st (*6 lps on hook*), yo, draw through all 6 lps on hook, ch 1.

Shell: (2 tr, ch 5, 2 tr) in indicated st.

Beginning shell (beg shell): (Ch 4, tr, ch 5, 2 tr) in indicated st.

First Motif
Rnd 1: Ch 6, sl st in first ch to form a ring, ch 3 (*counts as first dc throughout*), 23 dc in ring, join in 3rd ch of beg ch-3. (*24 dc*)

Rnd 2: Beg 6-tr cl (*see Special Stitches*) in next 2 dc, *ch 5, sl st in next dc, ch 5**, **6-tr cl** (*see Special Stitches*) in next 2 dc, rep from * around, ending last rep at **, sl st to join in top of beg 6-tr cl. (*8 petals*)

Rnd 3: Ch 1, (sc in top of cl, sc in next ch-5 sp, ch 5, sc in next ch-5 sp of next petal) around, join in beg sc. (*24 sc, 8 ch-5 sps*)

Rnd 4: (Ch 7, sl st in next ch-5 sp, ch 7, sk next sc, sl st in next sc) around. (*16 ch-7 lps*)

Continued on page 146

Blue Heaven Tablecloth

Design by Carol Decker

Make every day a special occasion when you top your table with this heavenly sky-blue tablecloth.

EXPERIENCED

Finished Size

56 inches in diameter

Materials

- J. & P. Coats Royale Classic size 10 crochet cotton (350 yds per ball):
  - 14 balls #479 bridal blue
- Size 7/1.65mm steel crochet hook or size needed to obtain gauge

Gauge

Center medallion = 3½ inches; 6 sc = 1 inch

Pattern Notes

Weave in loose ends as work progresses. Join rounds with a slip stitch unless otherwise stated.

Special Stitches

Picot: Ch 3, sl st in last st made.

2-double crochet cluster (2-dc cl): (Yo hook, insert hook in indicated st or sp, yo, draw up a lp, yo, draw through 2 lps on hook) twice, yo, draw through all 3 lps on hook.

3-double crochet cluster (3-dc cl): (Yo hook, insert hook in indicated st or sp, yo, draw up a lp, yo, draw through 2 lps on hook) 3 times, yo, draw through all 4 lps on hook.

Center Medallion

Rnd 1: Ch 6, sl st in first ch to form a ring, ch 1, (sc in ring, ch 5) 5 times, sc in ring, ch 2, dc in beg sc to form last ch-5 sp. *(6 sc, 6 ch sps)*

Rnd 2: Ch 5 *(counts as first tr, ch 1)*, dc in same ch sp as beg ch-5, (ch 1, (sc, ch 1, dc, ch 1, tr, ch 1, dc) in next ch-5 sp) 5 times, ch 1, (sc, ch 1, dc, ch 1) in same sp as beg ch-5, join in 4th ch of beg ch-5.

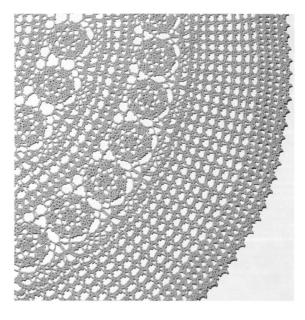

Rnd 3: *Ch 7, dc over side edge of ch-7 sp, ch 4, sc in next tr, rep from * 4 times, ch 7, dc over side edge of ch-7 sp, tr in same tr as beg ch-7, turn, sl st in next dc, sl st in each of next 3 chs, turn.

Rnd 4: Ch 4 *(counts as first tr)*, (tr, ch 4, sc, ch 4, 2 tr) in same ch sp as beg ch-4, ch 4, *(2 tr, ch 4, sc, ch 4, 2 tr) in next ch sp formed by working dc over edge of ch-7 sp, ch 4, rep from * around, join in 4th ch of beg ch-4.

Rnd 5: Sl st in next ch-4 sp, ch 2, (**2-dc cl**—*see Special Stitches*, ch 4, sc) in ch-4 sp, *ch 2, (sc, ch 4, **3-dc cl**—*see Special Stitches*) in next ch-4 sp, ch 4, (sc, **picot**—*see Special Stitches*) in next ch-4 sp, ch 4**, (3-dc cl, ch 4, sc) in next ch-4 sp, rep from * around, ending last rep at **, join in top of first cl.

Rnd 6: (Sl st, sc, picot) in ch-4 sp, *ch 3, 3-dc cl in next ch-2 sp, ch 3, (sc, picot) in next ch-4 sp, ch 2, (sc, picot) in next ch-4 sp, ch 6, (sc, picot) in next ch-4 sp, ch 2**, (sc, picot) in next ch-4 sp, rep from * around, ending last rep at **, join in beg sc, fasten off.

2nd Medallion

Rnds 1–5: Rep rnds 1–5 of Center Medallion.

Rnd 6: (Sl st, sc, picot) in ch-4 sp, ch 3, 3-dc cl in next ch-2 sp, ch 3, **sc in next ch-4 sp, ch 1, dc in opposite picot of medallion to be joined, ch 1, sl st in sc of working medallion to complete picot, ch 2, (sc, picot) in next ch-4 sp on working medallion, ch 2, sc in ch-3 sp, ch 1, dc in opposite picot on medallion to be joined, ch 1, sl st in sc on working medallion to complete picot**, ch 3, 3-dc cl in next ch-2 sp, ch 3, rep bet ** to join additional medallions or rep from * of rnd 6 of Center Medallion to complete medallion, fasten off. Rep 2nd Medallion until 6 medallions are joined in a circle around the Center Medallion.

Rnd 7: Attach crochet cotton in first ch-2 sp between picots on a medallion, ch 4, *(ch 4, tr in next sp) twice, (ch 4, dc in next sp) 7 times, (ch 4, tr in next sp) 4 times, ch 4, tr in last tr, sk next 3 sps (ch-3 sp on this medallion, joining sp between medallions and ch-3 sp on next medallion), tr in ch-3 sp before picot, ch 4**, tr in first ch-2 sp between picots on medallion, rep from * around, ending last rep at **, join in top of 4th ch of beg ch-4.

Rnd 8: (Sl st, ch 4, tr) in next sp, *(ch 5, 3-dc cl in next sp) 10 times, ch 5, 2 tr in next sp, ch 2, sk next sp, 2 dtr in ch-4 lp, ch 2, sk 1 sp, 2 tr in following sp, rep from * around, ending last rep with ch 2, dc in 4th st of beg ch-4 to create last ch sp.

Rnd 9: (Sc, picot) over dc sp, ch 3, sc in ch-5 sp, *ch 7, dc over side edge of same ch-7 sp, ch 4, (sc in next sp, ch 6, dc over side edge of same ch-6 sp, ch 3) 6 times, sc in next sp, ch 7, dc over side edge of same ch-7 sp, ch 4, sc in next sp, ch 3, (sc, picot) in next sp, ch 1, 3 tr in next sp, ch 6, dc over side edge of same ch-6 sp, ch 6, sc in next dtr, ch 3, sc in next dtr, ch 9, dc over side edge of same ch-9 sp, ch 3, 3 tr in next sp, ch 1**, (sc, picot) in next sp, ch 3, sc in next sp, rep from * around, ending last rep at **, join with sl st in beg sc, fasten off.

Rnd 10: Attach crochet cotton with sc in ch-3 lp of first ch 7, dc around ch-7 sp, ch 3, dc in same lp, *(dc, ch 3, sc, ch 3, dc) in next lp *, rep bet * 7 times, **(ch 3, dc in last dc) twice***, rep bet * 10 times**, rep bet ** around, ending last rep at ***, rep bet *, dc in beg ch-3 lp, ch 3, join in first sc of rnd.

Rnd 11: Sl st in next st, (sc, picot) in ch-3 sp, ch 3, (sc, picot) in next sp, ch 8, *(sc, picot) in next sp, ch 3, (sc, picot in next sp, ch 6*, rep bet * 3 times, (**(sc, picot) in next sp, ch 3, (sc, picot) in next sp, ch 8**, rep bet **, ***(sc, picot) in next sp, ch 3, (sc, picot) in next sp, ch 10***, rep bet *** twice, rep bet ** twice, rep bet * 4 times), rep bet ( ) 4 times, rep bet ** twice, rep bet *** 3 times, (sc, picot) in next sp, ch 3, (sc, picot) in next sp, ch 4. ending with tr in first sc of rnd to form last ch sp.

Rnd 12: (Sc, ch 3, dc) over tr sp, ch 1, (dc, ch 3, sc, ch 3, dc, ch 1) in next lp and in each ch-6, ch-8 and ch-10 lp around, ending with (dc, ch 3) in beg tr sp, join in beg sc.

Rnd 13: Sl st in next st, *(sc, picot) in ch-3 sp, ch 3, (sc, picot) in next ch-3 sp, ch 6, dc over side edge of same ch-6 sp**, ch 3, rep from * around, ending last rep at **, ending with dc in beg sc to form last ch sp, turn.

Rnd 14: Ch 1, sl st in next 2 sts, sc in the small lp created by ch-6 dc around the ch-6 sp, ch 3, turn, dc in same lp, ch 1, (dc, ch 3, sc, ch 3, dc, ch 1) in each lp around, ending with (dc, ch 3) in first lp, join in beg sc.

Rnd 15: (Sl st, sc, picot) in ch-3 sp, *ch 4, (sc, picot) in next ch-3 sp**, ch 6, dc over side edge of same ch-6, ch 3, (sc, picot) in next ch-3 sp, rep from * around, ending last rep at **, ch 6, dc over side edge of same ch-6 sp, tr in beg sc to form last ch sp, turn.

Rnd 16: Sl st in lp created by dc, sl st in next ch, sc in same lp, ch 3, turn, dc in same lp, ch 2, *(dc, ch 3, sc, ch 3, dc) in next lp, ch 2, rep from * around, ending with dc in first lp, ch 3, join in beg sc.

Rnd 17: Rep rnd 15.

Rnd 18: Rep rnd 16.

Rnd 19: Rep rnd 15.

Rnd 20: Sl st in lp created by dc, sl st in next ch, sc in same lp, ch 3, turn, dc in same lp, ch 3, *(dc, ch 3, sc, ch 3, dc) in next lp, ch 3, rep from * around, ending with dc in first lp, ch 3, join in beg sc.

Rnd 21: (Sl st, sc, picot) in ch-3 sp, *ch 5, (sc, picot) in next ch-3 sp, ch 7, dc over side edge of same ch-7 sp**, ch 4, (sc, picot) in next ch-3 sp, rep from * around, ending last rep at **, dtr in first sc of rnd, turn.

Rnd 22: Sl st in lp created by dc, sl st in next ch, sc in same lp, ch 4, turn, 2 tr in same lp, *(2 tr, ch 4, sc, ch 4, 2 tr) in next lp, rep from *

around, 2 tr in first lp of rnd, ch 4, join with sl st in first sc of rnd.

Rnd 23: (Sl st, ch 2, 2-dc cl) in ch-4 sp, *ch 5, 3-dc cl in next ch-4 sp, rep from * around, ending with ch 2, dc in top of first cl to form last ch sp.

Rnd 24: (Sc, ch 4, 2 tr) over dc sp, sc in next ch-3 sp, *(2 tr, ch 4, sc, ch 4, 2 tr) in next ch-5 sp, sc in next ch-3 sp, rep from * around, ending with 2 tr in same sp as beg sp, ending with tr in beg sc to form last ch sp.

Rnd 25: (Sl st, ch 6, sc) over tr sp, *ch 2, (sc, ch 3, dc) in next ch-4 sp, ch 2**, (dc, ch 3, sc) in next ch-4 sp, rep from * around, ending last rep at **, join with sl st in 3rd ch of beg ch-6, fasten off.

Small Medallions

Make 22.

Note: *Make a ring of 22 small medallions, rnds 26–31 to be joined to rnd 25 of tablecloth by rnd 31 of medallions.*

Rnd 26: Ch 6. sl st in first ch to form a ring, (sc in ring, ch 5) 6 times, sc in ring, ch 2, dc in beg sc to form last ch-5 sp. *(7 ch-5 sps, 7 sc)*

Rnd 27: Ch 4, (dc, ch 1, sc) over dc sp, ((sc, ch 1, {dc, ch 1} twice, ch 1, sc) in next ch-5 sp) 6 times, sc in next sp, ch 1, sl st to join in 3rd ch of beg ch-4.

Rnd 28: Sc in next sp, *ch 6, dc around ch**, ch 3, sc in ch-1 sp between dc sts in next petal, rep from * 6 times, ending last rep at **, tr in beg sc of rnd, turn.

Rnd 29: Ch 1, sl st in lp created by dc, sl st in next st, sl st again in lp, ch 3, turn, (dc, ch 3, sc, ch 3, 2 dc) in lp, *ch 4, (2 dc, ch 3, sc, ch 3, 2 dc) in next lp, rep from * 5 times, ch 4, sl st to join in 3rd ch of beg ch-3.

Rnd 30: Sl st in next dc, (sl st, ch 2, dc, ch 4, sc) in ch-3 sp, *ch 2, (sc, ch 4, 2-dc cl) in next ch-3 sp, ch 2, (sc, picot) in ch-4 sp, ch 2**, (2-dc cl, ch 4, sc) in next ch-3 sp, rep from * around, ending last rep at **, sk beg ch-2, dc in next dc to join.

Rnd 31: *(Sc, picot) in ch-4 sp, ch 3, 2-dc cl in ch-2 sp, ch 3, (sc, picot) in next ch-4 sp, ch 6*, rep from * to * 3 times, (sc, picot) in next ch-4 sp, ch 3, 2-dc cl in ch-2 sp, ch 3, (sc, picot) in next ch-4 sp, ch 3, tr in ch-3 sp of any (dc, ch 3, sc) group on rnd 25 of tablecloth, ch 3, (sc, picot) in next ch-4 sp on medallion, ch 2, dc in next ch-3 sp on tablecloth to left of previous joining, ch 2, 2-dc cl in next ch-2 sp on medallion, ch 2, dc in next ch-3 sp on tablecloth, ch 2, (sc, picot) in next ch-4 sp on medallion, ch 3, tr in next ch-3 sp on tablecloth, ch 3, (sc, picot) in next ch-4 sp on medallion** and leaving a 2-yd length to complete medallion and join to 22nd medallion in medallion rnd, fasten off.

Rnd 31: *(For medallions 2–22)*. Rep rnd 31 instruction for first medallion to ** placing first joining tr in the 6th ch-3 sp to the right of the first joining tr of the first medallion***, ch 5, sk 1 ch-2 sp, (dtr, ch 1, dtr) in next ch-2 sp on tablecloth, dtr in ch-3 sp of first medallion opposite ch-5 just made, ch 1, turn, (sc, picot) in ch-1 sp, sl st in next dtr and in each of 5 ch sts, ch 2, 2-dc cl in next ch-2 sp on new medallion, ch 3, (sc, picot) in next ch-4 sp, ch 3, 2 dtr in opposite ch-6 sp on first medallion, ch 3 and resume first medallion instructions from * to * in next ch-4 sp on new medallion to complete rnd, join with sl st in first sc of rnd, fasten off.

Complete first medallion by attaching with rem long thread to 22nd medallion.

Rnd 32: Attach crochet cotton with tr in 3rd free ch-6 sp on medallion, *ch 9, tr in next sp, ch 4, tr in last tr, sk 1 ch-3 sp on next medallion, tr in following ch-3 sp, ch 9, tr in next sp, ch 14, (dc, ch 3, dc) in next ch-6 sp, ch 14**, tr in next ch-6 sp, rep from * around, ending last rep at **, sl st to join in first tr of rnd.

Rnd 33: Sl st in each of next 3 sts, (ch 4, tr) in ch-9 sp, *ch 2, 2 dtr in ch-4 sp, ch 2, 2 tr in next ch-9 sp, ch 5, (3-dc cl, ch 5) 3 times in next ch-14 sp, 3-dc cl in ch-3 sp, (ch 5, 3-dc cl) 3 times in next ch-14 sp**, ch 5, 2 tr in ch-9 sp, rep from * around, ending last rep at **, ch 2, dc in 4th ch of beg ch-4 to form last ch sp.

Rnd 34: (Sc, picot) over dc sp, *ch 1, 3 tr in ch-2 sp, ch 6, dc over side edge of ch-6 just made, ch 6, sc in next dtr, ch 3, sc in next dtr, ch 9, dc over side edge of ch-9 just made, ch 3, 3 tr in next ch-2 sp, ch 1, (sc, picot) in next ch-5 sp, ch 3, sc in next sp, ch 7, dc over side edge of ch-7 just made, ch 4, (sc in next sp, ch 6, dc over side edge of ch-6 just made, ch 3) 3 times, ch 7, dc over side edge of ch-7 just made, ch 4, sc in next sp, ch 3**, (sc, picot) in next sp, rep from * around, ending last rep at **, join in beg sc, fasten off.

Rnd 35: Attach crochet cotton with sc in small lp of last ch 6, dc over side edge of ch-6 just made of a group, ch 3, dc in same lp, *(dc, ch 3, sc, ch 3, dc) in next small lp formed by working dc over the side edge of a ch*, rep bet *, (ch 3, dc around post of last dc made) twice, **rep bet * 7 times, ch 3, dc around post of last dc made**, rep bet ** 5 times, ***rep bet * 7 times, (ch 3, dc around post of last dc made) twice***, rep bet ** 6 times, rep bet ***, rep bet ** 6 times, rep bet * 4 times, dc in next small lp, ch 3, sl st to join in beg sc.

Rnd 36: (Sl st, sc) in ch-3 sp, *ch 3, (sc, picot) in next ch-3 sp, ch 3, sc in next sp, ch 10, sc in next sp*, rep bet * twice, **ch 3, (sc, picot) in next sp, ch 3, sc in next sp, ch 8, sc in next sp**, rep bet **, (rep bet * 3 times, rep bet ** twice), rep bet ( ) halfway around, rep bet * 4 times, rep bet ** twice, rep bet ( ) to end of rnd rep bet ** only once at end of rnd, ch 3, (sc, picot) in next sp, ch 3, sc in next sp, ch 4, dtr in beg sc of rnd to form last ch sp.

Rnd 37: (Sc, ch 3, dc) over dtr sp, *ch 4, dc, ch 3, sc, ch 3, dc* in next ch-10 sp, rep bet * in each ch-10 and ch-8 sp around, ch 4 dc in next ch-4 sp, ch 3, join in beg sc.

Rnd 38: (Sl st, sc, picot) in ch-3 sp, *ch 5, (sc, picot) in next ch-3 sp, ch 7, dc over side edge of ch-7 just made**, ch 4, (sc, picot) in next ch-3 sp, rep from * around, ending last rep at **, ending with tr in beg sc, turn.

Rnd 39: Rep rnd 22.

Rnd 40: Rep rnd 23.

Rnd 41: Rep rnd 24.

Rnd 42: Rep rnd 25.

Rnds 43–49: Rep rnds 26–31 of first small medallions making a ring of 37 medallions. At *** in rnd 31, ch 4, sk 1 ch-2 sp, (dtr, ch 1, dtr) in next ch-2 sp on tablecloth, tr in ch-3 sp of first medallion opposite ch-4 sp just made, ch 1, turn, (sc, picot) in ch-1 sp, sl st in next dtr and in each of 4 ch sts, ch 2, 2-dc cl in next ch-2 sp on new medallion, ch 3, (sc, picot) in next ch-4 sp, ch 2, 2 dc in opposite ch-6 sp on first medallion, ch 3, and resume rnd 31 of first medallion instructions bet * in next ch-4 sp on new medallion to complete rnd, join with sl st in first sc of rnd, fasten off.

Rnd 50: Attach crochet cotton with tr in first free ch-6 sp of a medallion, *ch 13, (dc, ch 3, dc) in next ch-6 sp, ch 13, tr in next ch-6 sp, ch 6, tr in next sp, ch 4, tr in last made tr, sk 1 ch-3 sp on next medallion, tr in next ch-3 sp, ch 6**, tr in next ch-6 sp, rep from * around, ending last rep at **, sl st to join in first tr.

Rnd 51: (Ch 4, tr, {ch 5, 3-dc cl} twice, ch 5, first and 2nd legs of 3-dc cl) in ch-13 sp, *3rd leg of cl, ch 5, first leg of another 3-dc cl in ch-3 sp, (2nd and 3rd legs of 3-dc cl, ch 5, 3-dc cl, ch 5, 3-dc cl, ch 5, 2 tr) in ch-13 sp, ch 2, 2 dtr in ch-3 lp**, ch 2, (2 tr, ch 5, {3-dc cl, ch 5} twice, first and 2nd legs of 3-dc cl) in ch-13 lp, rep from * around, ending last rep at **, dc in 4th ch of beg ch-4 to form last lp.

Rnd 52: Ch 4, 2 dc in dc sp, (ch 1, (sc, picot) in ch-5 sp, ch 3, sc in next sp, *ch 7, dc around side edge of same ch-7, ch 4, sc in next ch-5 sp*, **ch 6, dc around side edge of same ch-6 sp, ch 3, sc in next sp**, rep bet **, rep bet *, ch 3, (sc, picot) in next sp, ch 1, 3 tr in ch-2 sp, ch 6, dc around side edge of same ch-6, ch 6, sc in dtr, ch 3, sc in next dtr, ch 9, dc around side edge of same ch-9***, ch 3, 3 dc in ch-2 sp) rep between ( ) around, ending last rep at ***, dc in 4th ch of beg ch, turn.

Rnd 53: Ch 1, sl st in next 2 sts, sc in next lp, ch 3, turn, dc in same lp, *(dc, ch 3, sc, ch 3, dc) in next lp*, rep bet * 4 times, **ch 3, dc around last made dc**, (rep bet * 6 times, rep bet **), rep between ( ) around, join in beg sc.

Rnd 54: (Sl st, *sc, picot) in next sp, ch 2, (sc, picot) in next sp, ch 8, sc in next sp, ch 3, (sc, picot) in next sp, ch 3, sc in next sp, ch 8, sc in next sp, ch 3, (sc, picot) in next sp, ch 3, sc in next sp, ch 8, (sc, picot) in next sp, ch 2, (sc, picot) in next sp, ch 8, sc in next sp, ch 3, (sc, picot) in next sp, ch 3, sc in next sp**, ch 8, rep from * around, ending last rep at **, ch 4, tr in beg sc of rnd.

Rnd 55: Sc in same sp, (ch 3, dc) in same sp, *ch 3, (dc, ch 3, sc, ch 3, dc) in next ch-8 sp, rep from * around, ending with ch 3, (dc, ch 3) in first ch-8 sp, join in beg sc.

Rnd 56: Sl st in next st, (sc, picot) in ch-3 sp, *ch 4, (sc, picot) in next ch-3 sp, ch 6, dc around side edge of same ch-6**, ch 3, (sc, picot) in next ch-3 sp, rep from * around, ending last rep at **, tr in beg sc, turn.

Rnd 57: Sl st in next 2 sts, (sc, ch 3, turn, dc) in lp, *ch 3, (dc, ch 3, sc, ch 3, dc) in next dc lp, rep from * around, ending with ch 3, (dc, ch 3) in first lp, join in beg sc.

Rnds 58–61: Rep rnds 56 and 57.

Rnd 62: Rep rnd 56.

Rnd 63: Sl st in each of next 2 sts, (sc, ch 3, turn, dc) in lp, *ch 4, (dc, ch 3, sc, ch 3, dc) in next dc lp, rep from * around, ending with ch 4, (dc, ch 3) in first lp, join in beg sc.

Rnd 64: Sl st in next st, (sc, picot) in ch-3 sp, *ch 5, (sc, picot) in next ch-3 sp, ch 6, dc around side edge of same ch-6**, ch 3, (sc, picot) in next ch-3 sp, rep from * around, ending last rep at **, tr in beg sc of rnd, turn.

Rnds 65 & 66: Rep rnds 63 and 64.
Rnd 67: Rep rnd 63.
Rnd 68: Sl st in next st, (sc, picot) in ch-3 sp, *ch 5, (sc, picot) in next ch-3 sp, ch 7, dc around side edge of same ch-7**, ch 4, (sc, picot) in next ch-3 sp, rep from * around, ending last rep at **, tr in beg sc, turn.
Rnd 69: Sl st in next 2 sts, (sc, ch 5, 2 tr) in lp, *(2 tr, ch 5**, sc, ch 5, 2 tr) in next lp, rep from * around, ending last rep at **, join in beg sc.
Rnd 70: (Sl st, ch 2, 2-dc cl) in ch-5 sp, *ch 5, 3-dc cl in next ch-5 sp, rep from * around, ending with ch 2, dc in top of beg 2-dc cl.

Rnd 71: (Sc, ch 5, 2 tr) in dc sp, *sc in next ch-5 sp, (2 tr, ch 5, sc, ch 5, 2 tr) in next ch-5 sp, rep from * around, ending with sc in next ch-5 sp, (2 tr, ch 5) in first sp, join in beg sc of rnd.
Rnds 72–75: Rep rnds 70 and 71.
Rnd 76: (Sl st, *sc, ch 3, dc) in ch-5 sp, ch 2, (dc, ch 3, sc) in next ch-5 sp, ch 2, rep from * around, join in beg sc.
Rnd 77: (Sl st, *sc, picot) in ch-3 sp, ch 2, (dc, ch 4, sl st in 3rd ch from hook, ch 1, dc in last made dc, dc) in next ch-2 sp, ch 2, (sc, picot) in next ch-3 sp, ch 1, sc in next ch-2 sp, ch 1, rep from * around, join in beg sc, fasten off. ✂

Pretty Pineapples
Continued from page 123

Rnd 7: Ch 4, *(ch 1, tr in next tr) 6 times, ch 3, (tr, ch 1, tr) in sp between 2-tr groups, ch 3**, tr in first tr of 7-tr group, rep from * around, ending last rep at **, join in 4th ch of beg ch-4.
Rnd 8: Sl st into ch-1 sp, ch 1, *sc in ch-1 sp, (ch 2, sc in next ch-1 sp) 5 times, ch 2, ({tr, ch 1} twice, tr) in next ch-1 sp, ch 3, rep from * around, join in beg sc.
Rnd 9: Sl st into ch-2 sp, ch 1, *sc in ch-2 sp, (ch 2, sc in next ch-2 sp) 4 times, ch 3, (tr, ch 1, tr) in next ch-1 sp, ch 1, (tr, ch 1, tr) in next ch-1 sp, ch 3, rep from * around, join in beg sc.
Rnd 10: Sl st into ch-2 sp, ch 1, *sc in ch-2 sp, (ch 2, sc in next ch-2 sp) 3 times, ch 4, (tr, ch 1) twice in each of next 2 ch-1 sps, (tr, ch 1, tr) in next ch-1 sp, ch 4, rep from * around, join in beg sc.

Rnd 11: Sl st into ch-2 sp, ch 1, *sc in ch-2 sp, (ch 2, sc in next ch-2 sp) twice, ch 4, (tr, ch 1) twice in each of next 4 ch-1 sps, (tr, ch 1, tr) in next ch-1 sp, ch 4, rep from * around, join in beg sc.
Rnd 12: Sl st into ch-2 sp, ch 1, *sc in ch-2 sp, ch 2, sc in next ch-2 sp, ch 4, (tr, ch 1) twice in each of next 8 ch-1 sps, (tr, ch 1, tr) in next ch-1 sp, ch 4, rep from * around, join in beg sc.
Rnd 13: Sl st into ch-2 sp, ch 1, *sc in ch-2 sp, ch 5, sc in next ch-1 sp, (ch 2, sk next ch-1 sp, (tr, ch 1, tr) in next ch-1 sp) 7 times, ch 2, sk next ch-1 sp, sc in next ch-1 sp, ch 5, rep from * around, join in beg sc.
Rnd 14: Ch 1, *5 sc over ch-5 sp, (2 sc over next ch-2 sp, (sc, ch 3, sc) in next ch-1 sp) 7 times, 2 sc over next ch-2 sp, 5 sc over next ch-5 sp, rep from * around, join in beg sc, fasten off. ✂

Flower-Fresh Bookmarks
Continued from page 119

Using fabric glue, attach a Leaf to back of each Flower. Glue a Flower centered over each shell. Glue a pearl bead to the center of each Flower.

Tie picot-edged ribbon into a bow and glue to center top of Bookmark.

Peaches & Cream Bookmark

EASY

Finished Size
2¼ x 8 inches

Materials
- Size 10 crochet cotton (350 yds per ball):
    - 35 yds peach
    - 15 yds tangerine
    - 5 yds ecru
- Size 6/1.80mm steel crochet hook of size needed to obtain gauge
- 6 ivory 4mm beads
- Washable fabric glue
- 1½-inch piece cardboard

Gauge
1 sc and 7 tr = 1¼ inches

Pattern Notes
Weave in loose ends as work progresses. Join rounds with a slip stitch unless otherwise stated.

Bookmark

First Motif
Rnd 1 (RS): With peach, ch 7, sl st in first ch to form a ring, ch 4 *(counts as first tr)* 6 tr in ring, ch 2, 7 tr in ring, ch 4, 7 tr in ring, ch 2, 7 tr in ring, ch 4, join in 4th ch of beg ch-4, fasten off. *(28 tr)*

2nd Motif
Rnd 1 (RS): With peach, ch 7, sl st to join in first ch to form a ring, ch 4, 6 tr in ring, ch 2, 7 tr in ring, ch 4, 7 tr in ring, ch 1, sl st in ch-2 sp of previous Motif, ch 1, 7 tr in ring, ch 4, join in 4th ch of beg ch-4, fasten off. *(28 tr)*

3rd–6th Motifs
Rnd 1: Rep rnd 1 of 2nd Motif.

Trim
Row 1: With RS facing, attach peach in 4th tr before first ch-4 sp on side edge of Bookmark, ch 1, sc in same tr, *dc in next ch-4 sp, (ch 1, dc) 6 times in same ch-4 sp, sk next 3 tr, sc in next tr**, ch 2, sk first 3 tr of next Motif, sc in next tr, rep from * across edge, ending last rep at **, fasten off.

Row 2: With RS facing, attach tangerine in first ch-1 sp of previous row, ch 1, sc in same ch-1 sp, *(ch 2, sc in next ch-1 sp) 5 times, sc in next ch-2 sp between Motifs**, sc in next ch-1 sp, rep from * across, ending last rep at **, fasten off.

Rep rows 1 and 2 of Trim on opposite side edge of Bookmark.

Flower
Make 6.
Leaving a slight length of ecru at beg, form a ring, (ch 2, dc, ch 2, sl st in ring) 5 times in ring, fasten off. Pull rem beg length to close opening and secure end with a drop of glue. With RS facing, glue a Flower to the center of each Motif. Glue a bead to the center of each Flower.

Tassel

Make 2.

Wrap tangerine around cardboard 20 times, fasten off. Lp a piece of tangerine through top and tie ends in a knot, sl Tassel off cardboard. Wrap a length of tangerine ¼ inch down from top of Tassel. Cut bottom edge threads.

Attach a Tassel to each end of Bookmark. Secure knot with a drop of glue. ✂

Daisy Valance

Continued from page 129

Row 30: Attach white in ch-2 sp of beg shell of row 29, ch 6, **trtr** (see Special Stitches) in same ch-2 sp as beg ch-6, *ch 2, sk next petal on flower, (sc, ch 3, sc) in sp between center 2 dc sts of next petal, ch 6, sl st in 3rd ch from hook, sc in next ch, ch 2, sc in sp between center 2 dc sts of next petal, ch 5, sl st in 3rd ch from hook, sc in next ch, ch 1, sc in same sp between center 2 dc sts of same petal, ch 6, sl st in 3rd ch from hook, sc in next ch, ch 2, (sc, ch 3, sc) between center 2 dc sts of next petal, ch 2, 2 trtr in ch-2 sp of next shell, rep from * across, fasten off.

Top Curtain Trim

Row 1 (RS): Working over ends of rows of Curtain Top Band, attach white in end row, ch 1, sc in side edge of same dc, (ch 4, sc in side edge of next row) 128 times, turn. (129 ch-4 sps)

Row 2: Sl st into ch-4 sp, ch 5 (counts as first tr, ch 1), tr in same sp, (ch 1, tr) 3 times in same ch-4 sp as beg ch-5, *sc in next ch-4 sp, ch 5, sk next ch-4 sp, sc in next ch-4 sp, ({tr, ch 1} 4 times, tr) in next ch-4 sp, rep from * across, turn. (33 groups of tr sts)

Row 3: Sl st into ch-1 sp, ch 1, sc in same ch-1 sp, (ch 4, sc in next ch-1 sp) 3 times, *ch 2, working over ch-5 sp of previous row, work 1 sc into ch-4 sp of row 1, ch 2, sc in next ch-1 sp, (ch 4, sc in next ch-1 sp) 3 times, rep from * across, fasten off.

Finishing

Using photo as a guide, with WS of Curtain facing, attach a Leaf Group with crochet hook to top edge of each Flower. ✂

Flower Webs Table Topper

Continued from page 136

Rnd 5: Beg shell (see Special Stitches) in same st as joining, sl st next ch-7 sp, (**shell** (see Special Stitches) in next sl st, sl st in next ch-7 sp) around, sl st to join in 4th ch of beg ch-4. (16 shells)

Rnd 6: Sl st in next ch-5 sp of shell, ch 4 (counts as first tr throughout), 1 tr, (ch 7, 2 tr) 3 times in same ch-5 sp as beg ch-4 (beg corner), *(ch 7, 3 sc in next ch-5 sp of shell) 3 times, ch 7**, (2 tr, ch 7) 3 times and 2 tr in next ch-5 sp of shell (for corner), rep from * around, ending last rep at **, join in 4th ch of beg ch-4.

Motifs Joined on 1 Edge

Note: *The following motifs are joined to previous motifs across 1 edge, 2nd, 3rd, 4th, 5th and 9th.*

Rnds 1–5: Rep rnds 1–5 of First Motif.

Rnd 6: Sl st in next ch-5 sp of shell, ch 4, tr,

(ch 7, 2 tr) twice in same ch-5 corner sp, ch 3, sl st in 4th ch of corresponding ch-7 sp of corner on previous motif, ch 3, 2 tr in same ch-5 corner sp, (ch 3, sl st in 4th ch of corresponding ch-7 sp on previous motif, ch 3, 3 sc in next ch-5 sp on working motif) 3 times, ch 3, sl st in 4th ch of next ch-7 sp on previous motif, ch 3, 2 tr in next ch-5 sp of next shell, ch 3, sl st in 4th ch of corresponding ch-7 sp of corner of previous motif, ch 3, (2 tr, ch 7) twice and 2 tr in same corner ch-5 sp, *(ch 7, 3 sc in next ch-5 sp of shell) 3 times, ch 7**, (2 tr, ch 7) 3 times and 2 tr in next ch-5 sp of shell, rep from * around, ending last rep at **, join in 4th ch of beg ch-4, fasten off.

Motifs Joined on 2 Edges

Note: *The following motifs are joined to previous motifs across 2 edges, 6th, 7th, 8th, 10th, 11th and 12th.*

Rnds 1–5: Rep rnds 1–5 of First Motif.

Rnd 6: Sl st in next ch-5 sp of shell, ch 4, tr, (ch 7, 2 tr) twice in same ch-5 corner sp, *ch 3, sl st in 4th ch of corresponding ch-7 sp of corner on previous motif, ch 3, 2 tr in same ch-5 corner sp, (ch 3, sl st in 4th ch of corresponding ch-7 sp on previous motif, ch 3, 3 sc in next ch-5 sp on working motif) 3 times, ch 3, sl st in 4th ch of next ch-7 sp on previous motif, ch 3, 2 tr in next ch-5 sp of next shell, ch 3, sl st in 4th ch of ch-7 of corner of previous motif, ch 3**, (2 tr, ch 7, 2 tr) in same corner ch-5 sp, rep from * to **, ({2 tr, ch 7} twice, 2 tr) in same corner ch-5 sp, (ch 7, 3 sc in next ch-5 sp of shell) 3 times, ch 7, join in 4th ch of beg ch-4, fasten off.

Fill-In

Note: *At the junction of 4 motifs, 1 ch-7 sp rem from each motif. Work Fill-In over these 4 ch-7 sps.*

Rnd 1 (RS): Attach ecru in any rem ch-7 sp at junction of 4 motifs, ch 1, 5 hdc in same ch-7 sp, (5 hdc in next ch-7 sp) 3 times, sl st to join in first hdc, fasten off. *(20 hdc)*

Border

Rnd 1 (RS): Sk 3 motifs on any long side, attach ecru with sl st in first free ch-7 sp of corner motif and working to the left toward corner, ch 1, 3 hdc in same sp, *(ch 5, 3 hdc in next ch-7 sp) 14 times, 3 hdc in next ch-7 sp of next motif, (ch 5, 3 hdc in next ch-7 sp) 7 times, 3 hdc in next ch-7 sp of next motif, (ch 5, 3 hdc in next ch-7 sp) 14 times, 3 hdc in next ch-7 sp of next motif, (ch 5, 3 hdc in next ch-7 sp) 7 times, 3 hdc in next ch-7 sp of next motif, (ch 5, 3 hdc in next ch-7 sp) 7 times**, 3 hdc in next ch-7 sp of next motif, rep from * around, ending last rep at **, join in beg hdc.

Rnd 2: Sl st into 2nd ch of next ch-5 sp, ch 1, 3 hdc in same ch-5 sp, (ch 5, 3 hdc in next ch-5 sp) around, join in beg hdc.

Rnds 3 & 4: Rep rnd 2.

Rnd 5: Sl st into next hdc, ch 4, 6 tr in same st as beg ch-4, *sl st in next ch-5 sp, ch 7, sk next 3 hdc, sl st in next ch-5 sp**, 7 tr in center hdc of next 3-hdc group, rep from * around, ending last rep at **, join in 4th ch of beg ch-4. *(49 tr groups)*

Rnd 6: Ch 9 *(counts as first tr, ch 5)*, tr in same st as beg ch-9, *(sk next tr, (tr, ch 5, tr) in next tr) 3 times, sl st in next ch-7 sp**, (tr, ch 5, tr) in next tr, rep from * around, ending last rep at **, join in 4th ch of beg ch-9.

Rnd 7: Sl st into ch-5 sp, ch 1, 3 sc in same ch sp as beg ch-1, *9 sc in each of next 2 ch-5 sps**, 3 sc in each of next 2 ch-5 sps, rep from * around, ending last rep at **, 3 sc in last ch-5 sp, join in beg sc, fasten off. ✂

Hooked on Holidays

What is a holiday without colorful, handmade accessories to dress up your home or give as gifts? From fun to fancy, these delightful crocheted holiday accents are sure to add a festive and personal touch to special celebrations throughout the year.

Let It Snow! Afghan

Design by Katherine Eng

Big, fluffy snowflakes bordered by shades of sky and midnight blue bring to mind the season's first snowfall.

INTERMEDIATE

Finished Size
37 x 54 inches

Materials

- Lion Brand Homespun bulky (chunky) weight yarn (6 oz/185 yds/170g per skein):
    2 skeins each #302 colonial and #355 delft
- Lion Brand Chenille Thick & Quick super bulky (super chunky) weight yarn (100 yds per skein):
    3 skeins #098 antique white
- Size H/8/5mm crochet hook or size needed to obtain gauge

Gauge

Rnds 1–3 = 6 inches square; finished square = 7 inches

Pattern Notes

Weave in loose ends as work progresses.

Join rounds with a slip stitch unless otherwise stated.

Special Stitch

Shell: (2 dc, ch 2, 2 dc) in indicated st.

Square 1

Make 18.

Rnd 1 (RS): With white, ch 6, sl st in first ch to form a ring, (sc in ring, ch 4) 7 times, sc in ring, ch 2, dc in first sc to form last ch sp, turn. *(8 sc, 8 ch-4 sps)*

Rnd 2: Ch 1, sc in same sp as beg ch-1, (ch 3, sc in next ch sp) 7 times, join in beg sc, turn, sl st into next ch-3 sp.

Rnd 3: Ch 1, ((sc, ch 3, sc) in ch-3 sp, ch 3, sk next sc) 8 times, join in beg sc, fasten off.

Rnd 4: Draw up a lp of delft in any ch-3 sp above a sc of rnd 2, ch 1, sc in same sp, ch 2, sc in next ch-3 sp, *ch 1, (2 dc, ch 3, 2 dc) in next ch-3 sp, ch 1, sc in next ch-3 sp, (ch 2, sc in next ch-3 sp) twice, rep from * around, ending last rep with ch 2, join in beg sc, fasten off.

Rnd 5: Draw up a lp of colonial in first dc to the left of any corner ch-3 sp, ch 1,

Continued on page 171

Christmas Sachets

Designs by Diane Stone

Crochet a basketful of these dainty poinsettia and rose sachets as festive gifts for family.

INTERMEDIATE

Finished Size
4 inches in diameter

Materials
- Size 10 crochet cotton (350 yds per ball):
  1 ball each ecru, burgundy and green
- Size 6/1.80mm steel crochet hook or size needed to obtain gauge
- 24 inches ¼-inch-wide burgundy satin ribbon
- 4 x 4-inch square of ivory colored netting
- 3 cotton balls
- Scented oil
- Small gold safety pin
- 6mm ivory bead
- Washable fabric glue

Vintage Rose

Gauge
Rnds 1 & 2 = 1½ inches

Pattern Notes
Weave in loose ends as work progresses.

Join rounds with a slip stitch unless otherwise stated.

Front
Rnd 1: With ecru, form a ring with end of thread, leaving a slight tail at beg, ch 3 *(counts as first dc)*, 15 dc in ring, join in 3rd ch of beg ch-3. To close opening, pull rem beg length. *(16 dc)*

Rnd 2: Ch 3, dc in same st as beg ch-3, 2 dc in each rem dc around, join in 3rd ch of beg ch-3. *(32 dc)*

Rnd 3: Ch 1, sc in same st as beg ch-1, *ch 3, sk next st, sc in next st, rep from * around, ending with dc in beg sc to form last ch-3 sp. *(16 ch-3 sps)*

Rnd 4: Sl st into ch-3 sp, ch 1, sc in same ch sp, ch 3, (sc in next ch sp, ch 3) around, join in beg sc.

Rnd 5: Ch 3, 4 dc in next ch-3 sp, (dc in next sc, 4 dc in next ch sp) around, join in 3rd ch of beg ch-3. *(80 dc)*

Rnd 6: Ch 4 *(counts as first dc, ch-1)*, ({dc, ch 1} 4 times, dc) in same st as beg ch-4, sk next 3 sts, (sc, ch 3, sc) in next dc, sk next 3 sts, *({dc, ch 1} 5 times, dc) in next st, sk next 3 sts, (sc, ch 3, sc) in next st, sk next 3 sts, rep from * around, join in 3rd ch of beg ch-4.

Rnd 7: Sl st into ch-1 sp, ch 1, sc in same

ch-1 sp, *(ch 3, sc in next ch-1 sp) 4 times, sc in next ch-3 sp**, sc in next ch-1 sp, rep from * around, ending last rep at **, join in beg sc, fasten off.

Back
Rnds 1–5: Rep rnds 1–5 of Front. At the end of rnd 5, fasten off.

Rose
Rnd 1: With burgundy, form a ring with end of thread, leaving a slight tail at beg, ch 3, 9 dc in ring, join in 3rd ch of beg ch-3. To close opening, pull rem beg length. *(10 dc)*

Rnd 2: Ch 1, sc in same st as beg ch-1, sc in each rem st around, join in beg sc.

Rnd 3: Ch 1, sc in same st as beg ch-1, ch 3, sk next st, (sc in next st, ch 3, sk next st) around, join in beg sc. *(5 ch-3 sps)*

Rnd 4: (Sl st, ch 3, 4 dc, ch 3, sl st) in each ch-3 sp around. *(5 petals)*

Rnd 5: Ch 1, working between 2nd and 3rd dc of first petal, *insert hook from back to front over ch-3 sp of rnd 3, work a sc over ch-3 sp, ch 4**, working between 2nd and 3rd dc of next petal, rep from * around, ending last rep at **, join in beg sc. *(5 ch-4 sps)*

Continued on page 172

Friendly Scarecrow Door Decoration

Design by Belinda "Bendy" Carter

Hang this charming fellow on your door to welcome your holiday guests at Thanksgiving time.

INTERMEDIATE

4 MEDIUM

Finished Size

20 inches tall

Materials

- Red Heart Kids medium (worsted) weight yarn (solid: 5 oz/290 yds/141g; multicolor: 4 oz/232 yds/113g per skein):
  - 1 skein each #2845 blue, #2230 yellow and #2942 camper
  - 1 oz/58 yds/28g each #2001 white and #2390 red
  - 1 yd #2652 lime
- Red Heart Super Saver medium (worsted) weight yarn (7 oz/452 yds/225g per skein):

1 oz/56 yds/28g each #312 black, #776 dark orchid, #256 carrot, #360 café and 1 yd #778 light fuchsia

- Size H/8/5mm crochet hook or size needed to obtain gauge
- Fiberfill
- Nontoxic washable fabric paint: 1 bottle each black shiny, medium blue iridescent, medium orange shiny, red iridescent and strawberry iridescent
- 18-inch ¾-inch in diameter wooden dowel
- Tacky glue
- Stitch markers

Gauge

4 sc = 1 inch; 4 sc rnds = 1 inch

Pattern Notes

Weave in loose ends as work progresses. Join rounds with slip stitch unless otherwise stated.

Head

Rnd 1 (RS): With white, ch 2, 6 sc in 2nd ch from hook, do not join. *(6 sc)*

Rnd 2: 2 sc in each sc around. *(12 sc)*

Rnd 3: (2 sc in each of next 3 sc, sc in each of next 3 sc) twice. *(18 sc)*

Rnd 4: (Sc in next sc, 2 sc in each of next 4 sc, sc in each of next 4 sc) twice. *(26 sc)*

Rnd 5: (Sc in each of next 4 sc, 2 sc in each of next 2 sc, sc in each of next 7 sc) twice. *(30 sc)*

Rnds 6-12: Sc in each sc around.

Rnd 13: *Sc in each of next 4 sc, (**sc dec** *(see Stitch Guide)* in next 2 sc) twice, sc in each of next 7 sc, rep from * once. *(26 sc)*

Rnd 14: *Sc in next sc, (sc dec in next 2 sc) 4 times, sc in each of next 4 sc, rep from * once. *(18 sc)*

Rnd 15: *(Sc dec in next 2 sc) 3 times, sc in each of next 3 sc, rep from * once. *(12 sc)*

Rnd 16: (Sc dec in next 2 sc) 6 times, **change color** *(see Stitch Guide)* in last st to camper. *(6 sc)*

Shirt & Body

Rnd 1: 2 sc in each sc around. *(12 sc)*

Note: *For shoulders, mark 2 sts on each side of Head.*

Rnd 2: (Sc to marker, 3 sc in each of next 2 marked sts) twice, sc in each sc to end of rnd. *(20 sc)*

Rnd 3: (Sc in each sc to center sc of 3-sc group, 3 sc in center sc of 3-sc group) 4 times, sc in each rem sc around. *(28 sc)*

Rnds 4–7: Rep rnd 3. *(60 sc)*

Rnd 8: (Sc in each sc to center sc of 3-sc group, ch 3, sk next 12 sts, sc in center st of next 3-sc group *(Arm opening)*) twice, sc in each rem sc around. *(42 sc)*

Rnd 9: Sc in each sc around.

Rnds 10–23: Rep rnd 9.

Rnd 24: (Sc in each of next 5 sc, sc dec in next 2 sc) 6 times. *(36 sc)*

Rnd 25: (Sc in each of next 4 sc, sc dec in next 2 sc) 6 times. *(30 sc)*

Rnd 26: (Sc in each of next 3 sc, sc dec in next 2 sc) 6 times. *(24 sc)*

Rnd 27: (Sc in each of next 2 sc, sc dec in next 2 sc) 6 times, sl st in next st, fasten off. *(18 sc)*

Sleeve & Arm

Make 2.

Rnd 1 (RS): Attach camper at underarm, ch 1, work 15 sc around opening, do not join. *(15 sc)*

Rnds 2–21: Sc in each sc around. At the end of last rep, sl st in next st, fasten off. Lightly stuff Head and neck area with fiberfill. Cut 15 strands of yellow each

22 inches long, holding all strands tog, draw strands from cuff of 1 Sleeve, through both Arms and out through cuff of 2nd Sleeve, centering strands so that the same amount of excess is coming out through both cuffs. Stuff Body only *(not Arms)* with fiberfill until Scarecrow is pleasingly plump but not overstuffed. Holding front and back of bottom of Shirt tog and working through both thicknesses, attach camper to bottom of Shirt, ch 1, work 9 sc evenly sp across bottom to close opening, fasten off.

Hand

Make 2.

Rnd 1 (RS): With dark orchid, ch 2, 6 sc in 2nd ch from hook, do not join. *(6 sc)*

Rnd 2: Sc in each sc around.

Rnd 3: Sc in each sc around, ch 3, sl st in **back lp** *(see Stitch Guide)* of 2nd ch from hook, sl st in back lp of next ch, sl st in same st as last sc *(thumb)*.

Rnd 4: Keeping thumb in front of work, sc in each sc around. *(6 sc)*

Rnds 5–9: Sc in each sc around. At the end of last rep, sl st in next st, fasten off.

Apply glue to last 3 rnds on Hand, then insert rnds inside Sleeve. Cut a 10-inch length of café, tie length tightly around bottom of Sleeve over glued rnds of Hand, trim ends. Trim yellow stuffing around Hands as desired.

Leg Stuffing

Cut 2 strands of yellow each 26 inches long, holding strands tog, fold in half, insert hook in any st closing at bottom of Shirt, draw strands through at fold to form a lp on hook, draw cut ends through lp on hook, pull ends tightly to secure. Rep Leg Stuffing in each st across bottom of Shirt.

Hat

Rnd 1 (RS): With blue, ch 2, 6 sc in 2nd ch from hook, do not join. *(6 sc)*

Rnd 2: 2 sc in each sc around. *(12 sc)*

Rnd 3: (Sc in next sc, 2 sc in next sc) 6 times. *(18 sc)*

Rnd 4: (Sc in each of next 2 sc, 2 sc in next sc) 6 times. *(24 sc)*

Rnd 5: (Sc in each of next 3 sc, 2 sc in next sc) 6 times. *(30 sc)*

Rnds 6–10: Sc in each sc around. At the end of rnd 10, sl st in next st, turn.

Rnd 11 (WS): Ch 1, working in back lps only, (sc in each of next 4 sts, 2 sc in next st) 6 times, join in beg sc, turn. *(36 sc)*

Rnd 12 (RS): Ch 1, (sc in each of next 5 sc, 2 sc in next st) 6 times, join in beg sc. *(42 sc)*

Rnd 13: Ch 1, (sc in each of next 6 sc, 2 sc in next sc) 6 times, join in beg sc, fasten off. *(48 sc)*

Hair

*Cut 1 strand of yellow 10 inches long, fold strand in half, insert hook in st on rnd 9 on inside of Hat, draw strand through at fold to form a lp on hook, draw cut ends through lp on hook, pull tightly to secure, rep from * in each st of rnd 9 of Hat. Glue Hat on top of Head in desired position.

Neck Bow

Cut 3 strands of yellow each 24 inches long. Place strands around neckline, tie ends in a bow, trim ends to desired length.

Pants

Rnd 1 (RS): With blue, ch 42, sl st in first ch to form a ring, ch 1, sc in each ch around, do not join. *(42 sc)*

Rnd 2: (Sc in next sc, ch 1, sk next st) 21 times.

Rnds 3–9: (Sc in next sc, ch 1, sk next ch sp) around.

First Leg

Rnd 1: Sc in next st, ch 5, sk next 21 sts, (sc in next st, ch 1, sk next ch sp) 10 times. *(26 sts)*

Rnd 2: Sc in next st, (ch 1, sk next ch st, sc in next ch) twice, ch 1, sk next ch st, (sc in next st, ch 1, sk next ch sp) 10 times. *(26 sts)*

Rnd 3: (Sc in next sc, ch 1, sk next ch sp) around.

Rnds 4–6: Rep rnd 3.

Rnd 7: (Sc in sc, sk next ch sp) twice (*2-st dec*), *sc in next sc, ch 1, sk next ch sp, rep from * around. (*24 sts*)

Rnd 8: Sc, ch 1, sk next st, *sc in next sc, ch 1, sk next ch sp, rep from * around.

Rnds 9–23: Rep rnds 4–8.

Rnds 24–26: Rep rnds 4–6. (*18 sts*)

Rnd 27: Rep rnd 3.

2nd Leg

Rnd 1: With RS facing and working in unused lps of ch-5 going across crotch and then around Leg opening, attach blue in first ch, ch 1, sc in same st as beg ch-1, (ch 1, sk next ch, sc in next ch) twice, ch 1, sk next ch sp, (sc in next st, ch 1, sk next sp) 10 times, do not join.

Rnd 2: Rep rnd 3 of First Leg.

Rnds 3–27: Rep rnds 3–27 of First Leg. Place Pants on Shirt/Body, draw half of the Leg Stuffing through each Leg on Pants.

Waistline Trim

Rnd 1 (RS): Attach blue in opposite side of foundation ch of Waistline of Pants, ch 1, (sc, ch 3, sc) in same ch as beg ch-1, sk next ch, ((sc, ch 3, sc) in next ch, sk next ch) around, join in beg sc, fasten off.

Pants Patch

Make 1 each lime & light fuchsia.

Row 1 (RS): Ch 4, sc in 2nd ch from hook, sc in each rem ch across, turn. (*3 sc*)

Rows 2 & 3: Ch 1, sc in each sc across, turn. At the end of row 3, fasten off. Glue Patches to right Pant Leg.

Suspenders

Make 2.

Cut 1 strand of carrot 100 inches long, fold strand in half, tie ends in knot. Place knotted end onto a stationary object the diameter of a pencil. Place looped end on finger. Make strands taut. Twist strands 100 times. Place 1 finger in center of rope, fold in half letting the 2 strands twist tog. Tie a double knot in 1 end of rope 2 inches from end, tie a double knot in other end of rope 9 inches from first knot, trim tassel ends to 1½ inches.

Attach Suspenders, crisscrossing them in back, to Pants by pushing knots through ch-3 lps on Waistline Trim of Pants. If desired, glue Pants to Body and Suspenders in place.

Shoe

Make 2.

Sole

Rnd 1 (RS): With black, ch 9, 3 sc in 2nd ch from hook, sc in each of next 6 chs, 3 sc in last ch, working on opposite side of foundation ch, sc in each of next 6 chs, join in beg sc, turn. (*18 sc*)

Rnd 2: Ch 1, working in **front lp** (*see Stitch Guide*) of each st around, sc in each st around, join in beg sc, turn.

Tongue

Row 1: Ch 1, sc in each of next 3 sts, turn.

Rows 2–5: Ch 1, sc in each of next 3 sc, turn. At the end of row 5, fasten off.

Side & Heel

Row 1 (RS): Attach black in next st of Sole, ch 1, sc in same st as beg ch-1, sc in each st around to other side of Tongue, turn. (*15 sc*)

Row 2: Ch 1, (sc in next sc, ch 1, sk next st) twice, sc in each of next 7 sc, (ch 1, sk next st, sc in next st) twice, turn, fasten off.

Cuff

Rnd 1 (RS): Sk first 4 sts on Side and Heel, attach black in next st, ch 1, sc in same st as beg ch-1, sc in next 6 sts, sc in each of the 3 sts going across top of Tongue, do not join. (*10 sts*)

Continued on page 170

Halloween Checkers Game

Design by Belinda "Bendy" Carter

Your trick-or-treaters will enjoy a spirited game of checkers using colorful candy corn and friendly ghosts as play pieces.

EASY

4 MEDIUM

Finished Size
Checkerboard: 17 inches square
Candy corn: 2½ inches tall
Ghost: 2¼ inches tall

Materials
- Red Heart Kids medium (worsted) weight yarn (5 oz/290 yds/141g per skein):
    1 skein each #2001 white, #2252 orange, #2230 yellow and #2652 lime
- Red Heart Super Saver medium (worsted) weight yarn (7 oz/364 yds/198g per skein):
    1 skein #776 dark orchid
- Size H/8/5mm crochet hook or size needed to obtain gauge
- 24 black 4mm faceted beads
- 12 inches sewing thread
- 17-inch square ¼-inch thick board
- Tacky glue
- Stitch marker

Gauge
7 sc = 2 inches; 4 rows = 1 inch

Pattern Notes
Weave in loose ends as work progresses. Join rounds with a slip stitch unless otherwise stated.

Special Stitch
Bead single crochet (bead sc): Push 1 bead up against hook, insert hook in next st, yo, draw lp through, drawing bead through st to front of work, yo, draw through both lps on hook.

Ghost
Make 12.

Bead Preparation
Take sewing thread and fold in half so there is a lp at 1 end, draw white yarn through lp in sewing thread, string 2 beads onto sewing thread, draw beads down sewing thread and onto yarn, remove sewing thread.

Rnd 1 (RS): With white, ch 2, 4 sc in 2nd ch from hook, do not join, use a st marker to mark rnds.

Rnd 2: 2 sc in each sc around. *(8 sc)*

Rnd 3: Bead sc *(see Special Stitch)* in each of next 2 sc, sc in each of next 6 sc.

Rnd 4: Sc in each sc around.

Rnd 5: 2 sc in next sc, sc in each of next 2 sc, (2 sc in next sc) twice, sc in each of next 2 sc, 2 sc in next sc. *(12 sc)*

Continued on page 169

Bunny Faces Basket

Design by Belinda "Bendy" Carter

Puffy little bunny faces and cloth appliqué flowers add a whimsical touch to this darling, bead-handled basket.

EXPERIENCED

4 MEDIUM

Finished Size
5½ inches wide x 3¾ inches high, excluding handle

Materials
- Red Heart Kids medium (worsted) weight yarn (5 oz/290 yds/141g per skein):
  - 1 skein #2001 white
  - 3 yds #2652 lime
  - 20 inches each #2734 pink, #2680 jade and #2230 yellow
- Size H/8/5mm crochet hook or size needed to obtain gauge
- 12 black 4mm faceted beads
- 42 pink 4mm faceted beads
- 16 white 6 x 9mm pony beads
- 17 multicolored 6 x 9mm pony beads
- 5½ x 3¾-inch silver handle frame by Darice
- 12-inch length sewing thread
- 3 x 5½-inch floral clear plastic plant liner
- 6 mini 1-inch flower self-sticking patches
- Tacky glue
- Stitch markers

Gauge
4 sc rnds = 1 inch; 4 sc = 1 inch

Pattern Notes
Weave in loose ends as work progresses. Join rounds with a slip stitch unless otherwise stated.

Special Stitches
Bunny stitch (bunny st): *Note: All of bunny st is worked in 1 st. Beads will appear on WS of work.* Sl st in indicated st, ch 7, *push bead up to hook, sl st in **back lp** (see Stitch Guide) 2nd ch from hook, (push bead up to hook, sl st in back lp of next ch) twice*, (insert hook in next ch, yo, draw through) 3 times *(4 lps on hook)*, **insert hook in same st as beg sl st, yo, draw through, (yo, draw through 2 lps on hook) twice, push bead up to hook, yo, draw through 2 lps on hook**, ***yo, insert hook in first horizontal bar going down side of st just made, yo, draw through, insert hook in next horizontal bar going down side of st, yo, draw through***, insert hook in same st as beg sl st, yo, draw through, yo, draw through 2 lps on hook, push bead up to hook, (yo, draw through 2 lps on hook) twice, rep bet ***, rep bet **, yo, draw through all 4 lps on hook, ch 1 to close, ch 4, rep bet *, sk closing ch, sl st in first horizontal bar going down side of bunny

face, (sl st in next horizontal bar going down side of bunny face) twice, sl st in same st as beg sl st.

Bead Preparation for Handle

Unscrew end of handle, place 33 pony beads onto handle, starting and ending with a multi-colored bead. Screw end back onto handle.

Bead Preparation for Bunnies

Take sewing thread and fold in half so that there is a lp at 1 end, draw white yarn through lp in sewing thread, string beads into sewing thread, draw beads down sewing thread and onto yarn, when all beads have been placed onto yarn, remove sewing thread.

Place beads onto yarn in the following order: (3 pink, 1 black, 1 pink, 1 black, 3 pink) 6 times.

Basket Bottom

Rnd 1 (RS): With white, ch 2, 6 sc in 2nd ch from hook, do not join, place a st marker. *(6 sc)*

Rnd 2: 2 sc in each sc around. *(12 sc)*

Rnd 3: (Sc in next sc, 2 sc in next sc) 6 times. *(18 sc)*

Rnd 4: (Sc in each of next 2 sc, 2 sc in next st) 6 times. *(24 sc)*

Rnd 5: (Sc in each of next 3 sc, 2 sc in next sc) 6 times. *(30 sc)*

Rnd 6: (Sc in each of next 4 sc, 2 sc in next sc) 6 times. *(36 sc)*

Rnd 7: (Sc in each of next 5 sc, 2 sc in next sc) 6 times. *(42 sc)*

Rnd 8: (Sc in each of next 6 sc, 2 sc in next sc) 6 times, sl st in next st, turn. *(48 sc)*

Basket Sides

Rnd 1 (WS): Ch 1, working in **front lp** (see *Stitch Guide*) for this rnd only, sc in each st around, do not join, place a st marker. *(48 sc)*

Rnd 2: Sc in each st around.

Rnds 3 & 4: Rep rnd 2.

Rnd 5: (Sc in each of next 5 sc, sl st in next st, **bunny st** (see *Special Stitches*), sl st in next st) 6 times.

Rnd 6: (Sc in each of next 5 sts, sc in sl st, ch 3, sk bunny st and next sl st) 6 times.

Rnd 7: Sc in each st and each ch around. *(54 sts)*

Rnd 8: Rep rnd 2.

Rnd 9: (Sc in each of next 6 sts, *insert hook in next st, insert hook through any lp at base of bunnies' ears, yo, draw through lp in bunnies' ears and through st, yo, draw through 2 lps on hook*, sc in next st, rep bet *) 6 times.

Rnds 10-12: Rep rnd 2.

Rnd 13: (Working through end of handle and then through st, sc in next 3 sts to attach handle to basket, sc in each of next 24 sts) twice, sl st in next st, turn.

Rnd 14: Ch 1, **reverse sc** (see *illustration*) in each sc around, join in beg sc, fasten off.

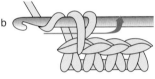

Reverse Single Crochet

Border

With RS facing, insert hook RS to WS through st of rnd 11, from WS, draw up a lp of lime and draw through to RS, *insert hook in next st on rnd 12, yo, draw lp through to RS and through lp on hook**, insert hook through next st of rnd 11, yo, draw lp through to RS and through lp on hook, rep from * around, creating a zigzag design, ending last rep at **, fasten off, secure ends.

Bow

Cut 2 strands each of pink, jade and yellow, each 10 inches long. Alternating colors, attach 1 strand of yarn to rnd 4 under bunny st, tie ends in a bow, trim ends to desired length, rep under each bunny st.

Finishing

Glue clear plastic liner inside of Basket. Insert a mini flower in sp between each bunny st. ✄

Black Cat Hot Mat

Design by Ruth Shepherd

Dress up your Halloween table with several of these fun, fanciful hot pads made extra thick with chunky yarn.

 BEGINNER

 5 BULKY

Finished Size

8¼ inches in diameter

Materials

- Bulky (chunky) weight yarn:
    1 ball each orange and black
- Size H/8/5mm crochet hook or size needed to obtain gauge

Gauge

3 hdc = 1 inch; 2 hdc rnds = 1 inch

Pattern Notes

Weave in loose ends as work progresses. Join rounds with a slip stitch unless otherwise stated.

Back

Rnd 1 (RS): With black, ch 5, join in first ch to form a ring, ch 2 *(counts as first hdc)*, 9 hdc in ring, join in 2nd ch of beg ch-2. *(10 hdc)*

Rnd 2: Ch 2, hdc in same st as beg ch-2, 2 hdc in each hdc around, join in 2nd ch of beg ch-2. *(20 hdc)*

Continued on page 168

Valentine Gift Bag

Design by Lori Zeller

Make a great presentation with this pretty purchased gift bag decorated with a beautiful crocheted ribbon heart.

EASY

Finished Size
Heart: 3½ x 3¾ inches
Bag: 5½ x 8½ inches

Materials
- Uncrimped ⅛-inch-wide curling ribbon:
    40 yds white
- Polyester ⅛-inch-wide ribbon:
    5 yds burgundy
- Size F/5/3.75mm crochet hook or size needed to obtain gauge
- 5½ x 8½-inch paper gift bag with handles
- Craft spray adhesive
- Craft glue
- 5 x 6-inch piece white mulberry paper
- 4¾-inch-square bright pink patterned heart paper
- 4¼-inch-square pale pink parchment card stock
- 4 white 20mm heart-shaped shank buttons
- Pliers
- Stitch marker

Gauge
5 sc = 1 inch; 5 sc rows = 1⅛ inch

Pattern Notes
Weave in loose ends as work progresses. Join rounds with slip stitch unless otherwise stated.

With pliers, remove shank from back of each button.

Heart
Row 1: With white, ch 2, 3 sc in 2nd ch from hook, turn. *(3 sc)*

Row 2: Ch 1, 2 sc in first sc, sc in next sc, 2 sc in last sc, turn. *(5 sc)*

Row 3: Ch 1, sc in each sc across, turn.

Row 4: Ch 1, 2 sc in first sc, sc in each sc across to last sc, 2 sc in last sc, turn. *(7 sc)*

Row 5: Rep row 4. *(9 sc)*

Rows 6 & 7: Rep rows 3 and 4. *(11 sc)*

Row 8: Rep row 3.

Row 9: Ch 1, sc in first sc, dc in next sc, 3 dc in next sc, dc in next sc, sc in next sc, sl st in next sc, sc in next sc, dc in next sc, 3 dc in next sc, dc in next sc, sc in next sc, do not turn. *(15 sts)*

Rnd 10: Now working in rnds, ch 1, work 9 sc down side edge of Heart, 3 sc in opposite side of foundation ch, sc in side edge of each of next 9 rows, working across sts of row 9, 2 sc in first sc, 2 sc in each of next 5 dc, sc in next sc, place st marker in last sc made, sl st over center sc of row 8 directly below sl st of row 9, sc in next sc, 2 sc in each of next

5 dc, 2 sc in last sc, join in beg sc, fasten off. *(48 sts)*

Trim

Rnd 11: Attach burgundy in center sc of 3-sc group at center bottom of Heart, ch 1, (sc, ch 1, sc) in same sc as beg ch-1, (ch 1, sc in next sc) around to marked sc, sl st over next sl st, (sc in next sc, ch 1) around, join in beg sc, fasten off.

Assembly

Adhere mulberry paper to front of bag. Center and adhere bright pink patterned paper to mulberry, center and adhere card stock to bright pink patterned paper. Center and glue Heart centered over card stock. Tie a small bow with burgundy ribbon and glue to front of heart centered between lobes. Glue a button to each corner of patterned paper. ✄

Tiffany Eggs

Designs by Katherine Eng

A woven web of ribbon yarn and glittering beads creates the illusion of stained glass in these pretty egg covers.

INTERMEDIATE

Finished Size

3¼ inches long x 7 inches around center

5 BULKY

Materials

- Lion Brand Trellis bulky (chunky) weight ribbon yarn (1¾ oz/115 yds/50g per ball):
    1 ball each #302 ocean, #304 rainbow and #305 stained glass
- Size G/6/4mm crochet hook or size needed to obtain gauge
- 3¼-inch jumbo neon plastic eggs: blue, green, pink and purple
- 12 each crystal 10mm beads: green, purple, pink and clear

Gauge

Rnd 1 = 1¼ inches

Pattern Notes

Weave in loose ends as work progresses.
Join rounds with a slip stitch unless otherwise stated.
Each ball of Trellis will make approximately 7 Eggs.
These Egg designs are as follows: ocean

with blue Egg and clear beads, rainbow with green Egg and green beads, stained glass with purple Egg and purple beads and stained glass with pink Egg and pink beads.

Egg

Rnd 1: Thread 12 beads onto ribbon, ch 4, sl st in first ch to form a ring, (sc in ring, ch 3) 6 times, join in beg sc, sl st into next ch-3 sp. *(6 ch-3 sps, 6 sc)*

Rnds 2 & 3: Ch 1, sc in same sp, ch 3, (sc in next ch-3 sp, ch 3) 5 times, join in beg sc, sl st into next ch-3 sp. At the end of rnd 3, pull beg tail, secure end by weaving into sts.

Rnd 4: Ch 1 ((sc, ch 3, sc) in ch-3 sp, ch 3) around, join in beg sc, sl st into next ch-3 sp. *(12 ch-3 sps)*

Rnd 5: Ch 1, sc in same ch-3 sp, ch 3, (sc in next ch-3 sp, ch 3) 11 times, join in beg sc.

Rnd 6: Ch 1, sc in same ch-3 sp, *ch 1, push bead down and forward, ch 1 over bead**, sc in next ch-3 sp, rep from * around, ending last rep at **, join in beg sc, sl st in next ch sp to the right of bead.

Rnd 7: Ch 1, sc in same ch sp as beg ch-1, ch 2, (sc in next ch sp to the right of bead, ch 2) around, join in beg sc, sl st into next ch-2 sp.

Rnds 8 & 9: Ch 1, sc in same ch-2 sp, ch 2, (sc in next ch-2 sp, ch 2) around, join in beg sc, sl st in next ch-2 sp.

Rnd 10: Ch 1, sc in same ch sp as beg ch-1, ch 1, (sc in next ch-2 sp, ch 1) around, join in beg sc.

Note: *Insert plastic egg into crocheted Egg.*

Rnd 11: Sl st into next ch sp, ch 1, sc in same ch-1 sp, sc in each ch-1 sp around, join in beg sc, leaving a 20-inch length, fasten off. *(12 sc)*

Hanging Loop

Weave rem length over and under sts of rnd 11, pull gently to tighten.

With rem length, insert hook in any st of rnd 11, ch 16, sl st in st opposite ch, weave rem length into a few sts, fasten off any excess length. ✂

Black Cat Hot Mat
Continued from page 163

Continued from page 163

Rnd 3: Ch 2, hdc in same st as beg ch-2, hdc in next hdc, (2 hdc in next hdc, hdc in next hdc) around, join in 2nd ch of beg ch-2. *(30 hdc)*

Rnd 4: Ch 2, hdc in same st as beg ch-2, hdc in each of next 2 hdc, (2 hdc in next hdc, hdc in each of next 2 hdc) around, join in 2nd ch of beg ch-2. *(40 hdc)*

Rnd 5: Ch 2, hdc in same st as beg ch-2, hdc in each of next 3 hdc, (2 hdc in next hdc, hdc in each of next 3 hdc) around, join in 2nd ch of beg ch-2. *(50 hdc)*

Rnd 6: Ch 2, hdc in same st as beg ch-2, hdc in each of next 4 hdc, (2 hdc in next hdc, hdc in each of next 4 hdc) around, join in 2nd ch of beg ch-2, fasten off. *(60 hdc)*

Front
Rnds 1–6: With orange, rep rnds 1–6 of Back. *(60 hdc)*

Cat Head
Rnd 1: With black, ch 5, join in first ch to form a ring, ch 2, 9 hdc in ring, join in 2nd ch of beg ch-2, (ch 3, sl st in next st) twice *(ears)*, fasten off.

Cat Body
Rnds 1 & 2: With black, rep rnds 1 and 2 of Back. *(20 hdc)*

Rnd 3: Sl st in each st around, ch 10, sl st in 2nd ch from hook, sl st in each rem ch across *(tail)*, sl st in next st of rnd 2, fasten off.

With tail at bottom and ears at top, sl st Head to Body. Working underneath edges of cat, sl st cat to front center of Hot Mat. Place a length of orange around cat's neck, tie ends in a bow.

Trim
Rnd 1 (RS): Holding WS of Front and Back tog, with Front facing and working through both thicknesses, attach black, ch 1, sc in same st as beg ch-1, ch 2, sk next hdc, (sc in next hdc, ch 2, sk next hdc) around, join in beg sc, fasten off. *(30 sc, 30 ch-2 sps)*

Rnd 2 (RS): Attach orange in any ch-2 sp of rnd 1, ch 4 *(counts as first dc, ch-1)*, dc in ch-2 sp before the sp that beg ch-4 was worked in *(beg cross-st)*, dc in next ch-2 sp, ch 1, dc in same ch-2 sp as beg ch-4, (dc in next ch-2 sp, ch 1, dc in previous ch-2 sp *(cross-st)*) around, join in 3rd ch of beg ch-4, fasten off.

Rnd 3 (RS): Attach black in sp between cross-sts, ch 1, sc in same sp as beg ch-1, ch 2, (sc in next sp between cross-sts, ch 2) around, join in beg sc, fasten off. ✂

Halloween Checkers Game
Continued from page 158

Rnds 6–8: Rep rnd 4.
Rnd 9: Sl st in each sc around, fasten off.

Candy Corn
Make 12.
Rnd 1 (RS): With white, ch 2, 4 sc in 2nd ch from hook, **change color** *(see Stitch Guide)* to orange in last st, do not join. *(4 sc)*
Rnd 2: Sc in each sc around.
Rnd 3: (2 sc in next sc, sc in next sc) twice. *(6 sc)*
Rnd 4: Rep rnd 2.
Rnd 5: (2 sc in each of next 2 sc, sc in next sc) twice. *(10 sc)*
Rnd 6: Rep rnd 2, changing color to yellow in last st.
Rnd 7: Sc in each of next 2 sc, (2 sc in next sc, sc in each of next 3 sc) twice. *(12 sc)*
Rnd 8: Rep rnd 2.
Rnd 9: Sl st in each st around, fasten off.

Checkerboard
Note: *Carry unused yarn loosely on WS, working over unused yarn every few sts to secure.*
Row 1 (RS): With dark orchid, ch 57, sc in 2nd ch from hook, sc in each of next 6 chs, changing to lime in last st, (sc in each of next 7 sc, changing to dark orchid in last st, sc in each of next 7 sc, changing to lime in last st) 3 times, sc in each of next 7 sc, turn. *(56 sc)*
Row 2: Ch 1, sc in each of next 7 sc, changing to dark orchid in last st, (sc in each of next 7 sc, changing to lime in last st, sc in each of next 7 sc, changing to dark orchid in last st) 3 times, sc in each of next 7 sc, turn.
Row 3: Ch 1, sc in each of next 7 sc, changing to lime in last st, (sc in each of next 7 sc, changing to dark orchid in last st, sc in each of next 7 sc, changing to lime in last st) 3 times, sc in each of next 7 sc, turn.
Rows 4–7: Rep rows 2 and 3.
Row 8: Rep row 2, changing to lime in last st.
Rows 9–14: Rep rows 2 and 3.
Row 15: Rep row 2.
Row 16: Rep row 3, changing to dark orchid in last st.
Row 17: Rep row 3.
Rows 18–23: Rep row 2 and 3.
Rows 24–64: Rep rows 8–23, ending last rep with row 16.

Edging
Rnd 1 (RS): With dark orchid, working around outer edge of Checkerboard, ch 1, (work 56 sc across side edge, ch 1 *(for corner)*) 4 times, join in beg sc, turn.
Rnd 2: Ch 1, working in **front lp** *(see Stitch Guide)* of each st, sc around, working (sc, ch 1, sc) in each corner ch-1 sp, join in beg sc, fasten off.

Finishing
Glue Checkerboard to wood board so that rnd 2 of Edging is over the edge of the board. To play, place Ghosts and Candy Corn on lime squares. ✂

Friendly Scarecrow Door Decoration

Continued from page 157

Rnds 2–6: Sc in each st around. At the end of last rep, sl st in next st, fasten off.

Laces
Make 2.

Cut 1 strand of white 20 inches long. Using strand and working through ch-1 sps on row 2 of Side and Heel, working over Tongue, lace up Shoe sides tog, tie ends in a bow, trim as desired.

Finishing

Stuff Shoe and Cuff with fiberfill. Holding front and back of top of Cuff tog and working through both thicknesses, attach black to top of Cuff, ch 1, work 5 sc across top of Cuff to close opening, fasten off. Apply glue to last 4 rnds on Cuff, then insert glued rnds inside Pant Leg. Cut 10-inch length of café and tie length tightly around bottom of Pant Leg over glued rnds, trim ends. Trim Leg Stuffing over Shoes as desired.

Facial Features

With fabric paint and following photo as a guide or as desired, , paint Facial Features on Head using blue for eyes and black to outline eyes and make pupils. Use orange for nose, red for mouth and strawberry for cheeks.

Swing Seat Cover

Rnd 1 (RS): With red, ch 10, join in first ch to form a ring, ch 1, sc in each ch around, do not join. *(10 sc)*

Rnd 2: Sc in each sc around.
Rep rnd 2 until Swing Seat Cover is 19 inches long, sl st in next st.

Rnd 3 (edging): Ch 1, ((sc, ch 1, sc) in next sc, sk next sc) around, join in beg sc, fasten off.

Rnd 4 (edging): Attach red in opposite side of foundation ch, ch 1, (sc, ch 1, sc) in same ch as beg ch-1, sk next ch, ((sc, ch 1, sc) in next ch, sk next ch) around, join in beg sc, fasten off.

Place Swing Seat Cover over wooden dowel so that rnds 3 and 4 extend out over each end of dowel. Cut 2 strands of café each 10 inches long, tie a strand to each end of Swing Seat Cover just inside edging worked on each end encasing the dowel.

Swing Rope

Cut 2 strands of café each 300 inches long, fold strands in half, tie ends in a knot. Place knotted end onto a stationary object the diameter of a pencil. Place lp end on finger and make strands taut. Twist strands 300 times. Put 1 finger in center of rope, fold in half letting the 2 strands twist tog. Tie a knot in each end of rope 5 inches from end forming tassels.
*Divide tassel threads on 1 end of rope in half, wrap ends around dowel stick 1 inch from end of stick and tie in knot, forming tassel at bottom of swing, rep from * for other end of rope. Trim tassel ends to 2 inches in length. Take center of rope and tie in knot forming a 3-inch lp at the top of the swing.

Finishing

Glue Scarecrow's bottom to swing sea. Cut 2 strands of café each 10 inches in length. Using 1 strand for each Hand, tie Hand to Swing Rope so that it looks like Hands are holding the rope, trim ends. ✄

Let It Snow! Afghan
Continued from page 150

(sc, ch 2, sc) in same dc, *ch 1, sk next dc, (sc, ch 2, sc) in next ch-1 sp, (ch 1, sk next sc, (sc, ch 2, sc) in next ch-2 sp) twice, ch 1, sk next sc, (sc, ch 2, sc) in next ch-1 sp, ch 1, sk next dc, (sc, ch 2, sc) in next dc, (sc, ch 4, sc) in corner ch-3 sp**, (sc, ch 2, sc) in next dc, rep from * around, ending last rep at **, join, fasten off.

Square 2
Make 17.
Rnd 1 (RS): With white, ch 4, sl st in first ch to form a ring, ch 1, (sc in ring, ch 1) 6 times, join in beg sc, sl st into next ch-1 sp. *(6 sc, 6 ch-1 sps)*

Rnd 2: Ch 1, ((sc, ch 2, sc) in ch-1 sp, ch 2, sk next sc) around, join in beg sc, sl st into next ch-2 sp. *(12 ch-2 sps)*

Rnd 3: Ch 1, (sc in ch-2 sp, ch 4) around, join in beg sc, turn. *(12 ch-4 sps)*

Rnd 4: Draw up a lp of delft in any ch-4 sp, ch 1, sc in same ch-4 sp as beg ch-1, ch 4, (sc in ch-4 sp, ch 4) around, join in beg sc, turn.

Rnd 5: Sl st into ch-4 sp, ch 1, *3 sc in ch-4 sp, ch 1, sk next sc, 3 sc in next ch-4 sp, ch 1, sk next sc, (2 dc, ch 3, 2 dc) in next ch-4 sp, ch 1, sk next sc, rep from * around, join in beg sc, fasten off.

Rnd 6 (RS) joining rnd: Draw up a lp of colonial in first dc to the left of any corner ch-3 sp, ch 1, (sc, ch 2, sc) in same dc, *ch 1, sk next dc, (sc, ch 2, sc) in next ch-1 sp, ch 1, sk next 2 sc, (sc, ch 2, sc) in next sc, ch 1, sk next ch-1 sp, (sc, ch 2, sc) in next sc, ch 1, sk 2 sc, (sc, ch 2, sc) in next ch-1 sp, ch 1, sk 1 dc, (sc, ch 2, sc) in next dc, (sc, ch 4, sc) in corner ch-3 sp**, (sc, ch 2, sc) in next dc, rep from * around, ending last rep at **, join in beg sc, fasten off.

After completing Square 1 through rnd 4 and Square 2 through rnd 5, arrange alternating Squares 5 x 7.

Work rnd 5 all around first Square, then work rnd 6 around Square 2. Join tog on 1 side, then join rem Squares on 1 or 2 sides as follows: to join corner ch-4 sps, ch 2, drop lp draw lp under to over through opposite ch-4 sp, ch 2 and continue with rnd. To join ch-2 sps, ch 1, drop lp, draw lp under to over through opposite ch-2 sp, ch 1, continue with rnd. Where 4 corners meet, ch 2, drop lp, draw lp under to over through opposite ch-4 sp, ch 1, drop lp, sk next ch-4 sp, draw lp under to over through ch-4 sp, ch 2 and continue with rnd.

Border
Rnd 1 (RS): Draw up a lp of colonial in any ch-2 sp on side edge, ch 1, (sc, ch 2, sc) in same sp, *ch 1, (sc, ch 2, sc) in next ch-2 sp *(or in ch-4 sp at seam)*, rep from * around, working at each corner, ch 1, (sc, ch 4, sc) in corner ch-4 sp, join in beg sc, fasten off.

Rnd 2 (RS): Draw up a lp of delft in first ch-2 sp to the left of any corner ch-4 sp, ch 1, sc in same sp, *ch 2, sc in next ch-2 sp, rep from * around, working at each corner, ch 2, ({sc, ch 2} 3 times, sc) in corner ch-4 sp, ending with ch 2, join in beg sc, sl st into ch-2 sp.

Rnd 3: Ch 1, sc in same ch-2 sp, *shell *(see Special Stitch)* in next ch-2 sp**, sc in next ch-2 sp, rep from * around, ending last rep at **, join in beg sc.

Rnd 4: *Ch 2, (sl st, ch 3, sl st) in next ch-2 sp, ch 2, sl st in next sc, working at each corner, ch 2, (sl st, ch 3, sl st, ch 4, sl st, ch 3, sl st) in next ch-2 sp, ch 2, sl st in next sc, rep from * around, ending with sl st in joining sl st of last rnd, fasten off. ✂

Christmas Sachets
Continued from page 153

Rnd 6: (Sl st, ch 3, 6 dc, ch 3, sl st) in each ch-4 sp around, fasten off. *(5 petals)*

Leaf
With green, (ch 7, sl st in 2nd ch from hook, sc in next ch, hdc in next ch, dc in each of next 3 chs) twice, fasten off.

Finishing
Place a few drops of scented oil on each cotton ball, wrap in netting and tie with a length of crochet cotton. Flatten and set aside.

Joining
Holding WS of Front and Back tog, working through both thicknesses of rnd 5, (weave burgundy ribbon over 2 dc and under 3 dc) around, inserting scented pouch inside before closing. Trim ends of ribbon and pin ends tog with small gold safety pin—this way the Sachet can be removed and fresh oil added. For hanging lp, cut a 6-inch length of burgundy ribbon, fold ribbon in half and glue to center top over ribbon weave. Fold rem length of ribbon into a bow and glue centered over base of hanging lp. Glue 6mm ivory bead to center of knot of bow. Trim ribbon ends as desired. Glue Leaves to back of Rose and glue Rose to center front of Sachet.

Poinsettia

Gauge
Size 6 steel hook: rnds 1 & 2 = 1⅜ inches in diameter

Pattern Notes
Weave in loose ends as work progresses. Join rounds with a slip stitch unless otherwise stated.

Special Stitches
Popcorn (pc): 3 dc in indicated st, drop lp from hook, insert hook in first dc of 3-dc group, pick up dropped lp and draw through st on hook.

Beg popcorn (beg pc): Ch 3, 2 dc in same sp, drop lp from hook, insert hook in top of beg ch-3, pick up dropped lp and draw through st on hook.

Front
Rnd 1: With size 6 steel hook and white, form a ring with end of thread, leaving a slight tail at beg ch 3 *(counts as first dc)*, 15 dc in ring, join in 3rd ch of beg ch-3. To close opening, pull rem beg length. *(16 dc)*

Rnd 2: Ch 1, sc in same st as beg ch-1, (ch 3, sc in next dc) around, ending with dc in beg sc to form last ch-3 sp. *(16 ch-3 sps)*

Rnd 3: Sl st into ch-3 sp, ch 1, sc in same ch-3 sp, ch 3, (sc in next ch-3 sp, ch 3) around, join in beg sc.

Rnd 4: Sl st into next ch-3 sp, **beg pc** (see Special Stitches), ch 1, **pc** (see Special Stitches) in same ch-3 sp, ch 1, *(pc, ch 1, pc) in next ch-3 sp, ch 1, rep from * around, join in top of beg pc. (32 pc)

Rnd 5: Sl st into ch-1 sp, ch 3, dc in same ch-1 sp as beg ch-3, 2 dc in each rem ch-1 sp around, join in 3rd ch of beg ch-3. (64 dc)

Rnd 6: Ch 1, sc in same st as beg ch-1, ch 3, sk next st, (sc in next st, ch 3, sk in next st) around, join in beg sc, fasten off.

Rnd 7: Attach green in any ch-3 sp, ch 1, sc in same ch-3 sp, *ch 4, sl st in 2nd ch from hook, sc in next ch, hdc in next ch**, sc in next ch lp, rep from * around, ending last rep at **, join in beg sc, fasten off.

EASY

Finished Size

3¾ inches in diameter

Materials

- Size 10 crochet cotton (350 yds per ball):
    - 100 yds white
    - 25 yds green
    - 3 yds red
- Sizes 4/2.00mm and 6/1.80mm steel crochet hooks or size needed to obtain gauge
- 1 yd gold embroidery floss
- 30 inches ¼-inch-wide gold ribbon
- 4 cotton balls
- Scented oil
- Small gold safety pin
- 6mm ivory bead
- Washable fabric glue

Back

Rnds 1–6: Rep rnds 1–6 of Front.

Poinsettia

Rnd 1: With size 4 steel hook and gold embroidery floss, ch 2, 8 sc in 2nd ch from hook, join in beg sc, fasten off. (8 sc)

Rnd 2: Attach red with sl st in any sc, *ch 6, sl st in 2nd ch from hook, sc in next ch, hdc in next ch, dc in next ch, hdc in last ch, sl st in next sc on rnd 1, rep from * around, fasten off. (8 petals)

Leaf

Make 4.

Row 1: With size 4 steel hook and green, ch 6, sl st in 2nd ch from hook, sc in next ch, hdc in next ch, dc in each of last 2 chs, fasten off.

Finishing

Place a few drops of scented oil on cotton balls, set aside. Holding WS of Front and Back tog, cut a 14-inch length of gold ribbon, weave through both thicknesses of rnd 6 over and under each ch-3 sp around inserting cotton balls before closing. Pin ends of ribbon on WS with small gold safety pin. Sachet can be removed and fresh oil added.

Cut a 6-inch length of ribbon, form a hanging lp and glue to center top of Sachet over ribbon weave. Fold gold ribbon into a bow and glue centered over base of hanging lp, trim ends as desired. Glue 6mm ivory bead over center knot of bow.

Glue Leaves to back of Poinsettia, glue Poinsettia to center front of Sachet. ✄

General Instructions

Please review the following information before working the projects in this book. Important details about the abbreviations and symbols used are included.

Hooks

Crochet hooks are sized for different weights of yarn and thread. For thread crochet, you will usually use a steel crochet hook. Steel crochet-hook sizes range from size 00 to 14. The higher the number of the hook, the smaller your stitches will be. For example, a size 1 steel crochet hook will give you much larger stitches than a size 9 steel crochet hook. Keep in mind that the sizes given with the pattern instructions were obtained by working with the size thread or yarn and hook given in the materials list. If you work with a smaller hook, depending on your gauge, your project size will be smaller, if you work with a larger hook, your finished project's size will be larger.

Gauge

Gauge is determined by the tightness or looseness of your stitches, and affects the finished size of your project. If you are concerned about the finished size of the project matching the size given, take time to crochet a small section of the pattern and then check your gauge. For example, if the gauge called for is 10 dc = 1 inch, and your gauge is 12 dc to the inch, you should switch to a larger hook. On the other hand, if your gauge is only 8 dc to the inch, you should switch to a smaller hook.

If the gauge given in the pattern is for an entire motif, work one motif and then check your gauge.

Understanding Symbols

As you work through a pattern, you'll quickly notice several symbols in the instructions. These symbols are used to clarify the pattern for you: brackets (), curlicue braces {}, parentheses () and asterisks *.

Brackets () are used to set off a group of instructions worked a specific number of times. For example, *(ch 3, sc in next ch-3 sp) 7 times* means to work the instructions inside the () seven times.

Occasionally, a set of instructions inside a set of brackets needs to be repeated, too. In this case, the text within the brackets to be repeated will be set off with curlicue braces {}. For example, *(dc in each of next 3 sts, ch 1, {shell in next ch-1 sp} 3 times, ch 1) 4 times.* In this case, in each of the four times you work the instructions included in the brackets, you will work the section included in the curlicue braces three times.

Parentheses () are used to set off a group of stitches to be worked all in one stitch, space or loop. For example, the parentheses () in this set of instructions, *Sk 3 sc, (3 dc, ch 1, 3 dc) in next st* indicate that after skipping 3 sc, you will work 3 dc, ch 1 and 3 more dc all in the next stitch.

Single asterisks * are also used when a group of instructions is repeated. For example, **Sc in each of the next 5 sc, 2 sc in next sc, rep from * around, join with a sl st in beg sc* simply means you will work the instructions from the first * around the entire round.

Double asterisks ** are used to indicate when a partial set of repeat instructions are to be worked. For example, **Ch 3, (sc, ch 3, sc) in next ch-2 sp, ch 3**, shell in next dc, rep from * 3 times, ending last rep at *** means that on the third repeat of the single asterisk instructions, you stop at the double asterisks.

Buyer's Guide

Bernat
P.O. Box 40
Listowel, ON N4W 3H3
Canada
(800) 265-2684

Caron International Inc.
P.O. Box 222
Washington, NC 27889
(800) 868-9194

Coats & Clark Inc.
Consumer Services
P.O. Box 12229
Greenville, SC 29612-0229

DMC Corp.
S. Hackensack Ave.
Bldg. 10F
South Kearny, NJ 07032
(800) 275-4117

Lion Brand Yarn Co.
34 W. 15th St.
New York, NY 10011
(800) 795-5466

Patons Yarns
P.O. Box 40
Listowel, ON N4W 3H3
Canada
(519) 291-3780

Stitch Guide

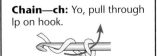

ABBREVIATIONS

beg	begin/beginning
bpdc	back post double crochet
bpsc	back post single crochet
bptr	back post treble crochet
CC	contrasting color
ch	chain stitch
ch-	refers to chain or space previously made (i.e. ch-1 space)
ch sp	chain space
cl	cluster
cm	centimeter(s)
dc	double crochet
dec	decrease/decreases/decreasing
dtr	double treble crochet
fpdc	front post double crochet
fpsc	front post single crochet
fptr	front post treble crochet
g	gram(s)
hdc	half double crochet
inc	increase/increases/increasing
lp(s)	loop(s)
MC	main color
mm	millimeter(s)
oz	ounce(s)
pc	popcorn
rem	remain/remaining
rep	repeat(s)
rnd(s)	round(s)
RS	right side
sc	single crochet
sk	skip(ped)
sl st	slip stitch
sp(s)	space(s)
st(s)	stitch(es)
tog	together
tr	treble crochet
trtr	triple treble
WS	wrong side
yd(s)	yard(s)
yo	yarn over

Chain—ch: Yo, pull through lp on hook.

Slip stitch—sl st: Insert hook in st, yo, pull through both lps on hook.

Single crochet—sc: Insert hook in st, yo, pull through st, yo, pull through both lps on hook.

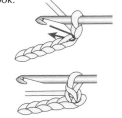

**Front loop—front lp
Back loop—back lp**

Front Loop   Back Loop

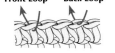

**Front post stitch—fp:
Back post stitch—bp:** When working post st, insert hook from right to left around post st on previous row.

Back   Front

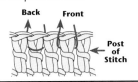

Post of Stitch

Half double crochet—hdc: Yo, insert hook in st, yo, pull through st, yo, pull through all 3 lps on hook.

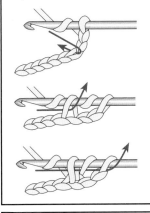

Double crochet—dc: Yo, insert hook in st, yo, pull through st, [yo, pull through 2 lps] twice.

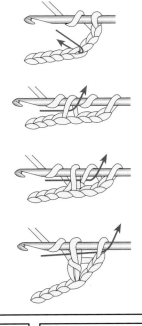

Change colors: Drop first color; with 2nd color, pull through last 2 lps of st.

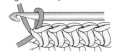

Treble crochet—tr: Yo 2 times, insert hook in st, yo, pull through st, [yo, pull through 2 lps] 3 times.

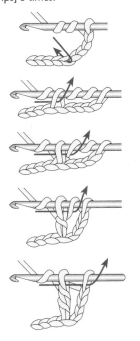

Double treble crochet—dtr: Yo 3 times, insert hook in st, yo, pull through st, [yo, pull through 2 lps] 4 times.

Single crochet decrease (sc dec): (Insert hook, yo, draw up a lp) in each of the sts indicated, yo, draw through all lps on hook.

Example of 2-sc dec

Half double crochet decrease (hdc dec): (Yo, insert hook, yo, draw lp through) in each of the sts indicated, yo, draw through all lps on hook.

Example of 2-hdc dec

Double crochet decrease (dc dec): (Yo, insert hook, yo, draw lp through, yo, draw through 2 lps on hook) in each of the sts indicated, yo, draw through all lps on hook.

Example of 2-dc dec

US		UK
sl st (slip stitch)	=	sc (single crochet)
sc (single crochet)	=	dc (double crochet)
hdc (half double crochet)	=	htr (half treble crochet)
dc (double crochet)	=	tr (treble crochet)
tr (treble crochet)	=	dtr (double treble crochet)
dtr (double treble crochet)	=	ttr (triple treble crochet)
skip	=	miss

For more complete information, visit

AnniesAtticCatalog.com

Special Thanks

Sandy Abbate
Charm-ing Bag & Belt, Heirloom Lace Bonnet & Booties

Svetlana Avrakh
Funky Fringe-Sleeve Jacket, Pretty in Pink Jacket & Purse

Bernat
Sweet Dreams Baby Blanket

Cindy Carlson
Desert Diva Crisscross Top

Belinda Carter
Bunny Faces Basket, Friendly Scarecrow Door Decoration, Halloween Checkers Game, Mango Lace Top

Coats & Clark
Funky Fringe Poncho

Donna Collinsworth
Furry Photo Frame

Carol Decker
Blue Heaven Tablecloth

Katherine Eng
Confetti Stars Pillow, Let It Snow! Afghan, Mixed Media Wrap, North Woods Throw, Peruvian Print Throw, Sparkling Jewels Scarf, Teen Tube Top, Tiffany Eggs

Kim Guzman
Amethyst Shell

Mary Jane Hall
Funky Stripes Leg Warmers, Heart Choker, Mocha Tweed Purse, Newsboy Cap & Medallion Belt

Jennifer Hansen
Techno Door Curtain

Tammy Hildebrand
Evening Elegance Capelet

Eleanor Miles-Bradley
Flirty Skirted Halter Top

Dora Ohrenstein
Black Magic Pullover, Midsummer Dream Skirt

Rose Pirrone
Bare Necessities Necklace Purse

Diane Poellot
Flowers & Lace Poncho

Josie Rabier
Flower Webs Table Topper

Fredricka Schuh
Gold Nugget Skirt-cho

Ruth Shepherd
Black Cat Hot Mat

Darla Sims
Girly-Girl Pillow

Mary Ann Sipes
Suede Luxury Scarf

Rena Stevens
Butterfly Lace Throw, Daisy Chain Throw, Flower Fields Rug

Diane Stone
Christmas Sachets, Daisy Valance, Flower-Fresh Bookmarks, Pretty Blossoms Pot Holders, Summer Breeze Throw, Sunflowers Pot Holder & Towel Topper

Judy Teague Treece
Dainty Lace Pot Holders, Pretty Pineapples

Amy Venditti
Lemon Squares Blanket

Margret Willson
Asian Mosaic Pillow

Lori Zeller
Rainbow Travel Set, Valentine Gift Bag